Jonathan Odell

Jonathan Odell

Loyalist Poet of the American Revolution

Cynthia Dubin Edelberg

Duke University Press
Durham 1987

© 1987 Duke University Press

All rights reserved

Printed in the United States of America
on acid-free paper ∞

Library of Congress Cataloging-in-Publication Data
Edelberg, Cynthia Dubin, 1940–
Jonathan Odell, Loyalist poet of the American
Revolution.
Bibliography: p.
Includes index.
 1. Odell, Jonathan, 1737–1818. 2. Poets, Canadian–
18th century–Biography. 3. Poets, American–
Revolutionary period, 1775–1783–Biography.
4. American Loyalists–Biography. 5. United States–
History–Revolution, 1775–1783–Literature and the
revolution. I. Title.
PR9199.2.O35Z64   1987   811′.3   [B]   87-6708
ISBN 0-8223-0716-2

*In loving memory of my mother and father,
Bertha Tarin Dubin and Jacob Dubin*

Contents

Preface xi
1 Odell's First Ministry 1
2 Burlington amid Violence 19
3 Revolution Comes to Burlington 33
4 Confrontation and Flight 53
5 Odell for the Loyalists and General Howe 63
6 Odell in Clinton's New York 79
7 Working in Vain for the Cause 93
8 Odell's Confidence Bolstered
9 Leaving the Colonies 131
10 From London to New Brunswick 147
Appendix 161
Notes 163
Bibliography 183
Index 191

Rebellion madly shakes the land,
And love is turned to hate and fear.

Preface

This book re-creates the Loyalist situation before, during, and immediately after the American Revolution by focusing on Jonathan Odell and his poems, essays, and letters. Although Odell was one of the most influential and gifted of the Loyalist writers, all of his essays and most of his poems were relegated to obscurity when the British army left the colonies in 1783. The few postwar Loyalists who felt compelled to set down their versions of events found neither publishers nor willing audiences in the colonies after independence. They would have acted unwisely had they tried. Tens of thousands of Loyalists had no choice but to leave America when the British withdrew. Those who remained worked hard to live with the new establishment, which meant relegating past allegiances to the past.

Nearly a century after the end of the war, Winthrop Sargent made a serious effort to reassemble Odell's writing. He selected poems from his own manuscripts and from those belonging to J. Francis Fisher and published two valuable but incomplete editions: *The Loyalist Poetry of the Revolution* (Philadelphia, 1858); and *The Loyal Verses of Joseph Stansbury and Doctor Odell* (Albany, 1860). Moses Coit Tyler, the distinguished literary historian, based his judgment of Odell's achievement on what he found in the Sargent editions. In his seminal work, *The Literary History of the American Revolution* (1897), Tyler called Odell "the most powerful and most unrelenting of the Tory satirists," his writing distinguished by "passionate energy of thought" and "pungency and polish of style. . . ." Tyler's discussion of Odell's work, the best to date, acknowledges its own limitation: "I am confident . . . that a considerable part of Odell's work as a song-writer and satirist during the Revolution has thus far escaped recognition as his."

Unknown to Sargent and Tyler, a remarkably rich collection of unpublished Odell Papers was housed in the New Brunswick Museum, Saint John, New Brunswick, Canada. In 1969 Joan Anderson edited a significant portion of these manuscripts for her M.A. thesis for the University of British Columbia; however, her work remains unpublished. In 1971 Pastora San Juan Cafferty edited "Loyalist Rhapsodies," fifty-one poems by Stansbury and Odell, for his Ph.D. dissertation for George Washington University. His dissertation, as well as the original manuscript of the poems held in the Library of Congress, also remains unpublished. The present book analyzes the contributions of Sargent, Anderson, and Cafferty and adds a substantial number of Odell's writings from 1767 to 1784, thereby doubling the canon.

Only a few scholars have seen even a portion of Odell's work. His poems, letters, and essays gleaned from manuscripts and newspapers, however, bring us closer to knowing what happened to a generation of Loyalists caught up in the Revolution. Here is a voice that should not be lost to us if we are to comprehend our own beginnings more clearly.

Odell discredited the Whig position early on. In his Episcopate Controversy poems of 1767–68, he denounced Whig mobs who were deluded by the few into believing that an Anglican bishop in the colonies would threaten their civil rights. As the Whigs moved toward revolution, Odell continued to accuse the few ambitious, upstart patriots, who deliberately brought the gullible multitude to an armed confrontation with the mightiest military in the world. These few alone were responsible for chaos, he asserted. To serve their selfish ends, they refused reconciliation with ever-lenient Britain, although such reconciliation would be in the best interests of all the colonists.

The bitter civil war between the rebels and Loyalists was under way in some places as early as 1774, when the Association, a congressional boycott pact, changed colonial life altogether. Prominent, visible Loyalists were openly harassed by provincial legislatures or victimized by mobs. When the highly respected William Howe became commander in chief of the British army, the Loyalists had every reason to believe they would win. Why then did they lose? From his vantage point as Superintendent of the Printing Presses, Odell tried to piece together Howe's rationale. Odell concluded that Howe purposely did not end the war despite numerous opportunities. He fought a war of containment; to crush Washington would have proved self-defeating in the long run. The rebels had repeatedly and convincingly demonstrated that they could bring to a halt the all-important trade relationship between Britain and her most profitable colonies. If Britain could not establish a "cordial" relationship with the rebels, the militant faction would continue to sabotage trade in a country too large to police. Britain had pressing commitments in Europe. Howe's determination to secure a negotiated settlement with the rebels cost the Loyalists their fortunes, their future in America, and often their lives.

Odell confided his frustration in letters and songs intended for friends. Publicly he deferred to Howe, asked the rebels to consider negotiations, and explained away the "hesitancies" of the British military. When Henry Clinton replaced Howe, Odell stayed on with the British military as a newspaper essayist. In an effort to turn the rebels against their leaders, he ridiculed the French Alliance and Continental fiscal policies.

A central figure in the Benedict Arnold intrigue, Odell believed this work his most important. Confident that West Point was about to fall into British hands, Odell wrote *The American Times*, the first sustained antiwar poem by an American. Once again, he berated the irresponsible, greedy few for forcing the naive multitude to war instead of contesting taxation issues on the floor of Parliament.

By the time Guy Carleton succeeded Clinton as commander in chief of the British army, the military aspect of the Revolution was essentially over. As Carleton's secretary, Odell was privy to his ill-fated negotiations with Washington. Carleton could neither persuade the Americans to remain within the British Empire, nor could he convince them to accept the Loyalists as citizens.

Between sixty thousand and a hundred thousand Loyalists had been forced into exile by the time the British army left the colonies in December 1783. Odell was one of the most privileged. The Loyalist Claims Commission appointed him Secretary to the Province of New Brunswick, a newly created Loyalist colony.

The Odell narrative gives us a human sense of what life was like for Loyalists caught between two inexorable enemies, the rebels and the British army. Although like all the Loyalists Odell lacked the power to determine his future, he had considerable resources to draw on. Highly educated, well connected, energetic, self-centered, lucky, and at times deceitful, he survived the "Wreck," as he called it. Odell and his wife, Ann, were apart from the time he fled Tory hunters in his Burlington, New Jersey, home in 1775 until their reunion in Fredericton, New Brunswick, in 1785. His letters to her put us in touch with his despair, confusion, and seething frustration.

I am indebted to the National Endowment for the Humanities for a fellowship that enabled me to devote full time to research, and to Cleveland State University for a grant to visit the New Brunswick Museum in Saint John, Canada, to study the Odell Papers. A substantial portion of chapter 1 was published as an article, "The Shaping of a Political Poet: Five Newfound Verses by Jonathan Odell," in *Early American Literature;* it is reprinted with the permission of the editor, Emory Elliott. I would also like to thank the staff of the New Brunswick Museum and the Special Collections curators at the New York Public Library and the Library of Congress.

Robert Calhoon read the entire manuscript. His advice on sources available and his editorial suggestions contributed significantly to the strength of this study. It is also a pleasure to thank Janice Potter, David Dubin, and Cecil Robinson for their critical observations. I am grateful to Kenneth Silverman and Barton Friedman for timely encouragement. David Larsen supplied information about Revolutionary Pennsylvania; other members of the English Department at Cleveland State University read individual chapters, and their pointed comments about style were most valuable. I am indebted to Peggy Broder, William Chisholm, Gary Engle, John

Gerlach, and Louis T. Milic. Sherri Van Camp typed the Britannicus essays from the *Royal Gazette*, and Evelyn Green answered text processor questions with skill and consummate patience.

And to my closest friends: my husband, Stu, and our children, Jay, Jacqueline, and Wendy, love always.

1 *Odell's First Ministry*

The Odell family was part of the Puritan migration in the 1630s to Massachusetts Bay. Through the years the Odells moved to Connecticut and acquired modest tracts of land. Jonathan's father, John, married Temperance Dickinson, the daughter of the Reverend Jonathan Dickinson, who was founder and first president of the college that now is Princeton.[1] John and Temperance settled in New Jersey, where they had three daughters and a son, Jonathan. No information survives about Jonathan's childhood or young adult years.

We do not know how John Odell lost his financial footing. Jonathan Odell spoke of its significance for him: "My father, having married in New Jersey, settled in that Province, where he lived but a few years and, at his death, left me, his only Son, a patrimony little more than sufficient to defray the expenses of a liberal education."[2] Jonathan graduated from Princeton in 1754. He tried the life of a schoolteacher, but returned to Princeton to study medicine and received his M.A. in 1757. Odell signed on with the British army in the West Indies as a surgeon, and, in the absence of further biographical information, we can guess that he earned his living as a physician during the next six years, briefly in the West Indies and then in New Jersey. He surely found it discouraging. Medicine as practiced in the colonies before the Revolution was largely a matter of collecting herbs and leeches.

His life took a different turn. In 1763 William Franklin, Benjamin's son, was appointed royal governor of New Jersey. He recognized Odell's ability, and he was in a position to be generous: "William sponsored him for Anglican orders, recommended him to his father in London, proposed him for elevation to become first bishop in America."[3] Odell decided on the Anglican ministry, despite family ties to the Congregationalist church that reached back for generations. We can only speculate on the motives and processes of Odell's conversion, if in fact he was the first of the family to convert. We do know that he left for England to prepare for ordination.

Every colonist who wished to take holy orders had to do so in London. No resident bishop was appointed to North America, although the Anglican church was well established in the southern colonies, strong in the middle colonies, and getting stronger in New England. There had been rumors since the start of the century that an appointment was "daily expected," but until Anglican colonists actually convinced the Church of England to complete its organizational hierarchy in North America, those belonging to the church were part of the diocese of the bishop of London.

The Anglican ministry had a particular appeal in 1763. Ezra Stiles, the cleric from Newport, Rhode Island, wrote about Thomas Bradbury Chandler's decision to become an Anglican minister in 1748 that he was "imbibing then an assurance that in his day the Hierarchy would be erected here and that the Young Adventurers had a fair chance of becoming Bishops and other Dignitaries in the Church. This same Bait was at that time offered to me."[4] Ten years later the odds were much better that a bishop would be settled in the American colonies. Dr. Thomas Secker became the archbishop of Canterbury in 1758, and his determination to complete the church hierarchy was well known. Odell had been offered the "Bait" by Franklin, and from time to time he referred to it in his poems. With wit and good nature, he denied any interest in personal advancement, although he was not completely convincing. In 1763 Odell and others who decided on a career in the Anglican ministry had personal ambition as one reason to celebrate imperial authority.

The Peace of Paris ended the French and Indian War and assured England's absolute dominance in North America. After seven years of war British regulars with the help of colonial militia had all but driven out France and its ally Spain. Under the severe terms of the peace, England almost doubled land holdings on the continent. For the colonists 1763 was a year of jubilation. Not only had the Catholic threat posed by France and the Indian alliance put together by King Philip been eliminated, but lucrative trade between the colonies and England had been restored to its normal peacetime level. Colonists predicted times of unparalleled prosperity. Odell's bits of verse, celebrating the British military—"Welcome Home After the Peace of 1763"—and the recent accession of twenty-two-year-old George III to the throne, were typical of the mood of the day.[5]

The Episcopate Controversy

Between 1763 and 1766 while Odell was in London preparing for ordination, the Episcopate Controversy became heated and changed his prospects. Congregationalists' fears that Anglican bishops would be introduced into the colonies reached the point of frenzy. Descendants of the first Puritan settlers driven from England by Archbishop Laud, these Congregationalists were adamant that bishops would use their authority to destroy a non-Anglican church as they had tried to do in the past. John Adams took note of long-standing suspicions among New Englanders of "lordships, temporal and spiritual": "Their ancestors fled to this wilderness to avoid them; they suffered sufficiently under them in England. And there are few of the present generation who have not been warned of the danger of them by their fathers and grandfathers, and enjoined to oppose them."[6]

Adams also made the connection between church and state: "The objection was not merely to the office of a bishop, though even that was dreaded, but to the authority of parliament, on which it must be founded. . . . if a parliament can erect dioceses and appoint bishops, they may introduce the whole hierarchy, establish tithes, forbid marriages and funerals, establish religions, forbid dissenters."[7] The Congregationalist ministers had for so long warned against episcopacy that they "had made the word *bishop* stand for everything hateful in the Yankee past."[8]

The likelihood that a bishop would be assigned grew with

the sheer number of Anglicans. Equally alarming to Congregationalists, the Anglicans were beginning to entrench themselves in traditionally Congregationalist areas.[9] When the Society for the Propagation of the Gospel (S.P.G.), the missionary arm of the Church of England, financed a mission in the Congregationalist heartland of Cambridge, Massachusetts, Congregationalists were outraged. Jonathan Mayhew, Boston pastor and seasoned veteran of the pamphlet wars concerning the ecclesiastical conspiracy, responded with *Observations on the Charter and Conduct of the Society*, in which he argued that the Cambridge mission made it apparent that the Church of England planned first to oppress all dissenters and then to usurp colonists' civil rights. So important was Mayhew's *Observations* that Archbishop Secker answered the tract himself. In January 1764 *An Answer to Dr. Mayhew's Observations on the Charter and Conduct of the Society for the Propagation of the Gospel in Foreign Parts* appeared in London. Secker's assurances were dismissed altogether when the Stamp Act went into effect in 1765. The furor caused by this unpopular legislation significantly lessened chances that the Church of England would send a bishop to the colonies.

Congregationalists like Mayhew characteristically defended themselves against religious and secular threats with the same argument. The Cambridge mission was evidence of a plan of civil oppression and the Stamp Act was a plan of religious oppression: "the stamping and episcopizing [of] our colonies were . . . *only different branches of the same plan of power.*"[10] Accordingly, an Anglican minister and a minister of Parliament could be viewed as interchangeable partners working for the single purpose of exploiting colonists now and enslaving them in the future. Odell predictably met with some degree of hostility when he returned to the colonies as an Anglican minister.

By 1767 Anglican clergymen up and down the seaboard, who had come to expect favor because of their close ties with England's church and therefore England's king, found themselves victims of open abuse because of those very ties. They had sworn the Oath of the King's Supremacy, and prayers for the king were part of the liturgy. Like royal appointees, with whom they were often compared, Anglican ministers were indissolubly identified in the public mind with the British government. Tensions mounted especially when Parliament issued new tax laws; in 1767 the Townshend duties were imposed. By now there were pockets of deep anti-British feeling throughout the colonies. Like others who would not shed their close ties with England, Anglican ministers felt the strain. Such was Odell's situation.

He had been ordained a deacon by the bishop of London in 1766, had taken the orders of priesthood, and on January 19, 1767, had been licensed by the bishop of London as a minister in the Province of New Jersey. Odell began his remarkable life as a minister in Burlington, New Jersey, a town of about 150 Quaker and fifty Anglican families.

Burlington played an ongoing part in the Episcopate Controversy. As early as 1712 Dean Jonathan Swift had been mentioned as the choice for the first American bishop.[11] By midcentury local tradition held that this town in western New Jersey had been designated as the site of the first American Episcopal See; acreage had been set aside for the bishop's residence.[12] Franklin considered Odell a serious candidate for bishop and at least another of Odell's friends, Margaret Morris, thought that the residence might one day be his.

The *Parish Register* of St. Mary's Church shows this entry in Odell's own hand: "Jonathan Odell, M.A., was appointed, by the Society for Propagating the gospel in foreign parts, to succeed Mr. Campbell, as Missionary at Burlington, Decem'r 25th, 1766, and he arrived at Burlington, the 25th of July, 1767, and was the next day regularly inducted into St. Ann's (now St. Mary's) Church, in the said city of Burlington, by his Excellency Wm. Franklin, Esqu., Governor of the Province of New-Jersey." As was the custom, Franklin ushered Odell into the church, turned over the key and property to him, and then tolled the bell to summon the parishioners.[13] The relationship between Franklin and Odell remained solid. As long as Franklin was in power, he used his influence to further Odell's career. For instance, he helped Odell to improve the building of St. Mary's. The sixty-four-year-old church needed extensive repair, and although many Anglican congregations were prosperous, St. Mary's was not. Odell turned to Franklin, who immediately proposed a remedy. Within months Odell wrote to the secretary of the S.P.G. about "a Lottery having been some time since granted by the Provincial Legislature in order to facilitate the necessary reparations."[14] Franklin's wife, Elizabeth, presented St. Mary's with elegant furniture for the pulpit. A new bell was installed in the belfry.

Odell began at once to work with prominent Anglican ministers in New York, New Jersey, and Pennsylvania. They established the Corporation for the Relief of the Widows and Orphans of Deceased Clergymen, an organization that Governor Franklin formally incorporated and that Odell served as secretary.[15] He fit into the circle of active and ambitious clerics, and when the controversy over policies of taxation and the introduction of bishops erupted into violent argument, Odell wrote poems in behalf of the Church of England.

Odell had written verse before and, had social and political circumstances been otherwise, he might well have continued as a serviceable poet of inconsequential themes. His first poems were occasional pieces such as "On the Anniversary of a Friend's Marriage" (1766); bagatelles such as "To the Ladies of Burlington Bank"; and conventional reflections on the changing seasons such as "The True History of the Golden Age."[16] He also wrote two poems of homage, "Pope's Garden at Twickenham" and "Song From Milton's Allegro, With Two Addition Stanzas Written At Sea, Anno 1767," which convey his admiration in their titles.[17] Neither of these poems is memorable in literary terms, but Odell's debt to Pope and Milton is considerable.

Odell's Augustan View of Society

The New Brunswick Society Museum houses hundreds of Odell's books, no doubt only a portion of his library. One can get a vivid sense of his intellectual assumptions and literary tastes by reviewing the list. Odell owned at least thirty-three volumes of Shakespeare and numerous classics and religious commentaries. He had a keen interest in science, in particular Isaac Newton's tracts. Educated colonists were avid readers of history. Odell had many ponderous works such as David Hume's *The History of England* in eight volumes and Richard Glover's twelve-book blank verse epic, *Leonidas*. We also find Sir William Blackstone's *Commentaries on the Laws of England*, which makes the four volumes of *De L'Esprit Des Loix* by the French materialist philosopher Loudon less of a surprise and suggests that Odell might have considered law as a career. He was also a student of French poetry and painting.

Most telling is his collection of the major Augustan humanist writers. University graduates would not necessarily own these texts. There are ten volumes of *The Works of Alexander Pope*. Jonathan Swift is represented by three volumes as well as a critique of his life and writings. Odell owned the two-volume 1741 edition of John Locke's *An Essay Concerning Human Understanding* and also the three-volume 1765 edition. There are poems by Thomas Gray and Matthew Prior, and two volumes of verse and prose by William Shenstone. Samuel Johnson does not appear, but Odell was aware of his work. His own ambitious effort, *An Essay on the Elements, Accents, and Prosody of the English Language,* was published in London in 1805 and again in 1806. According to the title page it was intended as the introduction to Jonathan Boucher's supplement to Dr. Johnson's *Dictionary*. Odell was indebted to the Augustans for specific themes and images for his own poetry, and he defined himself as an Augustan Christian humanist in general terms.

He subscribed to the major assumptions, rhetorical devices, and various images associated with the conservative eighteenth-century masters. As his writing attests, he was clearly one of them in spirit if not in genius. Odell believed, of course, that the moral man of social action necessarily values order and virtue and abhors chaos and fraud. As a devotee of Swift, he naturally did in the literary world of Burlington what all staunch humanists do: he inquired into the nature of man's attributes and found that man is flawed.

Odell's poem on the subject was printed in the *Pennsylvania Chronicle*. It is a sermon in verse called "UNTHANKFUL man, perversely blind." The poet introduces himself as a firm but kindly parson compelled to instruct a certain Lorenzo to confront his sin—the refusal to accept what is—and embrace resignation. "UNTHANKFUL man" is an Augustan lesson in patient understanding. Lorenzo "Calls life unhappy, GOD unkind!" because he envies *"the happy few.*" Having been advised by the minister that even the most blessed by earthly bounty are men "and therefore wretched still!" Lorenzo has a vision of "a radiant messenger of love!" descending from "her Father's awful throne." She, Celestial Truth, chides him for "senseless impious railing" and scolds him for presuming to "treat thy Maker with disdain!" Then she softens her tone and sets about to unravel the problem. The passage recalls Pope's "Essay on Man":

> Heav'n has kindled in thy frame
> An inextinguishable flame,
> A restless avarice of bliss,
> Which all pursue, yet all must miss!

It is man's fate never to be fully satisfied on earth. In heaven is *"endless joy"* and *"calm repose,"* but only those who are "to Heav'n's will resign'd" are so rewarded. The goddess, "Sweet smiling Peace from Heav'n," implores Lorenzo to cultivate virtue and content himself. Then she returns to "the realms of uncreated light" in accord with conservative, eighteenth-century Christian humanist thought.

Signed Veridicus, "UNTHANKFUL man" was printed by editor William Goddard in the March 7–March 14 issue of the *Pennsylvania Chronicle*. Odell uses the same pseudonym for his translation of La Fontaine's fable "Le Songe d'un habitant du Mogal," which appeared in the next edition of the *Chronicle*. The political overtones of this poem make it clear that he was caught up in the swirl of controversy concerning taxation and episcopate policies.

Odell prefaces his version of the La Fontaine poem by instructing the reader as to its context. It is a tale that "contains a lesson of no small importance. It may serve as a *terror* to those *evildoers*—who assume the garb of sanctity—*and a praise to those who do well*—without ostentation." He goes on to say that he has put the fable "into an *English* dress." Odell's translation actually reinterprets La Fontaine to convey a political message: knaves who plot "to join / In some intriguing dark design" while wearing "the *semblance* of a *saint*" have not gone unnoticed. The fable itself concerns an Indian who dreams of a vizier possessed of eternal joy,

and of a hoary hermit consigned to raging flames. Confused by the
judgment that a worldly vizier should go to heaven and a hermit
to hell, the Indian consults a Brahmin, who unravels the hidden
truth. Contrary to expectations, the vizier quietly studied the art
of good government, and the ambious hermit *"studied arts of dark
disguise":*

> Your vision wants not sense, and shows
> How apt *appearance* to deceive.
> In life the *Vizair* often chose
> The splendid pomp of state to leave,
> To seek the silent lonely shade,
> And study how to govern well.
> Far from the peaceful hallow'd cell
> The ambitious Hermit often stray'd,
> An *unsuspected* knave, to join
> In some intriguing dark design.
> He wore the *semblance* of a *saint*,
> That he might *sin* with less restraint.
> But *here*, you see, the judge defied
> The *studied arts of dark disguise*
> He saw the *truth*, and, to confirm it,
> The *Vizair* blest—and damn'd the *Hermit*.

Odell repeats the narrative sense La Fontaine provided in the opening lines, but in the final passage just cited he has thoroughly reworded the model. The original says nothing about the ambitious hermit and "the *studied arts of dark disguise,*" but rather, "Cet hermite auz vizirs allait faire sa cour."[18]

Following Pope's argument about revision, spelled out in the 1717 edition of *The Works*, Odell alters the fable to suit the occasion of rogues hiding behind the garb of sanctity. Since man's nature has essentially always been the same, the ancient genres are the most appropriate because they have stood the test of time. To alter an individual work to address the immediate circumstance was to do as Pope would have expected. The fable, as fable, would convey the general message; topical details would compromise the purity of the form. Odell's Augustan method in "Le Songe," as in "UNTHANKFUL man," tells us a great deal about his initial poetic aspirations, but 1768 was not a subtle year in New Jersey, and his fable, which requires careful reading by a schooled audience, probably did not make much of an impact. Perhaps pressure from colleagues, the response of his congregants and readers, or the increasingly blatant opposition of the vocal Whig faction was the reason that Odell changed his poetic strategy. He next came out with topical, vitriolic lines charging that Whigs, having lost all respect for authority, were being led by their baser instincts.

The Townshend duties brought Whig mobs back to the streets. These mobs had already proved effective in repealing the Stamp Act. Whig bands roving throughout the colonies learned that they could humiliate, harass, and even persecute Loyalists without fear of retaliation. "Be-flipp'd" (drunk on flip, a concoction of rum, heated molasses, and ale), they were familiar sights. Those who defended imperial policy, "whether sacred or civil," as Odell put it, had cause to be afraid. Anglican ministers, highly visible authorities within their communities, were prime targets.

Yet during the tense boycott months the first Episcopal convention of clergymen from New York, New Jersey, and Connecticut met and chose Thomas Bradbury Chandler to write *Appeal to the Public in behalf of the Church of England in America*, which called for a bishop to be settled in the colonies and refuted possible objections to the plan. The widely publicized statement drew support and criticism from Massachusetts to Virginia. In fact, discussion of the episcopate question took second place only to debates about the Townshend duties. Odell vigorously defended the purpose, members, and writings of the convention. He was particularly worried that Chandler's *Appeal* would cause dissenters to disrupt his congregation. Their riotous behavior must be curbed immediately.

The Seeds of Loyalist Ideology

In *The Liberty We Seek*, Janice Potter explains that "Loyalist spokesmen provided a comprehensive, consistent, and compelling explanation of the Revolution."[19] This ideology did not suddenly appear during the 1774-76 period but continued "warnings about attitudes and practices fostering anarchy. . . . [which] raged in the 1760s and early 1770s." Consider the abuse heaped on Governors Francis Bernard and Thomas Hutchinson during their administrations. To those who abhorred chaos, the men who showed wanton disrespect for Bernard and Hutchinson were liars, hypocrites, and "sons of contention," as Odell called them. These confused malcontents must return to law and order lest society collapse altogether. Odell's next two poems, "What the Deuce is the Matter?" and "When a Man of True Spirit, in Speaking or Writing," support Potter's thesis (which she notes has been "so far virtually ignored by historians").[20] That is, in 1768 Odell "warn[s] about attitudes and practices fostering anarchy," and he denounces unruly dissenters in precisely the same terms he will use to express his scorn for the rebels.

The April 4 *Pennsylvania Chronicle* carried Odell's angry, straightforward "What the Deuce is the Matter?" Veridicus takes the responsibility "to defend / The *Convention* from slander and groundless abuse." The opening lines are straight eighteenth-century British conservatism: A fixed social hierarchy is an absolute, and the satirist's role is to upbraid those who by greed or insolence failed to accept their place in the hierarchy. These same lines give us the sense that the war of words between denominations took attitudes as well as rhetoric from the strained relationship between the lower and upper classes.

> Ho! ye *Sons of contention*, pray whither so fast?
> Don't ye know that—"*a cobbler should stick
>   to his last?*"
> Then why, *ye pert Whigs, ye dull Centinels*, why
> Do ye fly in a passion and make such a cry
>   About *Church-men* and *Bishops*

Odell is quick to point out (though he contradicts himself later in the poem) that he is not calling all dissenters to task, but only those "insolent, meddling, *anonymous* vermin" who are bent on disrupting the "peaceable life." The speaker casts about for an effective way to deal with such "*dirty* work" and conjectures: "shou'd *we condescend* to repay you in kind." Gone are the hints about knaves and "*dark disguise*" from his wisdom piece about viziers and hermits. Instead we get confrontation—"why make such ado / About *other mens matters?* What is it to you / Whether Bishops are sent us or not?"—and a warning that the argument can and soon may take a violent turn: "Yet occasion may happen to call for a sprig / Not of *laurel*, but *birch*, for a *libelling Whig*." If the "*Convention*" is slandered again, he goes on, one may find that "we're not quite so tame / As not to repel an attack on our fame." And as a poet completely alert to the gossip of the day, he takes note of the proposed Whig-French-Spanish alliance against England and its church.

Rumors held that although France was heavily in debt after the Seven Years War, the French wanted to reestablish influence in the colonies and hoped to involve their ally Spain, forming a bloc of Bourbon powers against Great Britain. Throughout the seventeenth and eighteenth centuries France and Spain had contended with Britain for territory in North America, because to command these seemingly unlimited natural resources was in effect to command world trade. France was reluctant to admit that two centuries of military campaigns had ended in complete failure. In 1767, four years after the unforgiving Peace of Paris, France sent ambassadors to the colonies to monitor opinion about a rebellion against England. The timing was right. Colonists were enraged over the Townshend duties, and Congregationalists and other dissenters were furious about the Episcopate Controversy. Odell acknowledged the proposed alliance and denounced it:

> That the Church's request for a Bishop or two,
> And whether she gets them or not, is to *you*,
> And all *other Dissenters*, a matter in which
> You have no more concernment, than whether my Bitch
> Be a New-found-land Spaniel (and here—to be plain—
> *She comes in for the rhyme*) or a pointer from Spain.

Apparently Odell's poem of scorn and ridicule elicited anger. His next poem, which appeared three weeks later in the same newspaper, purports to be an apology for those "*harsh* rhymes." "When a Man of True Spirit, in Speaking or Writing" begins as a mock apology for earlier rhymes that friends told him exceeded "the limits of *due moderation*." Now the disdainful speaker, again Veridicus, exercises all patience. Having confessed to the absurdity of the "*bitch*" and "the pointer from Spain," as well as apologizing for the rudeness of his tone, he insists that Whigs also back down. Apologies aside, he declares that they must leave his congregation alone and thus show the world that they have retreated from their mistaken path.

As for the ungodly situation of April 1768, the poem speaks plainly: the Whigs are caught in a tangle of lies and contradictions. They indeed possess sacred and civil freedom, although they have wrongly "*spread an alarm*" that freedom was endangered and have appeared "*in armour*" to defend what was never assaulted. Odell hammers away at the point that the introduction of bishops would not interfere with matters of state, and he ridicules Whig inconsistencies. At the same time that they complain about supposed oppression by the British government, Whigs continue their attempt to deny Odell's congregation freedom. And this, pronounces Veridicus, is not only hypocritical but a "sin / Against *equity, truth,* and *the faith you profess.*" Whigs are dishonest, intolerant, and finally "*unchristian.*"

The poem ends with a string of invectives. Veridicus warns the Whigs to repent. If they ignore him, he threatens to delineate their demerits "*with the pencil of truth*" for the world to see. In this poem, as in the earlier "What the Deuce is the Matter," the Whigs' crime is "the rage of *intemperate zeal* / Against *Bishops* and *Chandler's pacific Appeal*":

> To your *Consciences* then let me hold up the glass.
> See! with *hearts full of rancour*, with *foreheads*
>   *of brass,*
> With *unbounded ambition, unlimited pride,*
> (Which *Hypocrisy* vainly endeavours to hide)
> With *suspicious distrust,* that appears to be fraught
> With *revenge* for what *ne'er was attempted or thought,*
> With *ferocity, perfidy, envy and spite,*
> And *implacable*—How! do you start at the sight?

The condescending tone of "When a Man of True Spirit" culminates in Veridicus's letter to the editor, which followed the printed poem. This brief letter, more than the poem itself, conveys the sarcasm characteristic of early Loyalist writing. Odell's references to disease, popular images with the Augustan writers, will become one of his own trademarks:

Mr. GODDARD,

Once more I must request you to publish, in your Chronicle, a few lines to those restless *Perturbed Spirits*, the *Whigs*, and *Centinels*. They seem, at present, to be troubled with *bad dreams*, which may probably arise from a *bad digestion* for a disorder'd *stomach* is apt to affect the *head:* But I hope they will, in a little time, become less *stomachful*, and then, I doubt not, they will *rest* better *themselves*, and be less given to disturb the repose of *others*.

I am, Sir your humble
Servant, Veridicus.

April 21, 1768[21]

After this poem Odell decided temporarily not to go on with political poetry, even though Archbishop Secker was hard at work to settle bishops in America and the Episcopate Controversy was still raging. Odell had more pressing matters to deal with. Franklin was in political trouble. To write inflammatory verse would have been ill-advised.

Between 1763 when he was appointed governor and 1766, Franklin had a good working relationship with the New Jersey General Assembly. Then in 1766 he faced a serious clash with the legislature over the Massachusetts circular dealing with the Stamp Act. Franklin tried to fulfill his responsibilities to the Crown, although he personally disapproved of the measure. He barely managed to avoid an "open confrontation."[22] Legislators became wary.

In April 1768 the assembly convened for the first time since the Townshend duties had been enacted. Legislators knew what they wanted to do, and this time they were not going to argue with Franklin. In response to the Townshend duties Massachusetts had drafted the famous circular letter that denied Parliament the right to tax colonists—no taxation without representation. The letter had been sent to the other colonies in the hope that they would follow suit.

While Governor Franklin was giving his assurance to Lord Hillsborough (the newly appointed secretary of state of the American Department) that he would curtail the influence of the Massachusetts circular letter in New Jersey, the New Jersey General Assembly drafted their own circular letter modeled after the Massachusetts one, immediately adopted it, and sent it to London for presentation to the Crown.[23] Not even his most trusted allies told Franklin about the actions taken by the assembly. He did not see the petition until the official minutes of the assembly meeting were printed two weeks after the session ended. Obviously he was furious, and more furious still when he was publicly censured by Lord Hillsborough. When he angrily answered Hillsborough and at the same time denounced the Stamp Act in a sincere attempt to placate the assembly, there were rumors that Hillsborough would use his influence to oust him from office.

In the next issue of the *Pennsylvania Chronicle* Odell offered a new version of "Pope's Garden at Twickenham," his homage to Pope written two years before. The original poem, signed V.S., records the poet's visit to the simple "consecrated Bowers" while he was in London preparing for holy orders. He reflects on Pope's inspirational genius, on his presence still felt—"And lo! the *ravish'd Lock* I see"—and on his consolation that Pope has been received in heaven with full favor.[24] (Odell had a sure sense of redemption that was "not readily accessible to the Augustans."[25] Otherwise he assumed what Augustans did about the proper social hierarchy and the instructive role of literature.)

The revised version, called "On MR. POPE'S (now SIR WILLIAM STANHOPE'S) garden at Twickenham," presents essentially the same narrative, although Odell has changed several details given the immediate situation. He tells his readers that he is, after all, a colonist. He introduces himself as "a native of AMERICA" and recalls not an actual visit to Twickenham but an imagined one. Often, when young, he was transported in imagination to the "once belov'd retreat":

> In mental rapture to survey
>   This soul-enchanting spot,
> This mingled scene of Shade and day,

> With your Muse-haunted Grot,
> Which still inspires the pensive mind,
> Which awes the fancy still,
> Though gushing now no more we find
> The sweetly-murmuring Rill,
>
> That echoed through the sounding cave,
> Responsive to the strain
> Which here the tuneful sisters gave
> Eternity to gain.

The speaker muses on Pope's "deathless song," the filial love that inspired him to show "divinely justified / The way of GOD to man," and again the consolation: "Heav'ns decree, / A God, a God appears."

In this poem about the delights of "pensive mind" and "mental rapture," the immortality that poetry of genius affords, and his own humility at Pope's grotto, Odell reaffirms his seriousness about poetry, and even if he does not completely reconcile with the dissenters he does nothing to infuriate them. Odell's part in the war of words surrounding Chandler's *Appeal* ended in the April 25–May 2 edition of the *Pennsylvania Chronicle*.

2 *Burlington amid Violence*

Chiefly because the Episcopate Controversy was emotionally charged, the S.P.G. instructed its missionaries to "take special care to give no offence to the Civil Government by intermeddling with affairs not relating to their calling or function."[1] This was a plea for tact, not a theological dictum. For Odell, the church and civil government were enjoined to work in harmony for the common good. They were "mutually supporting institutions" with a single purpose: to "sustain social order and stability."[2] This idea was not a problem for Odell during the late 1760s and early 1770s. There were no compelling reasons for him to give "offence to the Civil Government," and accordingly he wrote nothing of a political nature during these years. By the time the agitation involving Franklin, the assembly, and Hillsborough had settled down, Archbishop Secker had died and consequently the Episcopate Controversy had lost its momentum. On the political front, the Townshend duties that had spurred the legislators to action had little effect on daily life in agrarian West Jersey. Burlington, its major city and seat of government, "remained relatively quiet"[3] on the surface. There was tension, certainly, but the townspeople were not yet overtly polarized."[4]

The War Seems Far Away

In the comparative quiet of Burlington Odell considered his financial problems. Almost from the start of his rectorship he had complained to the secretary that the Society's contribution to his income was insufficient. He repeatedly urged the Society to recognize his accomplishments. He was a competent and energetic minister who had written vigorously in behalf of the Episcopal Convention. He baptized, married, and buried hundreds of parishioners, and he delivered sermons throughout New Jersey and, on occasion, in New York and Pennsylvania. With Franklin's help he transformed St. Mary's church into one of the "most handsome," and served as an administrator of regional church programs. He kept a wary eye on itinerant "methodistic Emissaries" (particularly the popular Calvinist George Whitefield), who were "taking uncommon pains to get footing in this Country."[5] In spite of all this service Odell claimed he could barely support himself.

Reluctantly, he resumed practicing medicine in 1771. In 1772 he married Ann de Cou, daughter of Isaac and Hannah Nicholson de Cou, whose family had lived in Burlington since 1678. The Odells' first child, Mary, was born one year later and their second child, William Franklin, eighteen months after that. Now Odell spoke of poverty. The Society appointed him minister to a second church, the Church at Mt. Holly, and instructed that parish to supplement his income. Odell was disappointed. He continued to press his case with the Society.

He had, he insisted, done all he could to earn a living. He had taken from his own salary to contribute to the church building fund, but justifiably so. The Society should note that he had managed to persuade his Burlington congregation to establish a fund, the interest of which would eventually go to maintain "an Orthodox Minister of the Church of England" there. He was convinced that he would someday profit from this arrangement and not need to depend quite so heavily on assistance from the Society. In the interim, it must come to his aid. The strength of his argument rested on the fact that the Society owned land that was reserved for the American bishop when one would be appointed. That land generated rental income, and Odell claimed that the money was his as it had been his predecessor's. His petitions were denied: ". . . the Society how much soever they might be inclined to indulge me, in this request do not at present think themselves at liberty to do so."[6] Odell felt misused, but his argument with the Society was strictly a private issue. Publicly, he supported passive obedience to the established church and established government—"Fear God and Honor the King"—and he did so with the tone of authority.

Odell was not an obscure minister holding forth in a remote place, cut off from debate and action. He was a scholar with the privilege of Benjamin Franklin's respect. In March 1768 he was inducted into the American Philosophical Society founded by Franklin to promote learning. For this society he translated "Directions for the Breeding and Management of Silk Worms," which was printed in Philadelphia by J. Cruckshank and I. Collins in 1770. Dr. Cadwalader Evans had asked Odell to translate the tedious French text and to "make such abstracts as his judgment may dictate." The American Philosophical Society's "first publication was Odell's translation of Boissier de Sauvages' memoir on the raising of silk worms."[7]

Odell was also more informed politically than most because his patron, William Franklin, was in close touch with Benjamin Franklin until 1774. The father-son relationship could not sustain William's refusal to support war with Britain. With the end of that relationship, Odell lost his inside track, temporarily.

The Association Changes Colonial Life

When the First Continental Congress passed the Association in 1774, by one vote, power shifted to the radicals, and colonial life changed entirely. While the conservative Whigs and the Loyalists pondered their options, many who "had never been deemed worthy of leadership were taking a prominent part in public affairs."[8] Loyalists lost ground by default.

The Association, a nonimportation, nonconsumption, nonexportation agreement, became "law" despite protests from the conservative merchant class. By congressional order the boycott pact was also used as a fidelity oath. Colonists had no alternative but to choose publicly between loyalty to the king or loyalty to the rebel cause. Affiliation became a matter of immediate decision although, according to Thomas Paine, most were confused and reluctant to take sides: "I found the disposition of the people such that they might have been led by a thread, and governed by a reed."⁹ Then as now, no doubt, the large majority simply wanted to be left alone. But the militant rebel minority had an enforcement network too strong to be ignored. Representatives of the First Continental Congress, whether members of a Committee of Safety or Sons of Liberty, offered the Association to every white adult male in every community. "To sign or not sign!—That is the question," as the anonymous author of "The Pausing American Loyalist" put it. Not to sign was to risk the consequences of radical fury. Known Loyalists, especially if at all prominent, were likely to be half-hung from liberty poles, tarred and feathered, paraded through the streets in a cage, and finally hounded out, their property destroyed or confiscated.

Violence was rampant and the prospect of boiling tar on naked skin or worse convinced many who would have stayed in the middle of the road to sign. Self-exile to Canada, Bermuda, perhaps the West Indies or return to England were possibilities, but there were obvious problems about safe passage and how to survive once there. "The Pausing American Loyalist," printed anonymously, weighs these practicalities:

> To fly—I reck
> Now where—and, by that flight, t'escape
> Feathers and tar, and a thousand other ills
> That Loyalty is heir to: 't is a consummation
> Devoutly to be wished. To fly—to want—
> To want?—perchance to starve! Ay, there's
>   the rub.¹⁰ (5–11)

An Anglican minister was considered a Loyalist unless he presented his case otherwise, and whether he went into exile or stayed in the colonies his future was hard. Jonathan Boucher, once a close friend of Washington's and the most articulate of the ministers who censured Whig ideology and tactics, was compelled to leave Maryland after being repeatedly harassed in his church. He returned to England. Even for someone of his prominence, the transition was difficult: his connections "with men of rank and in power . . . all came to nothing."¹¹ The Reverend Samuel Seabury remained in New York. He brought down the mob's wrath when he published "Letters of a Westchester Farmer": "If I must be enslaved, let it be by a king at least, and not by a parcel of upstart, lawless committee men. If I must be devoured, let me be devoured by the jaws of a lion, and not be gnawed to death by rats and vermin." Connecticut Sons of Liberty paraded him through the streets and imprisoned him for two months before friends could secure his release.

Harassment of Prominent Loyalists

By 1774 Loyalists of stature were unable to protect themselves. For instance, James Rivington, the influential colonial publisher who would print Odell's most important poems and essays, was unable to safeguard his press. Neither Rivington nor Odell signed the Association. Odell did not suffer serious consequences because it was his good fortune to live among Loyalists and Quakers, who were not violent in the prewar years. Burlington was also home to militant, radical Whigs such as Joseph Borden, Peter Tallman, and Daniel Coxe, who held Odell in contempt (and years later had their revenge), but in 1774 Burlington was generally peaceful.

As a result, Odell knew the details of the unfolding drama in the prewar period, but he lacked a visceral sense of clear and present danger. When William and his father broke off their relations, Odell, in response to his friend's bitterness, no longer participated in Franklin's American Philosophical Society. Perhaps Franklin would not have him. Either way, this was not harsh punishment. Odell was decidedly lucky. It is Rivington's story that gives us insight into the options that most Loyalists had in 1774.

Rivington had emigrated from England to the colonies in 1760 at the age of thirty-six. Within a few years he set up a successful printing office and bookstore in New York. In 1773 he began publishing the *New-York Gazetteer*, a newspaper for which he claimed the remarkable circulation of 3,600 throughout the colonies.[12] The figure is all the more impressive given that in a largely illiterate population newspapers were passed from household to household, tacked up on posts, and read aloud in countless taverns.

Like many of the other approximately two dozen printers in the colonies, Rivington announced an open press policy—"Open to all Parties, Influenced by None." He printed pro- and anti-Parliamentary opinions dealing with the Tea Act and all that followed it. He believed that an open-forum policy was manageable in 1773, that argument was accepted, and that a clash of ideas had to do with emphasis.

"Non-associators," especially those like Rivington who were well known in a community, suffered. In November 1774 a group of subscribers to the *New-York Gazetteer* issued a broadside explaining that Rivington was "very unfriendly, in our opinion, to the common cause of American liberty."[13] The printer was hanged in effigy and his papers burned. Four months later a group of tenacious Whigs from Loyalist-dominated Newport, Rhode Island, recommended "to every person who takes his paper to immediately drop the same" because Rivington, wickedly "impelled by the love of sordid pelf" has printed "in the dirty 'Gazette' . . . false representations" and "wrong sentiment respecting the measures now carrying on for recovery and establishment of our rights."[14]

The campaign against Rivington did not end with nonviolent assaults. The radical militant Issac Sears, whose reputation for terrorizing Loyalists was well earned, led a mob of two hundred Sons of Liberty from New Haven, Connecticut, and in broad daylight they demolished his press, carting off what they could not smash. Rivington took refuge on board a British man-of-war in New York harbor. Like other ambitious merchants who depended on the public's good will, he had resisted a "premature commitment to the Loyalists, but circumstances were forcing" him to take a stand.[15] At this juncture, he maintained his balance.

Rivington was tried in absentia by the Continental Congress in Philadelphia. On May 20, 1775, he wrote a letter to Congress in his own defense. He grounded his argument in the principle of freedom of the press: "[my] press had been always open and free to both parties." He appeared to his judges to look at his publications, "among which are to be reckoned all the pamphlets, and many of the best pieces that have been written in this and the neighboring colonies in favor of the American claims." He reminded the

Congress that he paid almost two thousand pounds annually for local salaries and locally made printing paper. Finally, he promised to give no "further offense."[16] And he signed the Association.

The Continental Congress accepted his loyalty oath and his apology for "ill-judged publications." They advised "the inhabitants of the Colony not to molest him in his person or property."[17] All the same Rivington abandoned his open-press policy and rightly understood that he had no future in the colonies. At most the recommendation by the Continental Congress assured him temporary safety; he fled to England.

Samuel Loudon, publisher of the "open press" New York *Packet*, stayed in the colonies. He had advertised that he would print and sell an answer to *Common Sense*. A midnight mob, led by the energetic Issac Sears and others, seized Reverend Charles Inglis's "The True Interest of America . . . Strictures on a Pamphlet Intitled Common Sense. . . ." They burned the first printing and ruined the entire first run. Loyalists and Loyalist sympathizers, whether they left or stayed, were victimized.

The British military was in no position to defend them. General Thomas Gage, commander in chief of British forces in North America since the Peace of 1763, repeatedly warned Parliament that the colonies were a powder keg about to explode and that the Loyalists were vulnerable. Given only minimal resources, he could do little about it. He had no more than four thousand men and insisted he needed twenty thousand. He judged that the Friends of Government constituted a majority, but the violent measures taken by the Continental Congress had terrified them into silence. Unless Britain decided on "Recourse to Force," he suggested, they had best establish and maintain a policy of no "new Laws" so that people would have "time to cool and hearken more to Reason."[18] Without a "respectable Force" that he could lead "in the Field," he could mount neither a case for reconciliation nor any military "Impression of Consequence."[19] Repeatedly, he described the volatile situation in the colonies as slipping beyond his control and warned Parliament to execute its responsibility.

In January the British ministers voted to send reinforcements, not the twenty thousand requested but the two thousand they deemed feasible. On February 2, 1775, they appointed Major

Generals William Howe, Henry Clinton, and John Burgoyne to join Gage. Gage saw these reinforcements as too little, too late. Parliament recalled him and named Howe commander in chief during the Siege of Boston. Gage continued to fault England for not acting with speed and force earlier on. Aboard the homebound ship he wrote to Colonial Secretary Lord Dartmouth that the rebels "give out that they expect Peace on their own Terms thro' the inability of Great Britain to contend with them; . . ."[20]

From the Loyalists' viewpoint, England did have the ability "to contend with them." The Continentals and militiamen who surrounded Boston and laid seige to it could not to be called an army—they were ill-equipped, inadequately fed, and paid by Continental dollars that were losing value almost daily. They "did not constitute an organized fighting force."[21] At best they were a hastily put together lot of farmers turned soldiers. Although the naive assumed that they would succeed by "virtue of their virtue," Washington, an experienced major in the Virginia militia during the French and Indian War, came closer to the truth when he first reviewed his troops in July 1775 and remarked, "Could I have foreseen what I have and am likely to experience no consideration on earth should have induced me to accept this command."[22] According to Washington, Howe also knew that the state of the Continental army was "truly alarming": ". . . General Howe is well appraised, it being of common topic of conversation . . . [in] Boston. . . ."[23]

The deep misgivings and apprehensions among the rebels at the onset of revolution are voiced by Odell's counterpart Philip Freneau, often called the "Father of American Poetry." His poem about the Siege of Boston, entitled "A Voyage to Boston," was printed in Anderson's *New York Constitutional Gazette* on October 25, 1775. It records a Continental soldier's dismal realization that Boston is on the verge of a bloodbath: "Stranger, in pity lend one pensive sigh, / For all that dy'd and all that yet may die, / If wars intestine long their rage retain, / This land must turn a wilderness again." (When Freneau revised this poem as "The Midnight Consultations," he deleted these sobering lines, which make poor propaganda indeed.)

"A Voyage to Boston" also focuses on the sheer hatred that

the militant Whigs felt for the Loyalists. The most savage lines of the poem are reserved for the torture of an unarmed Tory. Freneau's "dissection passage" contains some of the most starkly vicious lines written by an American poet:

> What is a Tory? Heavens and earth reveal!
> What strange blind monster does that name conceal?
> There: there he stands—for Augury prepare,
> Come lay his heart and inmost entrails bare,
> I, by the forelock, seize the Stygian hound;
> You bind his arms and bind the dragon down.
> Surgeon, attend with thy dissecting knife,
> Aim well the stroke that damps the springs of life,
> Extract his fangs, dislodge his teeth of prey,
> Clap in your pincers, and then tear away.—
> Soldier, stand by, the monster may resist,
> You draw your back-sword, and I'll draw my fist.[24]

To "part the sutures of his brazen scull" and then "rake his entrail" thus exposes the words "deep grav'd with iron pen": "To my country I'll a traitor prove." The "dissection" passage concludes with the final instruction forbidding burial of the Tory.

Jonathan Trumbull Argues against Anarchy

Freneau spoke for the militant Whigs. By contrast, the extraordinarily popular poet and future Federalist Jonathan Trumbull spoke for the moderate and conservative Whigs. Odell wrote nothing of a political nature during the crucial years 1774–76, but a brief look at Trumbull's *M'Fingal* makes us aware of just how close was the thinking of the two poets about the nature of man and the need for a stable society. Both wanted reconciliation and thought it possible. Both judged Parliament's taxation policies plain madness, and both, in William Franklin's words, deemed "the opposition of the colonists more mad than the measures of the ministry."[25] Like Odell, Trumbull held an Augustan world view. Predictably, then, he instructs his readers in the horrors of anarchy, and he sharpens his wit to serve his cause. In the preface to *M'Fingal* Trumbull states his intention: to expose "with as much impartiality as possible ... the follies and extravagancies of his countrymen as well as of their enemies."[26] To Trumbull, this meant that the rebels, akin to short-sighted anarchists, could not defeat the British military. In 1775 it was an act of national suicide to try.

M'Fingal speaks of the tenuous Whig position, "Seriously of their Danger." Squire M'Fingal angrily warns the same Whigs he accuses of recklessly forcing a conflict. Armed rebellion against Britain is not simply a matter of treason; it is a thoroughly irresponsible course of action, which will bring ruin to hundreds of thousands of gullible colonists who have just managed to settle down to a less primitive life. Britain had already shown strength after Lexington and Concord. M'Fingal's argument is grounded in the fear of defeat.

How could raw Whig recruits hope to prevail over the most powerful military machine in the world? The squire predicts that the mighty British navy will bring "Destruction on her canvas-wings." War is not a romantic story of "Stiled swords of death" as "novel-writers" present it. It is a nightmare of "horror thro' the land":

> 'Twould not methinks be labour lost
> If you'd sit down and count the cost;
> And ere you call your Yankies out,
> First think what work you've set about.
> (ll. 145–48)

The realities of violence must be confronted in earnest, M'Fingal contends in the poem, and the Tories who have suffered at the hands of Whig mobs can speak of the horror of anarchy: "For we're in peril of our souls / from feathers, tar and lib'rty poles." The central episode of canto two graphically describes the torture of M'Fingal. Captured by the mob, he is tarred and feathered, carted through the streets in a cage escorted by a band of drunken merrymakers, and finally half-hung from the liberty pole. Trumbull's narrator disapproves.

M'Fingal's radical opponent Honorius answers with essentially a fiction about England's military weakness. He argues that Britain is fit to be a lunatic asylum and Gage is a harmless incompetent; the "venal band" of impious Tories consumed with desire for money and position constitutes the only threat. He concludes with a call to arms. Even read with complete sympathy Honorius's speeches contain little that would convince a thoughtful, reasonable man to risk war with Britain in 1775.

The first half of the poem (cantos three and four were published in 1782) closes with the suggestion that Whig and Tory factions, more alike than not in their human weaknesses, share sufficient ground on which to build a working relationship. So close was Trumbull's assessment to Odell's that when the editor John Buel brought out the 1792 edition of *M'Fingal*, he felt compelled to note that "the Author is no friend to monarchy, nor aristocracy" although "the absurdities and misconduct of his own countrymen have not escaped his notice."[27] Trumbull's *M'Fingal* does indeed expose "the absurdities and misconduct" of the rebels. The poem, which ran through thirty pirated editions, is an explicit plea for a return to law and order. But instead tensions increased quickly.

The British Army Fails the Loyalists

The Loyalists depended on the British army for protection, and they had reason to expect a great deal from Howe, who had distinguished himself during the French and Indian War. Odell in particular would not have doubted his ability. Added to what he knew about Howe's leadership of the detachment that scaled the Heights of Abraham and Howe's victories at Belle Isle and Havanna would be the information he had gleaned as a surgeon for British soldiers in the West Indies. Howe was respected as a strict disciplinarian. He was a popular officer, praised for integrity, bravery, and energy. Ira D. Gruber concludes that William Howe "was considered in 1775 to be one of the most able men in his profession."[28] But he did not use his power to extricate the Loyalists, and the war was coming home to them.

In October 1775 Odell's trouble with the New Jersey Provincial Congress began. He had sent two letters to England expressing disapproval of "the measures of defence adopted by the continent." His envoy Christopher Carter, about to board ship for England, was arrested by a Committee of Inspection. Odell's letters were seized, opened, and sent first to the Committee of Safety of

New Jersey and then to the New Jersey Provincial Congress.[29] Odell was "compelled to appear as a Prisoner" before the congress on October 17. The following day congress declined "passing any public censure against him," having determined that the letters in question did "not clearly appear to have been intended to influence public measures."[30] Still, the harassment of Jonathan Odell had begun.

He later explained to the secretary of the S.P.G. that the local committeemen who sat in judgment of him had neither the legitimate right nor a sufficient cause to do so: ". . . I presumed it reasonable in me to expect I should be indulged in the unmolested enjoyment of my private sentiments so long as I did not attempt to influence the sentiments or conduct of other men, and that private sentiments ought not to be made a matter of public notice, much less of public censure."[31] All we know of the Society's response to the confrontation between Odell and the Provincial Congress comes from a brief note recorded by Reverend George Hills, in *History of the Church in Burlington, New Jersey:* "the Society had reason to believe that Mr. Odell has met with a disappointment of his wishes in his own person."[32]

The Church of England did not act decisively to protect Anglican ministers or colonists who supported imperial authority in 1775. Nor had it previously formulated a long-range plan. Thomas Bradbury Chandler, enmeshed in church politics since the Episcopate Controversy, spoke for those who believed that it was the church's responsibility to act at this juncture, as it had been during the Two Penny Crisis years before. He wrote to the Society: "[If] the interest of the Church of England in America had been a national concern from the beginning, by this time a general submission in the Colonies to the Mother Country, in everything not sinful, might have been expected. . . . Who can be certain that the present rebellious disposition of the Colonies is not intended by Providence as a punishment for that neglect?"[33]

3 *Revolution Comes to Burlington*

During 1776 Odell's tone shifted between flippancy born of despair and bristling arrogance. These changes were no doubt directly related to the successes and failures of the British military. Howe was appointed commander in chief in February 1775. While he occupied Boston for more than one year, Loyalists waited anxiously for him to secure Dorchester Heights, from which British soldiers could at least keep watch on the twenty thousand rebels surrounding the beseiged city. To the Loyalists' profound disbelief, Howe did not build fortifications. Instead, he moved the army to Halifax to wait for reinforcements.

Robert Calhoon in *The Loyalists in Revolutionary America* considers the impact of Howe's departure from Boston: "The British evacuation of Boston in March 1776 was the most massive and traumatic experience that befell the New England loyalists."[1] The rebels were so delighted that they overlooked their Puritan suspicion of theater, and "The Blockhead, or The Affrighted Officers," attributed to Madam Mercy Warren, enjoyed a brief run in Boston. The play celebrates Washington's successful takeover of the city, makes much of the cowardice and stupidity of "affrighted" British officers who were "forced" to give it up, and offers all "sympathy" to distraught Loyalists who could not believe that their protectors had deserted them.

The Howe Brothers and Their Rationale

Howe had a reputation as an aggressive, brilliant soldier. Every Loyalist needed to sift through the rumors to recognize Howe's plan and ascertain what his strategy would mean to the Loyalist community. In 1775 even the most insightful Loyalists could not have perceived the truth. Howe and his elder brother Admiral Richard Howe, in charge of the British fleet on its way to colonial waters, were determined to try for reconciliation, even though the king and the ministry then in place wanted to meet force with force: "The Admiral had long feared that a devastating offensive would permanently alienate the colonists and render them useless to Britain."[2] The resumption of trade was useful; a hostile British America would not supply it.

If the Howes were aiming for reconciliation, what would happen to the Loyalists? They were not part of the Howes' strategy for 1776.[3] The Howes would not support their efforts to organize into effective fighting units; nor would they grant them the status of British regulars. The Howes wanted a negotiated peace with the rebels and saw nothing to be gained by encouraging Friends of Government. Arming the Loyalists would fuel a bitter civil war.

To put it another way, if Admiral Howe and General Howe had wanted to use Loyalists as soldiers, nothing would have prevented them from doing so. Common sense argued for it. It would have been less expensive and more efficient than to send thirty-eight thousand British regulars across the Atlantic and to contract with German princes for an eventual eighteen thousand Hessians as well. It cannot be claimed that Loyalists refused to fight, that they simply assumed that the British regulars allied with Hessians, slaves, and Indians would fight for them.[4] While Loyalist leaders did come from the upper class in far greater proportion than did the rebel leaders, Loyalists could be found in every social and economic sphere. With the exception of Virginia, all the southern colonies were Loyalist blocs, chiefly because they had strong cultural and economic ties with England, which needed their raw materials, especially cotton and tobacco. For generations Parliament had enacted beneficial trade laws in behalf of the southern colonies, and wisely so. Loyalists also made up a substantial portion of the middle colonies' population. There is absolutely no reason to suppose that Loyalist soldiers would not have been at least as effective as the Continentals and militiamen who served under Washington. The British army's capability of training, outfitting, and paying Loyalist troops outweighed Washington's capability throughout.

In 1776 King George's and the ministers' "desire for a vigorous prosecution of the war was unmistakable."[5] Even a mediocre Loyalist force could have secured it. The question is why the king's faction did not take steps to put such a force in the field. Perhaps they wanted to avoid demands for privilege by Loyalist militiamen at the end of what they believed would be a short war. After all, during the taxation arguments that followed the French and Indian War, many colonists claimed that, because colonial militiamen fought alongside British regulars, to pay taxes for the war would be in effect paying twice.

By the time the "hawk" faction recognized its mistake of not arming the Loyalists before 1776 when they still had money, property, and stable positions within their home communities from which to operate safely, it was too late. To equip and train scattered refugees and to regain the confidence of moderate Loyalists, who had signed oaths of allegiance to insure their own well-being, would have required a massive financial and propaganda campaign. When Britain cut losses in 1783, the overwhelming majority of Loyalists were left completely to their own resources, and they had reason to conclude that Britain's decision to abandon them finally was the inevitable result of the decision to abandon them from the start.

War between the Rebels and Loyalists

During the early months of 1776 Burlington Loyalists, as a group more protected than most, were apprehensive. Their prospects brightened in May. Fifteen British officers and about seventy-five troops, captured by General Richard Montgomery in Canada and sent to Burlington as prisoners of war, reported firsthand that Governor Guy Carleton, defending the beseiged city of Quebec, had received reinforcements of ten thousand British regulars. In May Carleton drove the rebels out of Canada, although not in time to save these particular prisoners. I believe that British military activity prompted Odell to write "The Tory Hunt," his first political poem since 1768. The poem tells us two important facts: First, the Loyalists knew that they were entirely dependent on the British army, and second, Odell conspicuously looked to Commander Carleton, not Howe, for help. The subject of the "The Tory Hunt" is a battle called the Peacock Expedition, the official beginning of the civil war between Whigs and Loyalists.

While Howe was shut up in Boston during December 1775, the First Continental Congress capitalized on rebel momentum then underway, seized the initiative, and inaugurated a military campaign against the Loyalists. Congress ordered General Philip Schuyler to lead almost four thousand militiamen into upstate New York, where they mounted a full-scale attack on the Loyalists of Tyron County, who, it was rumored, had squirreled away "several thousand stand of arms." The defenseless Loyalists surrendered.

Schuyler offered his account of the Peacock Expedition in three letters printed in the February editions of the *Pennsylvania Evening Post*. He specifies that the aim of the "business" was not primarily to gather up arms but "to discourage the Tories in other parts of the country and give confidence to the Whigs in all parts. . . ."[6] In this end he succeeded.

Odell ridicules the Peacock Expedition—and Schuyler, who was a bit of a hypochondriac and thus an easy mark—but however flippant he could not dismiss the fact that the Loyalists were absolutely helpless. He refers to them as "destin'd Game," "affright'd," and "Defenceless." The fourth stanza of the verse describes Loyalists scattered throughout Tyron County as "the vanquish'd Train":

> By hounds pursu'd, the timid Hare
> Thus flies in vain; the tainted Air
> In vain She leaves her Foes behind
> They follow still, secure to find
>   And track her winding Maze!

The opening stanza of the poem speaks of Schuyler's power. On the one hand, Odell wants to dismiss "the valiant Hero" as an outlandish fool. On the other, he seems compelled to acknowledge that Schuyler's men are the "well-trained Pack":

> Hark, hark! the valiant Hero comes!
> With screaming Fifes, and roaring Drums,
> > To search the Vallies through!
> With clamorous Din, in eager chase,
> The well-trained Pack, from place to place,
> > The destin'd Game pursue.[7]

Odell's self-effacement—"And what but timid Hares are We, / O Schuyler, when compar'd to thee, / . . . Accept my feeble Praise"—is followed by a prediction that warns Schuyler: "The dauntless Tiger smiles at fear; / But when he sees the Lion near, / He smiles at fear no more." Odell relied exclusively on the British Lion. As "the Tory Hunt" has it, Schuyler prevailed because "no Carleton checks his bold career." Who would think of William Howe, settled in Halifax, Nova Scotia, as the British Lion?

Mockery in four-liners, such as Odell used to offer his "feeble praise" for Schuyler, was a worthless weapon against rebel attacks. Without an immediate and formidable show of force by the British regulars, "affright'd" Loyalists were on their own. Such strength did not materialize in early 1776; where was it going to come from? Had Carleton been instructed to mount an attack against the rebels *within* the colonies? With Howe gone, the Loyalists watched Washington, now with the field essentially to himself, begin to entrench in Brooklyn, Manhattan, Long Island, and Westchester. Howe's withdrawal, then, must have appeared the very embodiment of treachery.

For "The Tory Hunt" Odell uses the pseudonym "Yoric," the name of the parson and advisor in Laurence Sterne's *Tristram Shandy* and the sentimental parson in *A Sentimental Journey*. The choice shows us Odell's plan to handle grave matters with a light touch. Here and in future poems he bids the reader to look at the world in order "to laugh at its follies, to pity its errors, and to despise injustice," as Sterne wrote to a friend about Yoric's aim. Considering the mystery surrounding General Howe's inaction, Odell's choice of a genial persona is both politic and self-protective.

If Odell could not fathom Howe's plan, he did have opinions on why the country was in the midst of revolution when there was no clear reason for war, colonists were more prosperous than at any other time in their history, and disputes could be negotiated as they had been in the past. As Odell understood the situation, "a few" from the rising middle class had been consumed by "envy, malice and spleen." Having attained all the power and wealth they could through legal and quasi-legal means, ambitious mobsters were becoming dangerously restive. They were blocked from the highest circles of influence by the established families, almost all Loyalists, whose ties with England were lucrative and secure. The only way these ambitious few could advance, Odell predicted, was by forcing the old guard out and taking its place in government and commerce.

Thus Odell blamed the "few" who burned with misguided ambition and pride. To further their own interests, he maintained, they ruthlessly planned to lead the many to slaughter. Potter's study of Loyalist ideology instructs us: "The Loyalists also believed that there was no widespread, spontaneous discontent and no legitimate grievances of a magnitude to justify revolution. The Revolution came about because the masses, easily swayed and vulnerable by appeals to their passions or baser instincts, were duped by a crafty and unscrupulous cabal."[8] In "Song for a Fishing Party Near Burlington, On the Delaware, in 1776" Odell points an accusing finger at these few: "While thousands around us, misled by a few, / The Phantoms of pride and ambition pursue, / With pity their fatal delusion we see; / And wish all the world were as happy as we."

It is plausible that Odell sincerely hoped that a bloc of conservative and moderate Whigs, together with the Loyalists, could come to terms. Moderates on both sides were the majority and they agreed with each other more than not. The speaker of "Song" reflects on the possibility of truce. Here is peace, "Away from the noise of the fife and the drum, / And all the rude din of Bellona . . ." His message is plain: "A truce then to all whig and tory debate."[9] But the radicals made reconciliation impossible, and they controlled the streets if not always the Congress. Under the circumstances Odell's only realistic option was to press for reconciliation anyway.

Odell Censured

By the summer of 1776 the Continental Congress had an impressive "law"-enforcement network against which individual Loyalists, however prominent, could not mount effectual opposition. It is therefore surprising that Odell became more aggressive. Perhaps he felt emboldened to take a stand in loyalty's behalf by the news of Carleton's success, or even by the mere presence of almost one hundred unarmed British soldiers. Perhaps he was trying to measure the changing mood as the Revolution slowly came to Burlington.

The king's birthday became his occasion. Traditionally celebrated on June 6 with parades, fireworks, dinners, and toasts to the glory of the empire, it was observed with discretion, if at all, in June 1776. Nevertheless, Odell composed "Birth-day Ode," a public tribute to George III, for the captive British officers to sing in honor of "Great George's Royal Line." The officers "to avoid offence, had an entertainment in honor of that day prepared on an island in the river Delaware, and they dined under a tree." Whatever their intentions, they did not "avoid offence." Mud Island was only a few miles from Philadelphia, where the Continental Congress was in session. The arousing sounds of "Birth-day Ode," accompanied by regimental music that had "liked to have made a Rumpus," as a contemporary observer described it, were duly noted by the delegates.[10]

"Birth-day Ode," which refers to the French and Indian War when British regulars fought on behalf of the colonists, marks the occasion when Odell's relationship with the Whigs began to deteriorate without pause. In a stout ringing tone his verse defends British soldiers held captive by "Thankless Sons!" in a "hostile land":

> When by foreign Foes dismay'd
> Thankless Sons! ye call'd for aid,
> Then we gladly fought and bled,
> And your Foes in triumph led!
> Ever Sacred be to Mirth
> The Day that gave our Monarch birth!

> Now by Fortune's blind command,
> Captives in your hostile Land,
> To this lonely Spot we stray,
> Here unseen to hail this Day!
> Ever Sacred be to Mirth
> The Day that gave our Monarch birth![11]

When the British officers were transferred to Maryland by order of the Board of War, Odell honored them by composing "A Farewell." It is about blind "Fortune," who has "betray'd / The Brave" after the French and Indian War. The song was signed Yoric, a pseudonym with which Odell had come to be identified and which certainly fooled no one. The sobering footnote to the manuscript copy reads: "Observe—it was not without danger of being even persecuted as Enemies, that the Loyal Inhabitants ventured to entertain the British Prisoner with any hospitality or even civility."[12]

Apparently Odell was not censured for offering hospitality, but in this he was lucky. Loyalists were being viciously "persecuted as enemies." On June 25 former governor Franklin, who had urged the New Jersey Assembly to break away from other colonies bent on war and make a separate peace with England, was arrested, judged a virulent and dangerous enemy by the Provisional Congress, and sent under guard to Connecticut. There Odell's patron would remain a prisoner of war for two and one-half years, mostly in Simsbury Mines, a veritable hellhole—the Andersonville of its day.

All known Loyalists who traveled about the colonies were regarded with suspicion. Odell's critical views had already been scrutinized by the New Jersey Provincial Congress, and his comings and goings were carefully watched. Yet on July 18, 1776, Odell's family set out for Shrewsbury, forty miles away. "The General Warrant," his poem about the experience, begins: "A Lawyer and Parson, their Wives and little Brats [mere children] / Set out upon a Journey, far away, / Before the rising Sun had blinded Owls and Batts." What these opening lines lack in charm they make up for in provocative clues. We know that Odell's wife was fully four months pregnant. In 1776 it was considered most risky for her to travel, risky to the pregnancy and to her own life.

It is unlikely that Mary and William Franklin Odell, both under three, were delightful travel companions. In all likelihood Odell was trying to escape with his family to the protection of British lines.

Howe's army had arrived on Staten Island July 12. Within days frigates from Admiral Howe's fleet could be spotted crossing Sandy Hook, New Jersey, on the way to link up with the army in New York. Shrewsbury was about fifteen miles south of Sandy Hook, and from there it was relatively easy to get to Staten Island. Many hundreds of Loyalists from New Jersey, New York, and Connecticut did travel to greet Howe and supply him with news of Loyalist strength. Unaccompanied by their families at this early stage of the war, most probably did not plan to stay behind British lines. Odell, however, had clear motives for leaving Burlington. His church had been closed, Franklin had been arrested, and he had been censured by the New Jersey Provincial Congress. It was dangerous to remain in Burlington, and he felt defenseless. Thus he reported to the secretary of the Society that the times were at best precarious in the months before the Declaration of Independence, "difficult and dangerous" after. Most of the people in his mission remained loyal to the Crown but concluded that their only weapon was an arrogant silence, the rebels having conducted themselves "in such a manner as to preclude any effectual opposition."[13]

The Odell party was stopped by a member of the Provincial Congress carrying a warrant that directed the colonel of the militia to arrest and search them: "Congress had received well-grounded information that they had undertaken to convey some Letters of dangerous consequence on board a Man-of-War near Sandy Hook." The search, Odell said in the song poem, proved *"fruitless."*

"The General Warrant" is filled with flippancies. Odell ridiculed the search as he had ridiculed Schuyler's Peacock Expedition. A frightening confrontation is described as a rude interruption, which the knowing speaker, if tolerant enough, can dismiss as a droll diversion. Briefly, the song tells this sad tale. Silly, overanxious Mr. President has been tricked into thinking that an honest group of travellers "With cheerful hearts at ease" are agents of "the darkest Plot." So undiscerning and overzealous is Mr. President that he is taken in by a blind owl, "The Optics of Suscipion," who comes to him in a dream and bids him foil a "dark Design!" in progress. "Tories in disguise" are abroad, and it is up to him to save "the sinking *State*." Quickly he gives the order—"Pause, arrest and search them round"—and burns with impatience "till the Prize is found!" Odell nonchalantly reports the outcome that so disappointed Mr. President:

> The *Culprits* are pursued, your Orders are
>   obey'd,
> A Troop of Col'nels come, a *fruitless* search
>   is made;
> Their pockets all turn'd inside out,
>   Open'd locks,
>   Caps and Smocks;
> But not a Letter after all this rout![14]

Odell ends the song on a stoical note: those who insult majesty are more witless than evil, and the wise can hope for the time when "banish'd Laws" are restored.

Odell's song works hard to amuse, but it cannot conceal the fear that something is really wrong. Certainly Odell knew it. Yet it is not uncommon for war poets to present a confident posture, or even affect bravado, in their public writing at the same time that they express uncertainty, even despair, in writing intended to remain private. Odell spoke with several voices. His lighthearted poems are stays against chaos.

Odell's travel brought immediate censure. On July 20 the New Jersey Provincial Congress ordered him, "a person suspected of being inimical to American liberty," to "confine himself on the East side of the Delaware river, within a circle of eight miles from the Court House in the city of Burlington."[15]

By July 28 Odell found the lines he needed in Horace (book III, ode 3) to convey his fury with "Tyrant rage," and his resolve to stand "firm and steady" in the face of it. More copies of this piece are among the Odell Papers than anything else he wrote. His translation of the Latin INSTUM ET TENACEM PROPOSITI VIRUM appears in full:

> No civil frenzy, no dark frown
> Of Tyrant rage, no sweeping gale
> On Ocean fiercely rushing down,
> Can make the Good man's courage fail.
> Though Jove himself, with mighty hand,
> Should hurl his thunder round the land;
> Though Earth's foundations burst away,
> Unhinged at once the Starry Pole,
> Amid the Ruins no dismay
> Would shake his firm and steady Soul![16]
>
> J.O.
>
> July 28th, 1776

At the same time that he wrote about standing firm in the face of "civil frenzy," Odell petitioned the legislature for a more lenient punishment. His obligations extended well beyond the eight-mile limit. Parishioners came from Burlington and Mount Holly, and also "from the Country in the Neighborhood of the Towns." But his offer to sign a less stringent parole, a promise not to correspond with the enemy or to furnish them with provisions or intelligence, was denied on August 1 by the New Jersey Provincial Congress.[17]

Odell's poem about this eight-mile parole, "Tis Large Indeed—'Tis Monstrous Large He Cried," dated October 29, 1776, relies on mild, entertaining banter to serve his completely serious purpose. He takes Yorick (sometimes spelled Yoric) as his own persona; the character of Puff would have been known to the Loyalist audience as the "late Representative" in Jonathan Sewall's 1775 amusement called "A Cure for the Spleen." Puff is one of the deluded common folk, who comes to his senses when a Loyalist patiently enlightens him about England's legitimate demands based on precedent and justice and the colonists' obligations based on precedent and common sense. The opposing parties come to friendly terms over tankards and pipes. Considering Howe's New York strategy, which stunned the Loyalists, Odell would have been extraordinarily unwise to be argumentative. Nevertheless, he means to call attention to several alarming facts of colonial life now that loyalty has become a criminal offense.

First, the New Jersey Provincial Congress has made it impossible for him to continue public worship. St. Mary's and Mount Holly are but two of many churches in the area that have been closed. Anglican ministers who would not retract the Oath of the King's Supremacy had no choice but to shut their doors. Odell explains the "perplexing situation" to the secretary of the Society: "Since the declaration of Independency the alternative has been either to make such alteration in the Liturgy as both honor and conscience must be alarmed at, or else to shut up our Churches, and discontinue our attendance on the public worship." Odell did not "hesitate a moment," and like most of the Anglican clerics in Pennsylvania, and all but one in New Jersey, he elected "to suspend . . . public Ministrations rather than make any alteration in the established Liturgy."[18]

Second, the Provincial Congress has so restricted his activities that it is impossible for him to move freely among his parishioners, for whom he is both minister and physician. Odell may have been put on parole because of his letters censuring "the measures adopted by the Provincial Congress," his suspect trip to Shrewsbury, his part in the "Birth-day Ode" rumpus, or all three. He does not mention these embarrassing incidents in the poem. Peter Puff claims that Yorick's single, simple offense involves the recitation of the liturgy: "His *Oath* requires his praying for the King," a practice the "Rulers" forbid "so hard the present Times are grown."[19] Odell has always referred to dissenters and Whigs interchangeably. In this poem he implies that Whigs have fastened on the prayer as evidence of an Episcopate Conspiracy, and that they continue to believe that he aspires to become a bishop.

Third, those who have not identified themselves as rebels are easily and often intimidated. Open conversation between neighbors holding only slightly differing political views is becoming altogether impossible. These three issues, the "Pulpit barr'd," the "Pris'ner on *Parole*," and the climate of fear that have forced friends into enemy camps, make up the substance of the poem.

"Tis Large Indeed" is a dialogue between Peter Puff and an

unnamed neighbor. Puff sets out to describe and explain what has happened to Yorick, their mutual friend, a pseudonym for Odell. At first Puff's companion will not respond seriously. Who could "wear a Ring that double eight Miles wide!" he jokes. No mortal man, he must be "some huge Wight, to Brobdignags ally'd." Puff assures him that the "*Wearer*" of the Ring is "no more than common Size" and that without his "*Gown,* he looks like other Men."

So informed, the wag guesses that Puff is talking about "some Prelate," and he quickly concludes that the Ring "is for the *Diocess.*" Possibilities dawn rapidly. A bishop of a wealthy See must want a reward; perhaps this bishop "pants with Ardor" and thinks his "*Diocess*" too small. Perhaps he wants "to be call'd his *Grace.*" Puff reminds him that there are no bishops "within a Thousand Leagues" and as concerns the aspirations he ascribes to Yorick, he is flatly mistaken: "Your Fancy Sir runs wild with Court Intrigues." The sorrowful truth is that Yorick is "a Pris'ner on Parole!" The ring means that he cannot travel beyond the eight-mile radius "Drawn from the Center." Parodying Lovelace's "To Lucasta in Prison," Puff's friend quips that Yorick's body may be bound, but not his soul. Even if the Circle is guarded by "a *Chain* of *Kings,*" Yorick's soul is free to fly the place. Puff is determined to rescue Yorick from literary banter. Imprisonment is a "solemn Matter," not merely a subject for "sportive play." Yorick can be neither minister nor physician to those who have always counted on him. How can he bleed the pleuritic patient? Puff's companion holds to the "sportive" course and offers a flip remedy that reveals Odell's sophisticated understanding of medical possibilities, when most colonial practitioners had little acquaintance with more than homegrown elixirs. Yorick must "Adopt the *eastern* Mode to soften Pain." We can "Provide the *Doctor* with a *little* Bow / Plenty of Arrows, small & fine and neat." Thus equipped, he can "stand within his *Magic* Ring / And fire away."

Puff, who is running out of patience, takes up the most important issue of Yorick's imprisonment. How is he to execute the "Parsons Care?" How is he to perform a christening? Again Puff's friend has a ready answer: We can give him "A Speaking Trumpet, and an Engines Spout." He "may *speak* and *sprinkle* and the Things made out." Puff can listen to nonsense no more. Yorick is not to be laughed about, and his "woe" is not one of merely private implications. His church has been closed:

> His Pulpit barr'd—his Flock without the
>   Fold,
> Stand pensive, watchful till their Locks
>   grow Cold,
> The Threshold choak'd with Weeds, the Path
>   obscure,
> The rusty Hinges, 'speak the dormant Door,
> The Spiders web, with many a heedless Fly,
> Spread o'er the Key hold, and demands your
>   Sigh—   (74-79)

Now Puff's friend pays attention. What is the reason, he asks, for "this strange unheard of Case! / Are *Priest* and *People* too, devoid of Grace?" Puff has the answer: "His *Oath* requires his praying for the *King*." The liturgy had become the center of controversy.

Finally grasping the significance of Yorick's parole, and understanding the need to get at the heart of the matter, the jester leaves off jabbering and raises questions about a prelate's obligations to the king and to the people and, with an emphasis on deliberation and reason, he discusses priorities.

George may well be the lawful ruler, but are not "Men of Virtue" more important? Is it not right for the prelate to pray "for each *good* Man . . . Who wish again for Peace to rule the Land"? If the king can be counted among the well intended, then such prayers include him. If the king shows indifference while the "Country *bleeds*," then the prelate does not owe him a prayer. Puff recognizes the wisdom of a justifiable compromise and accepts its "Consolation." Odell may or may not have been willing to compromise, but "Tis Large Indeed" certainly acknowledges the complexity of the issue. Historically Anglican clergy had on many occasions exercised the right to take issue with a king.

Toward the end of the poem Puff has become confident. He chats on, convinced that he and his friend share common sense. With abandon and vigor, he dubs Yorick's "*eight Mile* Circle" a prison of disgrace and predicts that Yorick's "Prison-Makers . . .

soon will take his *Place*." Now Peter Puff has gone too far. His friend becomes frightened; he first admonishes Puff, then threatens him:

> How dare you utter such abhorrent Words,
> Presumes to talk of Prisons for your Lords;
> Your Lords & Masters Sir—my Pow'r I'd
>   show
> I'd lay such Chaps as you in Dungeon low.—
>   (122–25)

Puff fumbles for apologies. What he meant to say was that "soon their *Wisdoms* meet, where *he's confin'd* / And *then* you know, they're all in *Prison join'd*." The poem ends with Puff's whimper: "do not cuff, my Head till rough, / For this sad Stuff———."

Odell's "Tis Large Indeed" speaks of his parishioners' military and hence psychological weakness as tantamount to surrender now that "overt polarization" had become a reality in Burlington. Without organization and support provided by the British military, the Loyalists were beaten before they started.

Saviors of an Empire

By August 25, 1776, Howe had dispatched fifteen thousand British regulars and five thousand Hessians to Long Island. They outnumbered Washington's "untested" army by nearly two to one. Having "completely outmaneuvered the rebel forces," the British drove the remaining nine thousand Continentals into Brooklyn, but "On August 29, instead allowed Washington to escape during a providential fog to Manhattan."[20] Then Admiral Howe, in his capacity as peace commissioner, arranged a meeting with Franklin, Adams, and Rutledge on Staten Island. Howe was only authorized to issue pardons. Despite his off-the-record assurances that taxation policies would be changed, his instructions demanded that the rebels surrender before peace talks could begin. There was no way Howe could get around that stipulation, and with scorn the Continental Congress rejected his offer. The pattern continued.

Howe trapped nearly five thousand rebels on lower Manhattan, but allowed them to escape up the Hudson river.[21] Then

General and Admiral Howe brought their case to the people. They issued a joint declaration "not only inviting all colonists to converse with them on the means for restoring peace and reuniting the empire but also asserting that the king was disposed to revise royal instructions and acts of Parliament which the colonists complained of." This declaration received "the scorn of rebels, loyalists, and British officers alike."[22] It did not "trouble the Howes that they were sacrificing opportunities to gain decisive victories over the rebels; temporarily they were willing to subordinate all else to their hopes of finding a permanent reconciliation—to their dreams of a triumphal return to England as saviors of an empire."[23]

While Loyalists were "struck dumb" by what the Howes were doing during the fall of 1776, the Continental Congress issued orders quickly and with conviction. After the Declaration of Independence, merchants as well as ordinary citizens were required by law to accept Continental dollars, not sterling, in payment of debts. The Continental dollar, or Jo, as it was called, was the creation of the Continental Congress. This policy of issuing money by fiat, money backed by literally nothing tangible, led to an inflation bizarre by any standards. During October 1776 more than twenty-five million paper dollars were in circulation. The *New York Gazette* "contained a satirical advertisement calling for a quantity of Congress-dollars as a particularly cheap form of papering for the walls of a house; and, at about the same time, a lampoon insinuating that this money was then commonly used for kindling fires, lighting pipes, shaving, and still more ignoble uses. . . ."[24]

Odell probably saw the *New York Gazette*. A footnote to his poem, "The Law, in Days of Yore, How Harsh!" about the absurdity of Continental currency reads: "A Jo is now so highly priz'd, / I saw one lately advertis'd!"[25] This poem was probably written in October, on the heels of "Tis Large Indeed," but it is not dated. Both pieces share a similar jaunty tone born of necessity, and both present Puff as the abused, confused citizen unable to outwit the powers that be. Moreover, "The Law, in Days of Yore," which the narrator refers to as "the Sequel," talks about "the Bow / Trumpet and Pipe"—items that signified Yorick's inability to fulfill his responsibilities in the earlier poem.

This poem gives us further insight into Odell's understanding of what motivated the rebels. Loyalists typically described the Revolution as a plot to create havoc so that "dull Cobblers' sons" could wrest political power from those who supported imperial authority. Continental currency furthered the design by allowing debtors to erase their mortages and the like with worthless money. The penalty for refusing Continentals as "fair and legal tender" was jail. The poem begins by addressing the inverse relationship between creditor and tardy debtor and comments on the clerks' newfound status in church and state:

> The Laws, in Days of Yore, how harsh!
> When, in default of ready cash,
> The Creditor's Good-will to gain,
> The tardy Debtor oft was fain
> To beg, in humble terms, and pray
> The favor of a short delay!
> But now—to mortify your pride,
> The favor lies on t'other side:
> Now, in their turn, the Rich are roasted.
> "Your balance?"—"O, Sir, 'tis not posted—
> My Clerks have been employ'd, of late,
> To settle things in Church and State.
>
> (1–12)

Yorick, the penniless minister and physician, explains to Puff that although he is *"compell'd"* to settle his account in his favor, "As all true *Sons of Freedom* do" because "the *Laws direct*," he will not compromise his good name. A moral issue is at stake. Now people wear "rags along the Street," and should he take advantage of this? Let the "Legislators produce the Stone" and, by magic, remedy the situation they have created. He will not disappoint Peter Puff and forgo his *"gentle heart"* and *"manly mind."* In a word, he will not succumb to selfishness and "barter a good name for pelf!" Although Odell does accuse the rebels of being self-serving, he registers his disapproval with humor. The nature of the Howe brothers' activities dictated his moderate tone. His next poem, "Yoric's Address," though not dated by month, was probably written in late November 1776. It is significant that here Odell speaks with arrogance. By now he had reason to hope that all the feared "Mischiefs" would be prevented.

Odell Optimistic

Despite the Howes' plan not to devastate the Continental army, the British won decisive victories at Fort Washington and Fort Lee. With late November and early December came Washington's disastrous retreat through central and southern New Jersey with General Charles Cornwallis in pursuit: "So terrified did the Americans now seem that many British officers believed the Continental army would dissolve if pushed further."[26] Because the Continental army was on the verge of utter collapse, New Jersey neutrals and less-than-resolute rebels rushed to take the Oath of Allegiance to the British Crown offered by Howe. The state of panic was such that "almost three thousand Americans accepted the offer in a few weeks, including one signer of the Declaration of Independence."[27] On December 1, Cornwallis was in mid-New Jersey "awaiting General Howe's permission to follow Washington, who with the remnants of his army was seeking a refuge from the British on the west bank of the Delaware."[28] The war could not possibly continue.

Odell's brief piece called "Yoric's Address" makes its case in stern measures. His most personal statement thus far, it is actually a diatribe. Odell finds the worsening political situation repulsive, and he is not afraid to be candid, because the British army will be victorious after all. Such are the times that "Reptiles by Magic are fitted to fly / . . . While they, who by Nature were destin'd to soar, / Must creep into holes or be driven from Shore!" Stanzas 6 and 7 follow:

> How the Din of Bellona now roars in our Streets,
> And Discord usurps these once happy Retreats,
> Where Love and Simplicity lately were seen
> To dance on the primitive pastoral Green.
>
> Though Madness wou'd kindle implacable hate,
> And seems to be driving us on to our Fate,

> Let us hope Heaven still may restrain her career,
> And in mercy prevent all the Mischiefs we fear!

It is significant that Odell does not ask for revenge; rather, he wants a return to law and stability. "Yoric's Address" closes: "And hold to the end what we cherish'd in youth, / Chaste Love and Simplicity, Honor and Truth."[29]

Life quickly became more complicated for people throughout southern New Jersey, however. Burlington, set among the contested towns, the Delaware River, and Philadelphia, was in a pathway both armies needed for troop and supply movements. The Quaker Margaret Morris offers the best contemporary picture of Revolutionary Burlington in her *Journal*, and a good deal of what she tells us has to do with Jonathan Odell, its leading citizen.

4 *Confrontation and Flight*

In early December 1776 all advantage was with the British. Rumor had it that they planned to set fire to Philadelphia. The Continental Congress fled to Baltimore. Panicked residents in Philadelphia and nearby Burlington fled to the safety of the countryside. Odell's good friend the widow Margaret Morris trusted in Providence and determined to stand firm.

The people of Burlington were caught between substantial numbers of Hessian land troops pursuing Washington without effective opposition and rebel Gondola men protecting the Delaware River. If fighting broke out, Burlington was an obvious target. Odell knew that the Hessians intended to take post in Burlington for the winter. If that happened, the likelihood of violence would become a certainty. The citizens of Burlington were aware of their precarious situation. When numbers of Hessian riflemen came to town and demanded quarter for the night, several prominent spokesmen presented their case to the Hessian commandant, Colonel von Donop. Odell acted as the interpreter.

Speaking in French, Odell told von Donop that if the Hessians occupied Burlington, the galleys offshore would surely cannonade the town. Von Donop advised him to arrange a meeting with Commodore Thomas Seymour of the Pennsylvania fleet. It would be up to Seymour to guarantee the safety of noncombatants bound to suffer in the crossfire. The negotiating process got off to a quick and hopeful start. Captain Moore, a Gondola officer who happened to be on shore, agreed that the citizens ought to be spared and accepted the role of intermediary between the bargaining committee and Seymour.[1] He set off at once. Burlington waited for Seymour's answer.

Odell had reason to worry about a Hessian occupation. Soldiers had taken quarter in the area before. Even if the rebels left without a fight, the people of Burlington did not want the Hessians in their homes for the winter. However, they had no real way of persuading them to leave. All they could realistically hope for was that von Donop would treat them fairly. The first meeting between Odell and the Hessian commandant augured well. Mrs. Morris wrote in her *Journal* that Odell was pleased "that he might be of service to People of the Town" and that "the Commandant seemed highly pleased to find a person with whom he could converse with ease and precision."[2] Apparently Odell secured von Donop's concern for the people and property of Burlington. Given the Hessians' reputation for plunder, this was all-important. Von Donop promised that he would oversee discipline. If he could be assured that there were no men in arms against the king, he could give his word that Hessian troops would answer to him personally for any disorder they caused.

At this point Odell confessed to harboring a benign cache of rebel goods. He told von Donop that the wife of a longtime friend who was now a colonel in the Continental army left Burlington and before "her departure had begged of him on the footing of former friendship, to take into his house, & if he might be permitted, to keep as under his protection, some few things, which she could not remove. . . ."

Odell said that he was of course "ready to give him an exact account of such of her effects," to which the commandant replied without a moment's hesitation, "Sir you need not be at the trouble of giving further account of those things which you have so candidly mentioned, be assured that whatever affects have been entrusted with you in this way, I shall consider them as your own, & they shall not be touched." Odell and von Donop had thus established a relationship, for which the people of Burlington had cause to be grateful. Odell, Mrs. Morris concluded, "was encouraged to hope he might be still further Serviceable to his friends, in the full persuasion that nothing would happen to disconcert the peaceable disposition that was making. . . ."[3]

However, before the Gondola captain reached the galleys, Seymour received intelligence that a party of Hessians had entered Burlington. He "ordered up 4 Gallies to fire on the Town wherever any 2, or 3 persons should be seen together—."[4] While the opening cannonade was in progress, Seymour heard and refused the request made by the Burlington committee. John Jackson, the editor of Mrs. Morris's *Journal*, explains that Seymour was adamant because he knew that many Loyalists, neutrals, and lukewarm patriots resided in Burlington. Jackson supplies Seymour's answer: ". . . no mercy could be shown if Hessian troops were quartered in Burlington, but . . . he would order the destruction of the town by immediately opening fire with all the guns of the fleet."[5]

This information was promptly conveyed to von Donop who, being without heavy armament, realized that he would not be able to reply effectively to bombardment from the river galleys. He told Odell that "he should be sorry to be the occasion of any damage or distress to the inhabitants." Therefore he decided to withdraw the Hessian troops (to nearby Mount Holly according to Morris's account; to nearby Bordentown according to Odell).

Although von Donop's soldiers left Burlington, the gunfire continued, "cruelly insulting the Town and keeping it in Alarm." Most of those still in Burlington when the cannonade began joined those who had fled earlier in the countryside. Margaret Morris stayed, hid her four children in the cellar, and entrusted their "Safe keeping" to "the Guardian of the Widows & the Orphans." The Gondola men later claimed that they were sure they were firing at Hessians. Mrs. Morris called them "River Tyrants" and remained unconvinced: ". . . it was impossible to conjecture how such behavior could have happened, or suspect such a mistake, tis no wonder the Town was exceedingly alarmed, looking upon it in light of a cruel, as well as unprovoked piece of treachery. . . ."[6]

Odell Hunted

By morning the Gondola men occupied Burlington. They threatened to burn the town if the people did not reveal where the Hessians were hiding. Suspected Loyalists were more hated than mercenaries, and the Gondola men conducted a diligent search "in & about the Town for Men distinguished by the Name of Tories."

Mrs. Morris reports that the Tory hunters were especially anxious to find members of the bargaining committee who had been seen "entertaining" von Donop. In charming, idiosyncratic spelling, she writes that Odell, "*esteemed* by the *whole family* & very *intimate*, in it," had been informed that "a party of Armed Men were on the search for him": "The spirit of the Divil still continued to rove thro the Town in the shape of Tory Hunters—a Message was delivered to our intimate friend informing him a party of Armed Men were on the search for him, his horse was brought, & he retired to a place of safety."[7]

The two other committeemen "who entertained the foreigners were pointed out to the Gondola Men." They "were seized & dragged on board." Mrs. Morris hid Odell at Green Bank, a mansion to which Odell was no stranger. She had bought this home of Governor Franklin's, which was confiscated after he was forced from office. Odell and Mrs. Morris settled on an escape plan. The old mansion contained a "Secret Chamber" that included an augerhole, a serviceable hideout complete with a straw bed and a box partially filled with sawdust. Located in a room at the end of a long entry hall, the chamber was behind a trick closet. When the closet shelves were removed and the closet back pried off, the auger-hole appeared.[8] The closet had also been rigged with an alarm system connected to a warning bell wired to a knob on the inside of the front door. Someone in the house could ring the bell, even "violently," and the sound would not be heard by those standing outside. In other words, a person about to open the door to an enemy could ring the bell, giving the hunted person ample time to hide.[9]

Odell might have eluded the Tory hunters without incident had not Mrs. Morris's fourteen-year-old son become curious about a spyglass he found at the mill next door. The boy "took the glass

& resting it against a tree, took aview of the fleet—." Curiosity proved dangerous. He was observed by Gondola men on board their river galleys. They "suspected it was an Enemy that was watching their Motions—They Mannd aboat & sent her on Shore—." When the Tory hunters came to her door, Margaret Morris, for all her nervousness, distinguished herself as a scrappy conspirator. Her immediate task was to regain composure: "aloud knocking at my door brought me to it—I was alittle fluttered & kept locking and unlocking that I might get my ruffled face, alittle composd, at last I opend it." She found half a dozen men, all armed. They demanded the keys for the empty house next door so that they could search for the "D–d Tory who had been spyg at them from the Mill—."

Mrs. Morris rang the bell, the signal she and Odell had agreed on, and when she thought he had sufficient time to protect himself in the auger-hole, she began to chatter about her fear of Hessians. The Tory hunters were taken in by her dissembling:

> when I thought he had crept into the hole—I put on avery simple look & cryd out, bless me I hope you are not Hessians—say good Men are you the Hessians? do we look like Hessians? asked one of them rudely—indeed I dont know; Did you never see a Hessian? no never in my life but they are Men, & you are Men & may be Hessians for any thing I know— . . . but Ill go with you into Col co [Col. Coxe's] house tho indeed it was my Son at the Mill, he is but aBoy—meant no harm, he wanted to see the Troops—[10]

With Odell "concealed like athief in the auger-hole," Mrs. Morris led the party of armed men on a search of the vacant house next door, "but we could not find the tory—." Satisfied that Green Bank was above suspicion, they continued to search neighboring houses, "but no Tory could they find. . . ." The Tory hunters gone, Mrs. Morris worked more openly in Odell's behalf. The *Journal* resumes: ". . . in the Evening I went to Town with my refugee, & placed him in other lodgeings—." On December 18 she reported Odell's good luck: "our Refugee gone off today out of the reach of Gondolas, and tory hunters—."[11]

There was a great deal of talk in Burlington about making the area a "Neutral Island." Several attempts, all unsuccessful, were initiated by the townspeople in their effort to protect themselves from the vicissitudes of war. Only the heavy snows of December 20 and 21 brought them quiet days and the hope of more. Although troop movements had slowed, tension ran high. The Hessians quartered nearby had to be tended to. Mrs. Morris, apparently one of the few women who remained in Burlington, writes about the burden of cooking for them. There was the ever-present worry about pillagers: "put all things of gold & silver out of their way—& all linen too, or youll lose it," warned a friend.[12] And worse still was the "Number of Sick & wounded brought to Town. . . . There were several pritty innocent looking lads among them, & I simpathized with thier Mothers when I saw them preparing to return to the Army." The morale of the Continental army had reached near bottom. Mrs. Morris heard rumors that officers feared that most of their men planned to desert.

The outlook changed dramatically on that fateful Christmas night when Washington surprised the presumably drunken Hessian contingent camped in Trenton. The victory, desperately needed by the rebels, altered the course of the war. Burlington became a hub of activity. Hundreds, perhaps more than a thousand, soldiers passed through town offering accounts "Contradictory and various" about battle plans and consequences. Confusion reigned, but Mrs. Morris reported that Odell was safe.

Odell Critical of Howe

Odell survived "the rage of Tory Hunting" and fared better than most. On December 22 Mrs. Morris wrote that "he has got a Protection as its called," making it possible for him to travel with relative freedom. The *Journal* entry dated January 13, 1777, places him with his family in Burlington. Mrs. Morris is matter-of-fact about his return and amused to think that one day she will remind him of his anxious hours in the auger-hole. For her the possibility that Odell might one day become a bishop was still a reality: "The Earl of B———n, who quitted his Habitation of the first alarm of the Hessians comin in—is returned with his Family—We have some hopes that our Refugee will be presented with apair of lawn Sleeves, when Dignities become too Big to creep into his old Auger hole—but I shall remind him of the place, if I live to see him created first B——p of B——n."¹³

Mrs. Morris wrote that Odell was back with his family on January 13, but it is not possible to pin down his whereabouts during these turbulent days with any exactness. Whereas Loyalist diaries typically record the escape from a hunting party, and weeks of wandering to the safety of British lines, Odell was particularly skilled and lucky to get from place to place even with a "Protection." Tory hunters were extraordinarily determined in heavily populated Loyalist areas. New Jersey was treacherous territory.

In two letters Odell wrote from New York to the secretary of the Society he sums up what had happened to him during the terrible year just passed. On January 7 he chronicles the sequence of events that "obliged" him to leave his "wife & 3 children (the youngest not five weeks old) and to ramble as a Refugee God knows when to return." Writing in "great haste," he stresses the point that he has, from "the beginning of our troubles," acted as befit the character of a missionary, but became nonetheless the victim of "jealousy and misrepresentation." He continues with an account of the parole that was an obvious injustice, but he kept his oath until mid-December when, hunted by "River Tyrants," he escaped, "taking refuge among the King's Troops." He uses the opportunity to speak about his considerable financial losses during the last year: "You will oblige me by informing the Society that I lost almost all the Fence around the Point last Winter by the Soldiers quartered in the Barracks at Burlington, who made Fuel of the Rails, which after all will probably be again destroy'd this Winter."¹⁴ Odell goes on to say that he has no prospect of drawing "Salary from my Parishioners in [the] future, until this unnatural War is happily terminated, and when that will be God only knows, though I hope it may be nearer than many are apt to imagine."

In this letter for the first time Odell complains to the secretary about the "measures" that "brought the troops into the country" and he emphasizes the Loyalists' "defenceless condition": ". . . I believe every candid man will wonder why we should be punished for having been left defenceless and for having solicited safety from the Kings Troops in our defenceless condition, even supposing us to have assented to those measures which had brought the Troops into the country & even to our Doors. . . ."[15]

Odell's letter of January 25 is a brief, measured account of his situation, in which he repeats much of what he wrote in "great haste" in the earlier letter. He again emphasizes that the people of his mission, "almost unanimous in their aversion to independency," had been intimidated by Congress.[16] They depended on the British army, which failed them, in this case by not crossing the Delaware in pursuit of Washington and then by not capturing Philadelphia. Odell speaks plainly of his impatience: ". . . if the Kings Troops on their arrival at Trenton had crossed the River Delaware (which notwithstanding the want of Boats was most undoubtedly practicable) they would certainly have taken possession of Philadelphia without any opposition."[17] Instead, they yielded to inambition, camped at Trenton, and lost their opportunity.

Thomas Jones, a judge of the Supreme Court of New York and a contemporary observer, also discussed these amazing events. Like Odell, he successfully voiced the Loyalist perspective: "If only the British General, with his army, had passed the Delaware and gone to Philadelphia, from whence Congress, and all its warm advocates had fled! where the inhabitants were impatiently awaiting the British troops' arrival, wishing personally to congratulate them as their deliverers from the tyranny, the arbitrary power, and oppression, of Congress. All would have been safe." Washington's army, at crossing the Delaware, was reduced to less than three thousand men. Had the pursuit been continued, Washington would scarcely have stopped short of Maryland, and perhaps would have gone even into Virginia. Philadelphia stood ready to open its gates to the conqueror and to give him a hearty welcome as her happy deliverer.

> Had the General gone to Philadelphia . . . the whole country between Philadelphia and New York would have remained open and quiet, . . . Had this been done, the American rebellion, in all probability, would have closed with the year 1776. But unhappily for America, as much so for Great Britain, a victorious army, in full pursuit of a flying incon-

siderable enemy, was stopped upon the banks of the Delaware, and instead of taking necessary steps for the security of New Jersey. . . . [the campaign] ended in the loss of the province, the ruin of hundreds, and the lives of thousands.

In his own letter to the secretary of the Society, Odell referred to the British army's excuse for not crossing the Delaware because of a lack of boats. He and Jones agree that the excuse will not bear scrutiny. Jones denounces the claim that Howe did not have access to sufficient boats as nonsense. There was a full boat yard in the back of headquarters, and also barns, and thus wood and thus rafts, which could have transported the whole British army across.[18] Instead Cornwallis marched his army back to New York, stopping at towns on the way, including Burlington.

On February 3, 1777, Washington issued a proclamation from his Morristown, New Jersey, headquarters "ordering all persons who had taken protection from the Kings Commissioners, to come in 30 days & swear Allegiance to the united states of america, or else repair with their Families to the lines of the British troops." Mrs. Morris notes the ultimatum in her *Journal* and adds, "What will become of our Refugee now."[19]

Odell's painful dislocation helps to comprehend his circumstances, his mental processes, and his behavior. He was frustrated to the point of desperation, caught between two irreconcilable and inexorable forces, with no independent power to determine his fate. His predicament, assertive haste, and narrow escape with the heroic help of his Quaker friend Margaret Morris all dramatically exhibit his frustration, and that of other Loyalists.

5 Odell for the Loyalists and General Howe

For the overwhelming number of Loyalists who took refuge in New York, life was a constant struggle. Friends of Government who were once "lords of thousands" had to make do with dollar-a-day pensions begrudgingly allowed by the military. Cut off from their property and means of earning a legitimate income, bewildered refugees often became destitute. Penniless women and children from the surrounding colonies crowded into the city daily: "It was impossible to see them without pain, driving about the streets in the forlorn attitudes . . . making fruitless searches for the husbands and fathers."[1] The poorest subsisted among the ruins of the Burnt District, blighted sections caused by the great fire of September 1776, which leveled hundreds of homes. The most well intentioned of New York's wealthy Loyalists could not meet the needs of these incoming thousands.

The British army appropriated housing, and rents were high for what remained. Food and firewood were also scarce. Farmers near the British outposts on Long Island could supply only a fraction of the city's needs. Food brought in by the British fleet was often spoiled, and what there was went first to the army. Tensions mounted between the military and the Loyalists while proposals circulated announcing Howe's authority to grant pardons, and rumors abounded that Washington was to be rewarded with an earldom if he would negotiate. In sum, garrison New York was "a pathological environment."[2]

Whatever their situation, Loyalists had little choice but to indulge Howe, though among themselves they raged. For them, Howe's Sword and Olive Branch policy was a source of complete frustration. Yet in public they had to choose their words with discretion, and Odell spoke for them, carefully. He composed a "Song" for St. George's Day, April 23, 1777. Rivington, who had returned with Howe's troops, was now printer to the king. He renamed his newspaper the *Royal Gazette* and in it reported that the "Sons of St. George" would celebrate the birthday of England's patron saint with traditional banquets and attendant entertainments at Heck's Tavern and King's Head. At one place or the other, Odell used the occasion to register his anger over Howe's military "inepititude." A diplomat by necessity, he explained away his accusations.

The first two stanzas of "Song" offer standard praise of mighty Britain and close "Huzza! Huzza! Huzza! O ye Britons! the Ocean is yours, / Your Empire extends and your Glory secures!" Then follows an abrupt shift, a call to arms, which makes up the second part of this three-part song. What else, at the banquet table on that St. George's Day, would New Jersey Loyalists have been thinking vividly about but Trenton and Princeton? New York Loyalists no doubt fastened on the battles of Long Island and White Plains. Odell's message in the fourth stanza could not be more straightforward:

> 4
> Britons, strike home!
> Let Vengeance, Vengeance arm your hands!
> Arm, arm and pursue! Arm, arm and pursue,
>   And quell the frantic Bands!
> Now, seize and destroy! Seize, seize and destroy,
> Destroy, destroy the frantic Bands![3]

There was no getting around the hard fact that Loyalists had to cultivate Howe's sympathy. Military "inambition" must somehow be shown to be a virtue that would soon pay off. Yet it must have been with great difficulty that Odell wrote the politic part three of his "Song." Stanzas 5 to 10 praise Royal George who, ever mindful of justice and mercy and soft pity, sends his "gallant Chiefs"—"The name of Howe, so long revered"—to "Go heal despairing Freedom's wound, / and bid Rebellion cease!"

Within weeks New York Loyalists took heart, when Howe's campaign to overrun Philadelphia got underway. The largest city in the colonies as well as the seat of the Continental Congress, Philadelphia had long been a prize. The area had important businesses; its farms were productive suppliers; and eastern Pennsylvania was filled with Loyalists awaiting the protection of His Majesty's forces before they could identify themselves.[4] Odell records his optimism in a "Song" composed for the celebration of the king's birthday on June 4, 1777, in New York. This "Song" looks back to the time when, under British rule, the colonies "flourish'd . . . / And Plenty flow'd in with a yearly increase." Rebellion has changed all that, but the time when the "deluded . . . Multitude" holds sway is almost at an end. The fourth and final stanza of "Song," signed Yorick, signals hope and does not forget William Franklin in the Simsbury Mines:

> Though Faction by Falsehood a while may prevail,
>   And Loyalty suffers a Captive in Jail,
>   Britain is rous'd, Rebellion is falling!
>   God save the King!
> The captive shall soon be releas'd from his Chain,
>   And Conquest restore us to Britain again,
>   Ever to join in chaunting merrily
>   Glory and Joy crown the King![5]

Franklin's situation was indeed desperate. So bitter was the feeling between rebels and Loyalists that when Franklin appealed to Washington for permission to travel a few miles and visit his dying wife, Washington answered that he did not have the authority to approve such an action; he would send Franklin's request along to Congress. Congress refused.[6]

Odell, however, continued to escape real harm. When Howe's thirty thousand land forces, supported by Admiral Howe's British fleet on the Delaware River, moved on to Philadelphia, he went with them. Margaret Morris reported seeing Odell in mid-June on board a British boat, one of hundreds cruising the strategically important Delaware. Burlington was not secure and Odell did not come ashore. Mrs. Morris did have the satisfaction of seeing him point to her house and later hearing that he said: ". . . in that House lives a Woman to whom I am indebted for my life—She Sheltered me when I was driven from my home."[7] Mrs. Morris also wrote of a brief talk with him in Kensington, a town on the banks of the Delaware at the limit of the British lines, about two and one-half miles from Philadelphia, where she visited her aged father. This meeting is the subject of the June 14 entry, the last she wrote in the *Journal*. The Hessian commandant von Donop was killed in the fighting around Burlington. We do not know how Mrs. Morris fared.

It was probably about mid-June, and from the deck of a British ship on the Delaware, that Odell wrote "Canto," which begins "Twas on the twenty-fourth of May." The poem deals sarcastically with the rebels who came to power in Burlington after the battle of Trenton and with the Loyalists who switched sides to accommodate the new leadership and thereby protect themselves. Since that "well-fought day" at Trenton, Burlington citizens have scrambled to align themselves with the "Militia folks" who have invaded the town. To avoid fines and escape prison, numbers have pressed themselves on corporals, heretofore to their "muster-roles a stranger." Of course they will "run, / At any glimpse of danger," but they have satisfied their momentary purpose—to see to their own safety without thought of principle. This was not an unusual circumstance. Almost everywhere people pledged allegiance to the army that happened to be in power at the time.

The character of the rebels, created leaders on the spot, most "amuses" Odell. With "The People's Majesty" in charge, confusion reigns. "Nor Age, nor Wealth, nor Rank, nor Birth, / Avail'd with these true Sons of Earth." What these opportunists want most is Tory property. They keep a strict eye on such goods, thinking if they are "mov'd, / That they might share the booty." Power is in the hands of the mob:

> The mob tumultuous, instant Seize,
> With venom'd rage, on whom they please—
> The People cannot err.

> Can it be wrong, in Freedom's Cause,
> To tread down Justice—Order—Laws—
> When all the Mob concur?[8]

The consequence of mob rule is disastrous. Odell was from the start a resolute spokesman of Loyalist ideology holding that "deference and respect for authority were vital to the long-term health of the body politic." There was a "natural aristocracy of men of superior merit whose role it was to guide the community,"[9] and when respect for this authority breaks down, there is anarchy. In "Canto" Odell gives us a vivid picture of mob rule.

What a "grand Town Meeting" these mobsters make up: "Each Vagabond from whipping Post, / Or stranger, stranded on the Coast, / May here reform the State." Here a "motley train" wielding "Clubs and Bayonets" will not be persuaded by common sense; the worth of the Continental dollar is falling "like Lucifer, to lower Hell," and the people will lose all because they have tried to grasp too much. But the crowd is more interested in the chairman's motion "That Tories, with their Brats [mere children] and Wives, / Should flee to save their wretched lives. . . ."

If a Loyalist man had already fled behind British lines, Governor Livingston, who succeeded Franklin, had the authority to allow his family to join him. "Humane" motives aside, the policy evolved because dependents tended to "obstruct the Commissioners from seizing and disposing of the personal estate and effects of their husbands in the execution of the commission, by secreting and concealing the same."[10] The women must have had a hard time of it. We know that Ann Odell remained in Burlington with her three children, but we have no knowledge about her daily life.

Odell's hope that the British would retake Burlington came to nothing. The plan to trap Washington in New Jersey did not work, and Howe pulled out completely, "leaving the entire state in rebel control."[11] August 18 found Odell back in New York, writing to the secretary of the Society again about his bleak financial future: "Since my being driven from home I have been occasionally employed as a Deputy Chaplain in the Army which has afforded me some relief; but still my losses are very considerable and without the aids I have received from England my Family must have suffered greatly." He observes that the Society has docked his salary from the time he left Burlington at Christmas 1776, to the present. Assuming this to have been an oversight on their part, he has acted to rectify it. For the total "Sum I have this day drawn Bills on the Treasurer of the Society . . . in which I hope I shall have the approbation of the Society."[12] In further defense of his action, he informs the Society that the vestry of Burlington voted to continue his salary "notwithstanding my absense," and although they may not be able to carry the vote into effect, "it gives a pleasing proof of their friendly disposition in these times of Trial." Odell thus implies that he expects the Society to come forward with concrete proof of their own friendly disposition. But Odell was not able to work out a satisfactory financial arrangement with the Society. Whenever he writes about his income during the war years, it is to complain about its insufficiency, and never does he mention the Society's contributions.

Howe Moves to Occupy Philadelphia

Fearful of the risks of an overland march from New York to Philadelphia, Howe sailed with his brother Admiral Richard into Chesapeake Bay. Maryland, a Loyalist stronghold like the other middle colonies, received the British army with provisions, so that it was well fed and rested for the march into Philadelphia. Concentrating on occupying as much heavily populated territory as possible, Howe did not confront Washington until the Battle of Brandywine. For the rebels Brandywine was a loss. Once more Howe had the opportunity to pursue Washington in retreat, but once more he "showed no disposition to force an action."[13] Instead, he issued a declaration on August 27 that concluded with an offer of "a free and general pardon":

> Considering moreover, that many officers and private men now actually in arms against his Majesty, may be willing to relinquish the part they have taken in this rebellion, and return to their due allegiance, Sir William Howe doth, therefore, promise a free and general pardon to all such officers and private men, as shall voluntarily come and surrender themselves, to any detachment of his Majesty's Forces, be-

fore the day on which it shall be notified, that the said indulgence is to be discontinued.[14]

Whereas rebels in British territory had a viable option, the Loyalists, without military leadership, were trapped between their colonial enemies who despised them and the British generals who ignored them. After Brandywine, while Loyalists despaired, Washington appealed for and within two weeks received nine hundred Continentals and about twenty-two hundred militia from Maryland and New Jersey, so that he was prepared to fight with Howe again.

As this contest for superior position dragged on, Odell came to realize that he and his wife would not soon be reunited. In the fourth and final stanza of "The Way to keep him," dated New York, September 10, 1777, he affirms his affection and constancy though they remain apart: "Never can the fairest Face / Draw me from thy sweet Controul, / Nor the longest Absence chase / Thy dear Image from my Soul."[15]

Washington and Howe fought again. The "Paoli Massacre" threw Washington on the defensive, and on September 26, Howe marched into Philadelphia. Without control of the Delaware River—American forts blocked all traffic—the city would not be "full of comfort and ease."[16] Howe gained access to the river when Washington's attack on British-held Germantown failed.

With General Howe and Admiral Howe safe in Philadelphia, and British ships moving freely up and down the Delaware, Loyalists again became optimistic. On October 8 the Old Church and King Club met in New York, for the first time since the start of the rebellion. Odell composed a song for the occasion in which he relegates the "Perils and Pain" of recent years to the oblivion of a sick past. Despite false starts and so many failed opportunities, the British army had come through. Now, no longer terrified by "Congressional Tyrants,"

> We are once more assembled, all happy and free,
> In social good humour to drink, chat, and Sing,
> And toast—what we love in our hearts—Church and King.[17]

He speaks of their fears "When Honor was Baseness, and Loyalty Treason!" as well as of the contradictory rebel policy of demanding liberty for themselves while denying liberty to Loyalists, and of the time when "the Nation ran mad." Finally he prays that the "Leaders of Faction" be arrested, "And all the World love, in their hearts, Church and King." Victory seemed there for the taking. In the December 13, 1777, edition of the *Royal Gazette*, Rivington reported that Sir William Howe's army "were never since the commencement of the rebellion, in higher spirits and in better health than at present—."

Odell Works for Howe

Whatever Odell's thoughts about Howe's military hesitations, they remained private, and there is evidence that he had established himself in Philadelphia by the end of December. On January 5, 1778, Howe appointed him Chaplain to the First Battalion of Pennsylvania Loyalists[18] and named him Superintendent of the Printing Presses and Periodical Publications, for which Odell was paid fifty pounds.[19] Odell's immediate task was to persuade his old friend, the Philadelphia versifier Joseph Stansbury, to revise drastically his "New Year's Verses 1778," scheduled to appear in the *Pennsylvania Evening Post*, because the poem denounced Howe.

In Stansbury's manuscript version, Jove's mandate directs the gods on Olympus to give over to Howe the prized instruments of war, and they comply: Astraea presents her Sword, fierce Mars his Chariot, "Alcidies his Club and his Bow." By prolonging the war unnecessarily, Howe has squandered these gifts and made a mockery of the gods. Winthrop Sargent observes in the notes to *The Loyal Verses of Joseph Stanbury and Doctor Odell* (1860) that the unpublished version "offers renewed evidence of the disesteem Sir William Howe felt during his occupation of Philadelphia. . . ." It is indeed reasonable to assume that the fifth and final stanza of Stansbury's original echoes the feelings of the Loyalist majority.

    5
HERMES wand now was useless—no Snakes would unite,
    The Olive in vain was display'd,
For Blessings no longer attended the sight,
    And LOYALTY fled from its Shade:

> The Gifts sent to Burgoyne return'd to the Skies,
> 	Despairing he yielded his Arms,
> And VENUS disgusted perceived with surprize,
> 	A Mortal preferr'd to her Charms.

The afternote, which follows stanza five in the manuscript, reads in part: "This was alter'd by Yoric's advice, and a complimentary turn given to the whole of it."

Yoric's reworked version was printed as a broadside. The explanatory note to the title "New Year's Verses" tells us that it was "Addressed to the Kind Customers of the Pennsylvania Evening Post by the Printer's Lads who carry about the same." The poem with the "complimentary turn" was assured a wide circulation. Pennsylvania Loyalists publicly offered Howe a cordial welcome. In the printed poem the gods bestow the same gifts, but here Jove's instructions to Howe speak over and again of the dispensation of Mercy:

> This Balance and Sword to thy Hands we consign,
> 	Let Justice preside in thy Breast.
> But temper'd with Mercy let Justice appear,
> 	Majestic, yet mild and serene;
> And still in the Heat of your martial Career,
> 	Let the Prospect of Peace close the Scene.[20]

Had Odell not appeased Howe, he would surely have lost his income as well as his public voice. His most important contribution to the British cause while he was in Philadelphia was made in his capacity as Superintendent of the Printing Presses and Periodical Publications. A series of five political essays called "An Answer to the DECLARATION of the GENERAL CONGRESS" appeared in the *Pennsylvania Evening Post* between February 17 and March 25. These essays record what the Howe brothers wanted the rebels to understand about their options and, by implication, the military "hesitancies." As a peace commissioner, Admiral Howe had tried and failed to convince the Second Continental Congress to negotiate. The leaflets he distributed to the citizenry brought scorn. Now, for the last time, the Howe brothers brought their case before the people. The content of the essays all but states that the speaker's rationale is Admiral Howe's, although three of the essays are unsigned. Two are signed Britannicus, the pseudonym adopted by Odell and his collaborator, Samuel Seabury.

The first essay opens by challenging the assertion that "the body of men who lately sat in Philadelphia" are in fact "the representatives of a people," and defends the divisions of powers within the British government as well as its undeniable right to "tax all the subjects of the British empire." That "representation is inseparable from taxation" is a misguided principle: "Upon this principle, scarce one in twenty five of the people of Great Britain is represented." Historically "representation never accompanied taxation in any state," whether in ancient Rome or in the internal workings of the present New England colonies.

The British towns of Chester and Durham, "like the Americans, considered their being excluded from having representatives in an assembly by which they were taxed, a grievance." Accordingly, they petitioned the legislatures of Henry VIII and Charles II, respectively, "for the privilege of sending members to Parliament." Both petitions were successful. "Had the Americans, instead of flying to arms, submitted the same supposed grievance, in a peaceful and dutiful manner, to the legislature, I can perceive no reason why their request should be refused." Instead, they have "abrogated to themselves all the functions of sovereignty," and they affirm that they owe Britain nothing for the land on which they live. "Their very enemies could not meet them on more advantageous ground."

In the February 21 edition of the *Pennsylvania Evening Post* Odell publishes an account of sums expended by Britain in behalf of the colonies from their inception and an account of financial assistance rendered in the "last expensive war," which Britain fought to protect the colonies "not only from danger, but the very fear of danger." In return for a guarantee of "unlimited security" and "prosperity," the colonists have become "parricides." Britain "at the expense of *seventy* millions, and the lives of many thousands of her bravest soldiers, has removed every apprehension of the French and Indians." And "had Canada remained in the hands of the French, the colonies would have remained dutiful subjects" because of their "incapacity of defending themselves" against the habitually feared French. No one can effectively argue this point.

The treaty that ended the French and Indian War brought prosperity, not "public ruin," as the colonists deceitfully claim. It was "just and proper" for Mr. Grenville to assume that the colonists "should bear a proportionable share of the national burdens incurred by the war."

"An Answer" on February 24 blames the Stamp Act crisis on a divided Parliament, specifically on Lord Rockingham and his "motley junto" of "factious persons" so eager to "disgrace the minister" that they have defeated "the interest of the country" (a position Gage took in 1775). These bickering ministers, immersed in petty politics, abetted a war where there might have been none.

> The opposition in parliament, in short, committed themselves too far in favor of the prejudices of the Americans, with regard to the stamp act, to support it with vigor, when they themselves, very unexpectedly, came into office a few months after it passed into law. Though their view of the object changed with their elevation, they found that the flame which their own factious speeches, in the preceding session, had raised in America, was too vehement to be extinguished without either force or concessions. A natural timidity of disposition, joined to the common want of firmness which accompanies novelty in office, rendered them inclinable to purchase quiet for themselves, at the expence of the future advantage of their country.

The problem had been caused by a "disappointed faction in this kingdom" that encouraged Americans to reinterpret "judicial regulations." That "disappointed faction" had nothing to do with the present parliamentary administration as "the Americans falsely insinuate," and this present administration had the wisdom and authority to negotiate with mercy.

The "divided Parliament" essay probably did not have much of an impact. Between 1773 and 1778 life in the colonies had turned upside down. To castigate ministers embroiled in a 1765 crisis was to reach back to the distant past. The Britannicus essay that preceded this one deals with the never-trusted French, and the Britannicus essay that follows also deals with a current problem: money.

In the March 13 issue attention is given to "the abuses in the emission and circulation of paper money." Britannicus traces Britain's wise policy of prohibiting the colonists from issuing paper money. The Land Bank of 1741 is singled out as well as a 1763 Rhode Island attempt that reduced the worth of a dollar from eight pounds to six shillings and eight pence when "emission took place." Actually Britannicus had dozens of instances to choose from. Despite the prohibition, individual colonies had often printed paper money to extricate themselves from an immediate financial crisis. The long-term result was almost always confusion. Britannicus warns that the practice of substituting paper currency for silver and gold "has opened a gate for the entrance of public ruin." In the past, Parliament kept strict control over the financial health of the colonists: "Happy it would have been for the bulk of the colonists, that this uncontroulable authority had still extended itself with vigor over America, on the article of paper money."

The final installment of "An Answer to the DECLARATION of the GENERAL CONGRESS" appeared in the March 27 edition of the *Pennsylvania Evening Post*. The central issue is taxation, not relating to tea, which was of little concern, but relating to smuggling. The author (I assume Howe) goes to some length to establish as fact that "the right of the British legislature to bind the colonies in all cases whatever, is founded on long and immemorial usage, and uniform and uninterrupted practice." He comes close to dealing with the deep-seated grievances of the colonial merchant class, but he does not squarely confront them.

From 1763, when Parliament amended the Navigation Acts to restrict colonial shipping, colonists began smuggling. The illicit industry quickly thrived because it allowed colonial merchants to undersell English merchants by a substantial margin, and because England found it almost impossible to enforce the Navigation Acts from three thousand miles away. Molasses from the West Indies, the most profitable commodity smuggled into the colonies, reappeared as rum, which in turn was shipped to West Africa in return for slaves. Parliament passed the Molasses Act, which stipulated that molasses for the colonies could only be imported from England. In response to the Molasses Act, the smuggling trade flourished "and by the time of the American Revolution smuggling was an enterprise so respectable even the devout engaged in it without uneasy feeling."[21] "An Answer" names Mr. John Hancock "a most notorious smuggler." (Circumstantial evidence suggests that Hancock's shipping business was actually a smuggling operation, but both of the allegations brought against him were dropped for lack of evidence.)

A strong system of Vice Admiralty courts would have hurt the smugglers seriously. In the years immediately preceding the war, the British established a number of Vice Admiralty courts and enacted legislation, namely a general warrant called a Writ of Assistance, that gave custom agents virtually unlimited power to search ships carrying suspect cargo. "An Answer" charges: "Smugglers found themselves incapable of carrying on their contraband commerce; and they inflamed an ignorant rabble, to serve their own interest, or to gratify their own revenge."

One senses from "An Answer to the DECLARATION of the GENERAL CONGRESS" that Howe knew what at least one major problem was and how England might settle it: In the face of a growing colonial merchant class, Parliament needed to revamp the restrictive trade policies, or do away with the new Vice Admiralty court system and allow smuggling to continue. The Boston Tea Party had made it clear that colonial merchants were determined to trade for profit. In fact, John Adams claimed that the damnable Writs of Assistance gave birth to the American Revolution in the first place.[22]

While Howe reasoned with opponents from his comfortable headquarters in Philadelphia, where he commanded more than thirty-eight thousand troops, Washington with several thousand freezing and half-starved troops was penned in at Valley Forge, less than twenty miles away. Daily, Washington begged the Continental Congress for supplies; daily, deserters straggled into Philadelphia and surrendered. Without question Howe had his most obvious chance to end the war. His explanation that a spring offensive would prove more effective because that "season should afford a prospect of reaping" success sounds like empty talk, particularly when we know that Howe planned to return to England in May.[23] From the Loyalists' viewpoint, if Howe had wanted to win the war, it could have been over quickly. Judge Jones considered Howe's advantage over Washington and fumed: "and to the surprise of everybody, General Howe never attempted to beat up the rebel quarters."

To compound this abomination, Jones continued, Admiral Howe and General Howe indulged themselves and senior staff with every wanton possibility imaginable. A pageant called a *Mischianza* that took place in late spring capped the season and summed up its character. Jones described this exhibition of dissipation, luxury, and wantonness with its faro tables, songs, plays, Philadelphia belles decked out in Turkish costumes, fruits shipped up from the West Indies, and cockfights, as "something before unknown to the New World, perhaps to the old." He concluded that the *Mischianza* was "laughed at by one-half the army, ridiculed by the inhabitants, damned by the Loyalists, and made a mockery of, by the rebels." He offered his substitute: "Had the General been properly rewarded for his conduct while Commander-in-Chief in America, an execution, and not a *Mischianza*, would have been the consequence."[24]

Early in May Sir Henry Clinton superceded Howe as commander-in-chief. Lord Germain, orchestrating the war effort from London, ordered Clinton to send almost half his army to the West Indies in preparation for a French assault. The rest of his army, too small to defend Philadelphia, returned to New York. Odell went with them, believing Howe had recommended to Clinton that he retain his fifty-pound commission to write in behalf of the British cause.

When the British army settled into New York, Washington installed Benedict Arnold as the ranking military officer in Philadelphia. With the British out of the area, the rebels convened an Inquisition for High Treason in Burlington County during November 1778. Jonathan Odell was named as one of the defendants. The document, signed by Tallman, Borden, and Coxe, among others, reads in part: "To wit—on or about the 1st day of January 1777, [Odell joined] the Army of the King of Great-Britain; against the Laws; of their Allegiance to this State; and against the Peace of this State; the Government and Dignity of the same." The document also notes that the inquisition duly "Ordered that the Defendants be called, which was done—and they not appearing Ordered that their second Default be Mark'd against them, and the Judgment finally be entered on Behalf of the State."[25] Odell's property was confiscated, one of twelve hundred estates that rebels had taken by 1778 in New Jersey.[26]

6 *Odell in Clinton's New York*

New York City is a mix of the privileged and the poor, and so it was in the winter of 1778–79. Hundreds of well-paid British officers milled about; apart from the successful Charleston campaign, they had little to do but amuse themselves. Commander in Chief Sir Henry Clinton set a hedonistic pace. Living in grand style in Dr. Beekman's mansion on the corner of 52nd Street and First Avenue, he immersed himself in hard drinking and gambling.[1] Enthusiasts could bet on horse races, cricket matches, and cock fights.[2] The port stayed open and the ongoing round of dinner parties stayed well supplied. Fashion-conscious gentlemen wore two watches, "the custom esteemed highly polite."[3]

Loyalists found the British command inaccessible. The rebels were quick to note that Clinton regarded civilians as an annoyance; his military government all but ignored their pitiful situation. Philip Freneau's "Sir Harry Invitation" begins:

> Come, gentlemen Tories, firm, loyal, and true,
> Here are axes and shovels, and something to do!
>   For the sake of our king,
>   Come, labour and sing;
> You left all you had for his honour and glory,
> And he will remember the suffering Tory:
>   We have, it is true,
>   Small work to do;
>   But here's for your pay

Twelve coppers a day,
And never regard what the rebels may say,
But throw off your jerkins and labour away.[4]

Refugee Loyalists were more alienated in Clinton's New York than they were in Howe's garrison town. Rivington's *Royal Gazette* barely paid any attention to them. Apart from lists of military promotions and offers of pardon, almost every issue contained news about slave matters—private sales, rewards for runaways, or auction dates. There were ads for cock gaffs, silver or steel, Madeira wine, rum, and tea just unloaded from British ships. Rivington announced the dates for the Dancing Assembly and inevitably advertised the imported, celebrated pills from Dr. Keyser's London laboratory for the cure of venereal disorders.

The theater was ever active. Rivington continuously advertised plays, complete with instructions as to which streets theater goers should enter and exit to avoid a traffic snarl. Some plays, such as *Richard III*, *Macbeth*, and *Beaux Strategem*, were well known, and some, such as *The Tragedy of Douglas*, were written by a member of the cast. Officers acted in the major parts. When on occasion young women took the minor roles, Rivington took notice of the attraction. Clinton's New York was alive with "amateur theatricals."

Odell, resourceful and accomplished, managed to live on the periphery of the Clinton circle. He had been introduced by William Howe and recommended by William Franklin, who was in New York because of a prisoner-of-war exchange. Possibly more important, Odell was John André's friend. He and André met in Burlington in 1776, when André was a prisoner of war. André was then transferred to Philadelphia in an exchange. A central figure in the *Mischianza*, he was one of Howe's "leading thesbians." Probably it was André who shaped Odell's immediate future.

Prologues for the British Stage

Throughout 1778 André was Clinton's tremendously popular aide-de-camp. Admired apparently by everyone, including the Loyalists to whom he gave sympathetic attention, he wielded considerable influence. An officer's power to curry favor had much to do with his position in Clinton's fast-paced social scene, and within that whirl André was "the most attractive and romantic of them all."[5] Particularly involved with the theater, André wrote prologues and acted in lead roles. Perhaps through his help, Odell took up residence on Wall Street, "where the best people then lived,"[6] or perhaps Franklin, who had been awarded a government pension of twelve hundred pounds, had something to do with Odell's enviable address. By Odell's own account, he was financially destitute.[7]

We know nothing of Odell's whereabouts between June 1778, when the British army left Philadelphia, and January 3 of the next year, when he delivered a sermon at St. Paul's in New York.[8] We do know that at about that time, he followed André's lead and wrote a prologue called "The World's A Stage and All the Men and Women Merely Players." It was more a sermon in verse than a prologue.

There was no lack of "Vice and Folly" in New York. Whatever the nature of the play on the bill, Odell cast a critical eye on his audience: "The Muse holds up her Glass, and if it shows / Our image there reflected," the wise course would be to reform.

> Yes—from the days of Mother Eve till now,
> We've been playing, and—the Lord knows how!
> The Stage of Life presents, at every view,
> A thousand shifting Scenes; and yet how few,
> Among the busy millions do we find
> Content to play the part by Heaven assign'd!
> Whoever turns to view the motley scene
> Must wonder what this crouded play can mean.
> Bless me! what running, panting, pressing, raving!
> What scrambling, grasping, hoarding and still craving!
> How much cajoling, coaxing, cheating, huffing!
> And then what lying, tatling, caneing, cuffing!
> Here all is dangling, whining, tearing, kissing;
> And There is peeping, prating, sneering, hissing;
> And all for what can any Mortal tell?
> Because, alass, Men know not when they're well.
> In love, in politics, in peace or war,

One day they covet, and the next abhor.
In this alone they seem to act by rule;
In every shifting scene to play the fool.
In every Scene, unsatisfied, unblest,
They languish still for "something unpossess'd;
  "And to the Coffin from the cradle
  'Tis all a wish, and all a ladle!"
Then let the mimic Scene, to candid eyes,
Exhibit Vice and Folly as they rise.
The Muse holds up her Glass, and if it shows
Our image there reflected—I suppose
The wiser way would be, instead of railing,
To take the hint, and rectify the failing.[9]

Described as "running, panting, pressing, raving! . . . scrambling, grasping, hoarding and still craving," Clinton's coterie would probably not have appreciated the scorn. Odell changed tactics.

"Immediately After the Tragedy of Chrononhotonthologos, A Prologue Intended for the Farce called Taste," refers to itself as "the Second Course" and differs completely from the "First Essay."[10] The narrator, not steadfast Yoric but frivolous Peter Puff, presents a bit of froth better suited to the inclinations of the audience. He calls himself "Your Caterer" and "De gustibus," claiming that he would search "Town and Country" to "feast the Connoisseur" and gather delicacies to "furnish" the "savory Dish." His aim is to please all: Rake, Virtuoso, "roaring Buck, and sober Penseroso."

Odell now had a clear sense of his audience. He did not return to the somber tone of "The World's a Stage," but offered next "Colonel Buckeridge's Prologue," a brief version of a Rising Glory poem "to beguile one Winter's Evening." Recognizable at once to colonial Americans, the always popular Rising Glory poem promised that the colonies would be a religious haven, and, without contradiction, a commercial center of unparalleled prosperity and repository of culture. In prewar poems Odell, like Freneau in "On the Rising Glory of America" and Trumbull in "An Essay on the Uses and Advantages of the Fine Arts," assumed that artistic achievement and prosperity depended on peace and order under British rule. Freneau deleted references to British guidance and substituted

Washington and Franklin in his revised edition. Predictably, Odell in 1779 sees the source of these treasures still as Britain, as he indicates in "See Britain's Sons approach the Western World":

> And time may come when this expansive Field
> An Ovid and a Horace here be found,
> And classic authors stamp this classic Ground;
> May charm with Homer's Spirit, Pindar's fire,
> A Maro's majesty, Anacreon's Lyre.
> . . . .
> Prosperity from colonizing came
> With Commerce which rich Industry awakes,
> "And blesses him who gives and him who takes."
> Say too, each art, each Science loves to roam
> And gad—like other Ladies, far from home.[11]

In the recent past "the woods hung waving round our Ears"—but in the future the colonies may boast a "Second Shakesp[e]ar[e]."

Odell's prologue focuses attention on one of the curious facts of the American Revolution: the colonists were united in many of their aspirations and these aspirations were becoming realities. No one yet earned a living from pen or palette, but a cultural life was beginning to emerge. At the onset of rebellion the general population was more financially secure and militarily safe than at any other point in their history. Odell associates these gains with Britain. Central to Loyalist ideology was the basic belief in a mutually beneficial union between Britain and America. It was folly to jeopardize the advantageous relationship.[12]

The Britannicus Essays

With Clinton's approval, Odell and Seabury wrote essays for the *Royal Gazette* throughout 1779 under the signature Britannicus.[13] The first Britannicus essay, entitled "To the Inhabitants of the revolted Colonies in America. On the Alliance with France," was printed in the January 6 edition. The essay deals with the French Alliance, a controversial subject for all parties concerned. For generations France had been the enemy. Highly placed rebels did not actually want an alliance with France, but they had no alternative. John Adams, for instance, was completely suspicious: "Receive no troops from her."[14] France was a monarchy, and the colonists were fighting for independence; France was Catholic, and anti-Catholic feeling in the colonies was pervasive; France was the enemy that the colonial militia had fought on and off for two centuries. Yet the colonies' need of France prevailed. The Continental Congress, issuing money by its own fiat, created a worthless currency that was not accepted on the world market. Too, the Continental Congress had no way of manufacturing munitions or gun powder on a large scale. Congress yielded to necessity. All the rebels could do was take France's word that it only wanted to gain the colonial market, to weaken England, and to regain prestige lost after the French and Indian War, and not to reclaim territory in North America, either in Canada or the Mississippi Delta.

France secretly financed the war from the start, but would not formally enter without assurance that Washington could win. His decisive victory over General Burgoyne at Saratoga was convincing. In March 1778 the Franco-American Treaty was signed, and a substantial French fleet commanded by Count d'Estaing set sail for the colonies. D'Estaing arrived in the summer of 1778. In January 1779 Britannicus addressed the situation.

The question was whether French assistance would ensure a rebel victory. Britannicus concludes that, given d'Estaing's performance at Rhode Island during the summer of 1778, "at present appearances are much against her, whatever your Congress and news writers may tell you to the contrary." Newport was a test case for the French fleet and it did in fact fail. Washington was furious: "I do most devoutly wish that we had not a single foreign officer among us except the Marquis de Lafayette."[15] The strained feeling was mutual. When d'Estaing left, he did not bother to tell Washington where he was going.[16] Britannicus is not surprised by their inability to work together. He notes d'Estaing's track record—"but no success, except his escape from the British fleet has yet attended him"—and points out that the British fleet has a history of superiority.

Britannicus reminds rebels nervous about the alliance with France and Spain that they ought to know what to expect: "and you may rest your hopes on them if you can be foolish enough to trust to a broken reed, on which you cannot bear your weight without piercing your hand." He dwells on France's reputation for deceiving her allies and challenges the French minister to Congress, Monsieur Conrad Gernard, to deny it. He concludes: "France will deceive you, unless you are cunning enough to deceive her, and expeditious enough to get the start in the blessed work of deception."

Britannicus stays with his theme—the danger of the French Alliance—and links it to his disgust with Parliament's misrule. He refers to the rebels' many "friends in England." Without naming members of the Opposition, he tells rebels that "your greatest success has been owing to them." They have impeded reconciliation. "Nay worse, they have kept up the most vigorous opposition to the measures necessary to the re-establishment of order & peace in the colonies, they have supported your cause at home, they have encouraged you in your opposition, and have given you all necessary advice."

Now that rebels have formed an alliance with France, "Your friends in England must, therefore, join in the national resentment against France, or they will lose their influence and popularity, which to them is the loss of everything. Your connection with France has, therefore, served to unite the British nation against you. . . ."

Britannicus concludes with an emotional "explanation" of England's Sword and Olive Branch policy. The British army's failure to end the war has become his obsession. He begins calmly enough, "Consider also, that the endeavour of Great-Britain has hitherto been to reclaim, and not to punish; to convince you of the superiority of her arms, and the moderation of her views, that she might invite and prevail upon you to return to that state of union with her, in which you formerly experienced so much happiness."

But while he recounts Britain's "mercies," Britannicus gives us nothing less than a wholesale indictment of the British army. Beginning with Howe's failure at Long Island and culminating with Clinton's failure in New Jersey, we hear the cry of Loyalist outrage:

> But why else has the British army been so often checked in the instant of victory? Witness Long-Island, York-Island,

White Plains—Why have no sacrifices been made to political justice, when you on your part so cooly and shamefully murdered so many of his Majesty's liege subjects, under the course of a formal trial? Why were the inhabitants of New-Jersey, when the whole province lay at the mercy of Sir William Howe permitted to remain quietly at home after taking an oath of fidelity to the King, instead of being brought to trial, and thence to the gallows. Compare, in this instance, your conduct and ours. Why were so many proclamations of pardon issued and such noble and generous terms of reconciliation offered? Why again were not Boston and Philadelphia burned when the Royal Army left them? Why was not New-Jersey ravaged when Sir Henry Clinton led the army through it last summer? You know those things could have been done; and you are foolish enough to attribute the forebarance to timidity. I tell you, it was because Great-Britain wished to reclaim and not to punish, to save, and not to destroy, to re-unite you to her empire, and not to desolate your country.

The British army did, in fact, stop "in the instant of victory" because too many ministers wanted reconciliation, not conquest. As Edmund Burke explained: ". . . the use of force alone is but *temporary*. It may subdue for a moment, but it does not remove the necessity of subding again: and a nation is not governed which is perpetually to be conquered."[17] What Britain wanted was trade, which could not exist if British America was filled with rebels "perpetually to be conquered." If need be, the Loyalists would be sacrificed. Although Britannicus was constrained by the nature of his public task, his voice virtually trembles with indignation.

Perhaps Britannicus envisioned the following scenario. A more realistic trading policy would have placated the Hancocks, and the repeal of the Intolerable Acts, which made it illegal to develop land in the Ohio Valley, would probably have placated the Washingtons and Franklins, who had substantial landholdings there. Members of street bands such as the Sons of Liberty would have been lucky to escape with their lives, but there the matter might have ended. Whether this sequence of events would have played out successfully is not the issue; the point is that, from all Odell wrote, we can assume that the Loyalists expected some such strategy on the part of the British army working in concert with Parliament in their behalf.

On February 27, 1779, the *Royal Gazette* printed the second essay signed Britannicus, and curiously numbered No. 5. The "missing" three essays can be accounted for only if Britannicus meant to include the "Treaty of Amity and Commerce" as part of his contribution. He probably did. Rivington printed this Franco-American pact, by which France virtually declared war on England, in the January 13 issue. The newspaper column begins not with the title, "Treaty of Amity and Commerce," but thus: "(The French Treaty, concluded, from our last)." This suggests a connection with Britannicus. No other material published in the *Royal Gazette* between January 6 and February 27 seems to be the work of Odell and Seabury. Further, the essay in question takes note of "an interruption of several weeks, owing to some unavoidable avocations" left to the reader's imagination. Like the first essay, this one is addressed "To the Inhabitants of the revolted Colonies in America," and subtitled "On the Continental Money."

Britannicus begins, "Many things remain to be said on the subject of your *French Alliance*, but at present I shall defer them, and proceed to discuss the affair of your paper money." Odell had written about Continental money in October 1776 in a poem called "The Law, in Days of Yore, How Harsh!" Between the appearance of that poem and the publication of this essay, worthless Continentals had created havoc throughout the colonial economy. Britannicus observes that the "Gazette very often *creeps out* among the Rebels, in spite of all the care that is taken by their leaders to prevent the *deluded* multitude from knowing *the truth*."

He appeals to his readers to consider their own financial interest "and the interests of . . . posterity." The Congress has compelled colonists to accept paper dollars in lieu of silver or gold even for the "payment of long standing debts, bonds, and mortgages." To refuse paper dollars is a most serious offense with severe punishment. Men of property have "no remedy." Britannicus charges that the congressional leaders, consumed with ambition, knew in the first place that "it is impossible, by the mere dint of compulsive authority, to give a real and permanent credit to paper money." Despite the fact that paper money "must sink to no thing," Congress continues to issue money by its own authority: "The press, which had been so long employed, was still kept going, and is to this *moment groaning with the labor of increasing the unknown amount of those promissory notes.*" Britannicus goes on with basic lessons in economics: money has a relative value depending on the worth of the gold or silver that backs it; the value of these metals has been accepted throughout the world as the basis of doing business; paper money that obviously cannot be exchanged for real specie has no value at all outside this country.

Britannicus presents a detailed account of Pennsylvania's economy between 1760 and 1764 and contrasts that prosperous time with the dismal present. The Continental dollar has depreciated at the rate of "more than *twenty for one.*" Consider that this depreciation was entirely "unavoidable," and that the congressional leadership was completely aware of this at the start:

> And now let me ask you, do you think your Congress were ignorant of this necessary and inevitable consequence at the very time when they began this blessed work of *creating* money, as they call it? Surely they were not. They knew it well, but your distress and ruin was an argument of little weight in opposition to the views of their ambition. If they knew, as they certainly did, from the very first, that their bills must unavoidably and speedily depreciate, in proportion to their increasing amount, where was their honor, their justice and humanity, when they forced the circulation of those bills upon you with such cruel and bloody penalties?

The victims are the thousands born to affluence who have been "brought to beggary" by this "inhuman policy." In his later poems Odell continues to insist with still more vigor that Continental leadership is deliberately and maliciously leading the colonists to certain ruin. In this essay he argues that they know it is impossible to restore "in any degree the credit of these nominal dollars." Their plan "to *borrow* five or six millions sterling money in gold and silver" can come only to nothing: "Even if the Congress should, by a miracle, find the nation who is mad enough to lend them such a sum, not one farthing of it could be appropriated to the redemption of the Continental money. It must go towards defraying the expences of this ruinous, this fatal war. . . ."

Odell delivered a sermon at St. Paul's and St. George's on March 21, but during these months he was most active as an essayist.[18] The next Britannicus piece appeared in the April 21 issue of the *Royal Gazette*. Again it is addressed "To the Inhabitants of the revolted Colonies in America." Again Odell and Seabury contend that a tyrant Congress falsely promises "relief from the pressure of the present calamity." Congress's continued effort to convince the rebels that the British army is about to withdraw from the colonies has been overturned by clear and present facts.

Here Britannicus overstates his case. The British were getting tired of the war. Merchants, having sustained severe losses, pressured Parliament to offer the Continental Congress a treaty that would end it. It gave the rebels all they originally asked for except complete independence. They would enjoy self-rule, but they would remain within the empire. Congress rejected the proposal. Britannicus glosses over this reality and focuses on the worrisome French Alliance.

"They now persuade you that a large French fleet and army will soon be upon this coast—that the British army will then be obliged to submit, and your independency will be fully established." From where, Britannicus asks, is this French fleet to come? After his failure at Newport, d'Estaing sailed to the West Indies, where he is "scarcely able to secure himself; not to mention the strong reports that he has been defeated and his fleet ruined." Supposing France were able to send another fleet, why should it? D'Estaing has made it known that the Americans failed him. They could provide him neither provisions, not even bread, nor an army capable of cooperating with him. Supposing again that France was able to send another fleet, how would the rebels pay for it? They have arranged to compensate in produce, but "can you get your produce to her markets? Your trade is nearly ruined."

France claimed to finance the Revolution for the purpose of capturing the colonial market after the war. Britannicus asks, will the French king "for no other advantage than a share for his subjects in the trade of America, run every risk, and bear every expence, to secure you in that Independency which your ambitious leaders have planned as the basis of their own aggrandizement?" He closes the essay by answering the question: "But to suppose that she will risk every danger and incur every expence, without any prospect of reward, or for such rewards as you can *afford to give*, is an opinion, of all others, the most weak and childish."

7
Working in Vain for the Cause

Odell's writing is of particular value because he viewed the Revolution from many angles. He believed that his "private correspondence" about the Benedict Arnold conspiracy, from May 1779 and later, would be "essentially useful" and more effective than his "political publications."[1] The loss of West Point, the rebels' most famous fortress, which had cost three million dollars and three years of continuous labor to repair, would mean the loss of the Hudson River. Apart from the logistical blow, the seriously weakened Continental army might not sustain the psychological assault.

Arnold secured the command of West Point because Washington liked him, trusted him completely, and supported his never-ending battle with politicians. Arnold's bickering with committees and conventions began when he could not account for all the monies he laid out to supply the regiment that overran Fort Ticonderoga in 1775. The legislature would not reimburse him to his satisfaction. Washington was impressed by Arnold's attempt to capture Quebec, although it failed. Arnold's leadership of a pitiful group of ragtag Continentals against Sir Guy Carleton's disciplined troops during a freezing winter displayed the sort of charisma Washington admired. Arnold's next major effort also failed. He lost a substantial part of the rebel fleet on Lake Champlain, and though he succeeded in discouraging Carleton and boosting rebel morale by the very audacity of his plan, critics in the First Continental Congress tagged him, at best, foolhardy. Nevertheless

Washington named him military commander of Boston when the British evacuated the city after the Siege of Boston. Soon after Congress released Arnold from command; Washington reinstated him. Congress passed him over for promotion; he resigned and reenlisted as a volunteer, and Washington promoted him. When Clinton pulled his troops out of Philadelphia, Washington appointed Arnold military governor of the city.

Arnold lived there in the mansion recently vacated by Howe, and he approved of the indulgences Philadelphians were determined to hold onto despite the absence of the pacesetting British army. Arnold welcomed the ambassador from the Court of Louis XVI in grand style. He attended the theater often and with enthusiasm. His élan quickly brought down the wrath of the Second Continental Congress. John Adams, shocked at such goings-on, put the case before Congress. They resolved firmly that "any person holding an office under the United States" should be dismissed if he "shall act, promote, encourage, or attend such plays."[2] The matter did not end there. Evidence accumulated that Arnold bought foreign goods for what they cost during the British occupation and sold them to the long-blockaded rebels at a tremendous profit. The Pennsylvania Council indicted Arnold on eight charges for actions that were at least inappropriate and at worst illegal. Predictably Arnold did not want a civil trial. A military man, he pressed Washington to arrange for a court-martial. Arrangements dragged on. Apart from feeling that he had long been abused by the Continental Congress, both he and his bride Peggy Shippen assumed that a British victory would ensure a bountiful postwar era. A rebel win would probably mean subsistence.

The Benedict Arnold Intrigue

Arnold contacted Clinton in New York by sending for Joseph Stansbury, who sold china and pottery in a shop on Front Street. Stansbury, like so many others in Philadelphia, had taken the Oath of Allegiance and Adjuration to Washington's government once the British army withdrew. As an established merchant, his comings and goings to the Arnold house with gifts and samples for Peggy to peruse caused no suspicion. Arnold gave Stansbury a message addressed to Clinton announcing an intention to offer his services. He instructed Stansbury to act alone. Once in New York, an overwhelmed Stansbury immediately confided in Odell. Because Clinton was inaccessible, Odell and Stansbury appealed to André, who agreed to take the part of liaison.

Following Arnold's first meeting with Stansbury the principals worked out an intricate correspondence system. Letters would contain columns of figures keyed to various editions of Blackstone's *Commentaries* or Bailey's *Dictionary*. The first number in the figure would stand for the number of the page, the second for the number of the line, and the third for the number of the word on that line. When this was not possible the letters were to be written with invisible ink: an "A" signaled that the letters were visible by water, "F" by fire.[3] For pseudonyms, André chose Mr. Joseph Andrews or Mr. John Anderson, Arnold chose Mr. Moore or A.C. or Monk, and Odell first used the familiar Yoric, then Mr. James Osborne, and finally Jasper Overhill. Of all the conspirators Odell did most of the coding and decoding.

Odell's first experience with these "confidential services" showed him to be a completely overanxious bungler. Arnold delivered a letter to Stansbury, who slipped it through the lines to Odell. Odell was to carry it to André. That he opened it instead was an obvious mistake that he could not hide. His handling of the letter rendered it "one indistinguishable blot," and he had no choice but to explain to André:

> I am mortified to death, having just received (what I had been so anxiously expecting) a letter from S——, and by a private mark agreed on between us, perceiving it contained an invisible page for you, I assayed it by the fire, when, to my inexpressible vexation, I found that the paper, having by some accident got damp in the way, had spread the solution in such a manner as to make the writing all one indistinguishable blot, out of which not the half of any one line can be made legible.[4]

The letter, now "toasted," became "too brittle for folding." Odell speaks of Stansbury mischoosing the paper and then confronts his own guilt. He promised "to guard against the like accident in the future," and by way of apology offered to decode Arnold's letters for André and code Clinton's dictated letters to André for André's convenience. André accepted.

Odell did more than simply interchange words and numbers. He worked to keep the conspiracy going, encouraging Arnold to think of the British commander's generosity. Clinton had rejected Arnold's initial offer to defect; he wanted Arnold to secure a command that he would then betray. In mid-June André wrote to Arnold: "Join the Army, accept a Command, be Surprised, be cut off—these things may happen in the Course of Manoeuver, nor you be censured or Suspected a Compleat Service of this Nature involving a Corps of 5 or 6000 men would be rewarded with twice as many thousand Guineas." In response to Arnold's previously stated concern that Congress and Parliament were on the verge of negotiating an end to the war, André was insistent, saying that Clinton "informs you with the Strictest Truth that the War is to be prosecuted with vigour and that no thought is entertained of giving up the dependency of America, much less of harkening to such a claim as you have been told by Congress affect to debate upon."

Arnold was keenly disappointed. First of all, he could not secure a command until he was acquitted of the charges brought against him by the Pennsylvania Council. Second, he wanted to be paid a specific fee whether or not his efforts proved successful. Time was important. André's assurances aside, there was much speculation that new parliamentary proposals similar to the one Congress rejected in 1778 were in the offing. The intrigue inched forward. Letters got lost. Stansbury became separated from his code book when he fled Philadelphia in fear of Tory hunters who were not convinced by his Oath of Allegiance to the rebel cause.

When negotiations resumed in July, Arnold continued to ask for a fee of ten thousand pounds to be paid him "whether this contest is finished by sword or treaty." Now André became impatient. Odell reasoned with him in a letter dated July 18, 1779, urging Andre to write "once more": "It gives me much pain to find my Friend's Friend has misunderstood your letter, and disappointed (I apprehend) your expectations—yet, if I might take the liberty to suggest my own opinion, I could wish you to write once more at least—as it cannot do any harm, and *may* possibly be still worth while." Three days later, Odell followed up his suggestion with another persuasive letter to André: "I am glad to find you are still patient enough to continue the Correspondence—something surely may be expected from it, and I am, I confess, still in hopes of something 'on a large scale—' otherwise the conduct already shown is utterly unaccountable to me."

At the end of July André wrote to Arnold to ask specifically for "an accurate plan for West Point." Arnold replied with inconsequential news about the fortress because "there was no Assurance given that his property in this Country should be indemnified from any loss that might attend unfortunate discovery." Odell suspected that this would be the last communication with Arnold.

Although in an earlier Britannicus essay he argued that an impoverished French government would not replace d'Estaing's damaged and ineffectual fleet, privately Odell worried about d'Estaing's strength. In possibly his last letter to Arnold via Stansbury, he asked for information "and especially accurate accounts of the French Fleet—where are they? what have they done? what do they meditate? what is the real State of affairs to the Southward? . . . It is of importance that we should know with certainty whether there is any serious plan formed of any *joint* exertions of the French and the Rebels, and if so, what may the plan be, &c *Authentic* information on these points, I beg you. . . ."[5] In the works was a joint venture by the rebels and d'Estaing's fleet to capture Savannah, Georgia, but Odell did not get the specific information he wanted. The Arnold intrigue itself had come to a halt.

Patriot Cabal and the "Deluded Multitude"

Odell turned his attention to political verse. His first major satire, "The Word of Congress," appeared in the *Royal Gazette* on September 18, 1779. It was a humorous piece intended to "mock, till mirth be stirr'd / In every vein." Odell could afford to relax a little. Comparatively speaking, this was not a time of utter urgency for the Loyalists. The Continental army was faring poorly, and the French Alliance was not going well. Although the British military had indeed dragged out the war longer than anyone in the colonies expected, the assumption had merit that superior British forces would prevail if given, finally, clear instructions from Parliament.

Odell was always critical of Parliament's indecisiveness. In "The Word of Congress" he registers his contempt by first allowing himself a few lines that exploit the anti-Catholic sentiment rampant in the colonies. Who would believe that "Congress should proceed in pomp to Mass?" "But still, in Britain, many disbelieve— / I own, 'tis hard such baseness to conceive." By now it was typical for Odell to accuse Britain of being inadequate to the occasion, and then to explain away the accusation. Under the circumstances he must have felt that he had little choice but to be prudent.

He begins this long poem by urging his friend P——n to free himself from the "painful task of thought," to take the poem that follows as an occasion for rest:

> Oft has thy lib'ral, thy capacious mind
> Griev'd for the wicked, sorrow'd for the blind;
> Deplor'd past errors, present ills bemoan'd,
> And anxious for the future deeply groan'd.
> Were it not best to quit these gloomy views,
> And join the sportful sallies of the Muse?
> Smile at those evils we must both endure,
> And laugh at follies which we cannot cure?
> Come, friend, and let us mock, till mirth be stirr'd
> In every vein, the many colour'd Word.[6]

While not all of the poem is "sportive sally," it can usefully be described as a roast of congressional leaders. Bedrock Loyalist ideology held that the naive multitude had been betrayed by a conspiracy of the "unprincipled" few "Patriot upstarts who did not merit the respect of discerning citizens."[7] Although by 1779 the conspiracy theory would not change the minds of citizens, "discerning" or otherwise, it was easy for Odell to scorn the "Patriot upstarts" then in power. As a group they were not of the caliber of the First Continental Congress. Jefferson was now governor of Virginia; Franklin and Adams were negotiating in Paris. Their often incompetent replacements must "undergo the lash of wit," and is it not fitting that these evil doers should "sustain / The glance of anger mingled with disdain?" At the command of Congress "Contagion seiz'd and uproar filled the land." These ambitious men "Law turn'd out of doors" and "the tumult fann'd." Ordinary people are their victims: "O hapless Land! O People void of brains! / My heart bleeds for you, tho' my soul disdains."

The congressional "Word" itself is seductive, opportunistic, ruthless: "I've known it suit itself to ev'ry plan— / I've known it lie to God, and lie to Man." "Truth's unerring pencil" has portrayed Congress as a group Satan would at once recognize as his own:

> she draws
> An hydra-headed form, with harpies' claws—
> Lo! num'rous mouths hiss, chatter, bark, or croak;
> One like Cacas belches fire and smoke;
> The second like a monkey grins and chats;
> The third squalls horrible, like angry cats:
> Here, you've the growls and snarlings of a dog;
> And there the beastly gruntings of a hog.
> Others affect the puritanic tone;
> The whine, the caut, the snuffle, and the groan.
> In Candour's accents falsehoods some disguise;
> While others vomit forth essential lies—
> All sounds delusive, all disgustful notes,
> Pour like a torrent from their brazen throats,
> To fill with rage the poor distracted crowd;
> Whilst Discord claps her hands, and shouts aloud.

While Congregationalist clergy convinced their congregants that they were rightfully, dutifully throwing off Pharaoh's yoke by taking up arms, Loyalists presented the rebel leadership as villains who would find company on the burning lake. Odell deals with individual congressmen less severely, however, and at times "The Word of Congress" approaches droll monologue.

In the poem, each has heard the word promising power and fortune, and each, for absolutely selfish reasons, has made it his own. One, the famed mathematician David Rittenhouse, resigned his genius to become a "paltry statesman," the "Vice-President elect of rogues and fools." Others, more typically, had nothing what-

Working in Vain for the Cause

soever to lose. When the vagrant Tim Matlack—"Game-cocks and Negroes were his sole delight"—obeyed the "factious Word," he was "Restor'd to Consequence." Mifflin "owed ten thousand pound. / Great thanks to Congress, and its doughty Word, / He cancell'd his debt by flourishing his sword!" Murder is saluted, illiterates become justices, paupers turn statesmen. Remarkably, Sullivan, a malcontent farmer, is named a general: "Head of a shirtless, shoeless gang he strides, / While Wisdom stares, and Folly shakes her sides."

The rebel propagandists were extraordinarily effective, and here Odell pays them homage after his fashion. He is building up to a sustained attack on that "scribbling imp," Thomas Paine:

> Swarms of deceivers, practis'd in the trade,
> Were sent abroad to gull, cajole, persuade;
> Scoff with the scoffer; with the pious pray;
> Drink with the drunkard; frolick with the gay:
> All things to all with varied art become,
> And bribe with paper, or inflame with rum.
> Others, apart in some obscure recess,
> The studied lie for publication dress:
> Prepare the vague report, fallacious tale;
> Invent fresh calumnies; revive the stale;
> Pervert all records sacred and profane:
> And chief among them stands the villain Pain[e].

When the thirty-eight-year-old Paine arrived in Pennsylvania from England in 1774, carrying a letter of introduction from Benjamin Franklin, his most immediate business was "to procure subsistence at least." He was not wise; he was not educated. His life had been a series of failures. When *Common Sense*, the first open and unqualified argument for independence, was published anonymously in January 1776, some guessed the author to be John Adams, others Franklin. According to "The Word of Congress," written two and one-half years after that "work like wildfire through the Country ran," Franklin was its prime mover: "He caught at Paine; reliev'd his wretched plight; / And gave him notes, and set him down to write. / Fire from the Doctor's hints the miscreant took; / Discarded truth, and soon compos'd a book."

It is tempting to consider Odell's judgment seriously because of his close ties with William Franklin. Although William and his father Benjamin did not speak to each other during the war years, William's son, William Temple Franklin, served as his grandfather's secretary while Franklin was in France. Perhaps the line of communication between Temple Franklin and his father remained open. It is not completely unlikely that someone of Benjamin Franklin's brilliance would have had a hand in Paine's masterpiece.

In the closing stanzas of "The Word of Congress," Odell asks for a "stouter champion," a "Genius" to "rise and deal the fatal blow." His "endeavour" has been but to "amuse the Foe." As things now stand, "Genius, careless of his charge, sits still, / And lets the monster Congress rage at will: . . . / Arrests not those who sell the land to France." Until "some favour'd mortal raise his voice, / I must go on—'tis duty, and not choice." He appeals to the Goddess of Song, the Sister of Wisdom, for "poetic ardour" and "strength of thought" when next "the feather'd weapon I prepare, / Once more to lay the villain's bosom bare." If the final lines of the poem are taken out of context, Odell sounds positively vicious:

> Ask I too much? then grant me for a time
> Some deleterious pow'rs of acrid rhyme:
> Some ars'nic verse, to poison with the pen
> These rats, who nestle in the Lion's den!

But the poem itself has little to do with "acrid rhyme."

Odell's next effort, "The Congratulation, a Poem," printed by Rivington on November 6 and again on November 24, 1779, deals with the worthless Continental dollar and the failure of the French Alliance. The French fleet, having been dispersed by the storm Odell discussed in the Britannicus essay, is nowhere to be found. "Sir Washington" now has no alternative but to blame those who put their faith in France, which is to say, "Franklin's artifice." Confused members of Congress must confess, "Brother, we sinn'd in going to the Mass." Perhaps these "hide-and-seek Allies" are on their way to "the Chesapeak? Martinique? Boston? Sandy Hook?" The rebels will need to look elsewhere for encouragement.

Clearly the dismal state of Continental currency is not the answer. By November the Continental was worth about two cents, and more than 140 million certificates were in circulation. Odell scoffs:

> Dollars on dollars heap'd up to the skies,
> Their value sinks the more, the more they rise;
> Bank notes of bankrupts, struck without a fund
> Puff'd for a season, will be at last shunn'd.[8]

As Odell had said often before, Congress's only hope to keep "the deluded people" in line is to keep them drunk with lies and nonsense. But whatever the congressional strategy, the end is in sight: "Mock-money and mock-states shall melt away, / And the mock-troops disband for want of pay." It was true enough that by the end of 1779 desertion was a staggering problem for the Continental army. By the simple arithmetic of superior numbers, the British army must win. Odell includes a cryptic reference to Arnold's treason: "Seen or unseen, on earth, above, below, / All things conspire to give the final blow." "The Congratulation" ends with the prediction that soon "Abhorr'd rebellion [will] sicken and expire"; the rebels who looked to France and Spain for "succour" are fated to be "A ruin'd People."

Odell was not as convinced as "The Congratulation" suggests. That the French fleet was potentially stronger than the British caused obvious apprehension. In the November 13 issue of the *Royal Gazette*, Britannicus, responding to rumors about an impending French assault, offers an account of Sir Francis Drake's capture of a large Spanish fleet. The moral is clear: "the courage of Britons is not to be daunted or subdued by the superior force or number of their enemies." Britannicus introduces his history of Drake's experience by warning the discouraged that the Continentals together with the French might constitute a *"superior force"* if sympathy for the war effort lags:

> At this important crisis, when the avowed enemies of Britain, exert their utmost efforts to effect our destruction,— when their united and formidable fleet is reported to be actually upon our coast, and when an insidious and malignant faction, assuming the mask of patriotism, and basely

combining domestic treachery with foreign force, attempts to depress native valour by exaggerated estimates of our weakness and danger, and of the strength of our adversaries, it must afford consolation and encouragement to the real friends of this country, to reflect on the illustrious deeds of their ancestors, and the contempt with which the patriots of Elizabeth's reign regarded the superior force of their enemies.

Almost as soon as this was printed, news reached New York of the Franco-American defeat at Savannah, Georgia—the most severe battle of the war since Bunker Hill. Odell celebrates the victory in a poem called "Le Feu de Joie." The battle was indeed a series of errors. In October d'Estaing had come to Savannah at General Lincoln's request. The two commanders disagreed on how best to take the well-fortified garrison where Loyalist contingents and British regulars were entrenched. D'Estaing caused further problems by insisting that the garrison surrender "to the arms of the King of France."

Reportedly their communications were so confused that the French and the Continentals actually fired at each other. In the mix-up d'Estaing was wounded. The garrison held out, Lincoln retreated to South Carolina, and d'Estaing returned to the West Indies, never to take part in the Revolution again. Loyalists had particular cause to celebrate. It was not the British army but Loyalist militiamen—the Georgia Tory militia, the Tory North Carolina Volunteers, and a South Carolina Tory regiment—who prevailed, although they were far outnumbered.[9]

"Le Feu de Joie" appeared in the November 24 issue of the *Royal Gazette*. The title refers to the rebel practice of signaling a victory with a round of rifle shots,[10] a custom that infuriated Washington, who worried constantly about the shortage of gunpowder and shells. Odell makes much of the Continentals' inability to supply provisions for their Gallic allies. The Gallic chief himself, "the lost sheep," returned from the West Indies to Savannah only to be wounded in the confusion of battle by his own allies. To compound matters, Lincoln's men refused to fight: "What ails these braggadocios of the land? / Won't they come forward? Stiff as posts they stand. . . ."

Odell had long been sensitive to the toll war takes on non-combatants, and increasingly he calls attention to their vulnerability. Here he describes citizens caught by war and again asks them to recognize that their ambitious congressional leaders are using them as pawns. They themselves have the power to correct this disastrous situation by reconciling with Britain for their own interest and safety:

> Sore sigh'd the mother, for her babes afraid;
> And anxious for herself the blooming maid;
> The merchant trembl'd for his crouded store;
> One dreadful pause, and all perhaps is gore.
> . . . .
> Ye poor deluded owners of the soil,
> For other's good who labour, and who toil;
> Ye wretches doom'd to sorrowful mistake,
> Who hunger, and who thirst for Congress sake,
> Arouse for shame—like men your rights resume,
> And send your tyrants to the land of gloom;
> If shame prevails not, still let wisdom plead;
> If both are slighted vengeance must succeed.
> Your parent state grows stronger every hour,
> As yet its mercy far exceeds its power:
> Your Congress every moment weaker grows,
> Rags are its treasure, honest men its foes,
> Its building cracks, tho' butress'd by the Gaul,
> It nods, it shakes, it totters to its fall.
> O save yourselves before it is too late!
> O save your country from impending fate!
> Leave those whom justice must at length destroy.
> Repent, come over, and partake our Joy.[11]

Rivington printed Odell's afterword to "Le Feu de Joie," which questions the intentions of the French government. The Continental Congress had reason to fear that the French wanted to repossess colonial territory lost to Britain during the French and

Indian War, despite assurances to the contrary and the Treaty of Amity and Commerce that had corroborated them. The fact that d'Estaing planned to claim Savannah for the French king is introduced in the poem—"The sworn confed'rates manfully advance / In quest of glory, and the good of France. / Go, summon, Trumpeter, you haughty town, / Bid them surrender to the Gallic Crown." This issue is the focal point of the afterword. Odell finds the situation "astonishing" and concludes:

> It can only be accounted for by supposing, that France was determined to take possession of the Southern Provinces, to reimburse herself for sums and supplies advanced to the Congress. Had the combined arms been attended with success, it is probable, that the Comte would have put a garrison into Charles-Town, &c. An event, that no doubt would have afforded much speculation to their Allies at Philadelphia.

Britannicus Essays Resumed

Odell continued his indictment of the French Alliance in general and d'Estaing's inconstancy in particular in the last of his essays addressed "To the INHABITANTS of the several (revolted) British Colonies in AMERICA." The essay is signed "A Loyal American," but internal evidence strongly suggests that it is the work of Britannicus. In the December 8 issue of the *Royal Gazette*, the author advises that the defeat at Savannah, "the moment of affliction and disappointment" for the rebels, become "the moment of wisdom" when "the calm voice of sober reason and conscience" is heard with attention. His purpose is to warn the rebels of the dangers surrounding them and point out the means yet in their power "to avoid impending destruction." He has spoken out before and been ignored, yet "duty and principle" urge him "*once more*" to appraise his countrymen of their "truly critical situation."

The French court, acting with "unparalleled duplicity," sent "secret supplies" to America while giving "every public assurance of continued amity and peace" to Great Britain until the Battle of Saratoga. This alone should warn the rebels as to "the principles upon which French politics are founded." France acts only in its own interest, and yet Congress has offered France "the sole trade and commerce" of the country.

A brief study of the Treaty of Amity and Commerce shows that France has gained "the *sole* direction, regulation, and monopoly of all your trade." The colonies cannot allow other nations to participate in "your commerce and navigation, be it ever so advantageous to your interest," and are not allowed to refuse any nation a share in "your commerce and navigation, be it ever so disagreeable to you." France has complete control; "The Lord have mercy upon you, for it is plain Louis the 16th will have none." Under the fourth article of the treaty France also has the right to compel the colonies to join in any enterprise to advance the French interest. Simply put, France is more powerful than the rebels, who are "*dependant* upon her to all intents and purposes."

Under the sixth article of the treaty France renounces all possessions in North America as in the Treaty of Paris. Yet in August 1778 d'Estaing landed his marine troops on Connanicut Island and solemnly took possession of it and, no less incredible, "the *whole* province [Rhode Island] . . . *in the name of the French King his master!*" On October 9, 1779, in Georgia, "in the presence and hearing of your own army," he summoned the town of Savannah "to surrender *in the name of and to his Most Christian Majesty.*"

Is there anyone foolish enough to believe that France sent "her fleets and armies to this country, at a vast expence of blood and treasure, merely to retake towns and provinces for the united states?" Britannicus asks. Congress has deceived the rebels; the "French have at length shown the cloven foot." It is plain that they mean "to hold any and every part of this continent for themselves." The remedy is to dissolve Congress and "petition his Majesty's Commissioners for leave immediately to call a *free election.*" The "free" Congress will be able to negotiate satisfactorily with England.

By this time the Britannicus essays had been circulating for almost a year, yet Odell had not been paid for them. He understood that Howe had recommended him to Clinton, "from whom I flattered myself that I might hope the continuance of this additional allowance" for his newspaper work. Even if Howe had forgotten his promise "as a matter of no public moment," Odell knew that Franklin had written to Clinton in his and Seabury's behalf. On November 19, 1778, Franklin offered Clinton "the services of two loyalist writers who had been employed by Howe, did not expect more than £50 a year a piece, and could 'keep the paper full of decent, well-meant essays.' "[12] By December 1779 Odell, still unsalaried, wrote to André about the events of the last two years, describing his desperate financial situation now that his property had been confiscated and his hope that Clinton would come to his aid. The letter, dated from Wall Street, December 18, 1779, reads in part:

> My pay, as Chaplain to one of the Provincial Corps, after the deductions that are made for agency, &c, is about six shillings a day. With this (which is all that I receive at present from Government) and the precarious appointment of Deputy Chaplain to the Royal Fuzileers, I have to defray my own expences here and to support a Wife and three Children at Burlington, where my property has been confiscated by present usurpation.
>
> When Sir William Howe gave me this appointment, in January 1778, at which time I had been thirteen months Exile from my family, he was pleased to add, in the way of a contingent gratuity, fifty pounds a year to my Subsistence, which gratuity was paid up to the time of his return to England; and I had an intimation that it was intended to recommend me to Sir Henry Clinton, from whom I flattered myself that I might hope the continuance of this additional allowance: but the intended recommendation was probably forgotten, as a matter of no public moment.

Odell added that he was also a competent master of Spanish and would be happy to be of service to the army or navy, or possibly act for the commander as an interpreter. Speaking for himself and Seabury, he most humbly thanked André for bringing their situation to Clinton's most gracious attention.

André responded at once. He probably asked Odell to be more specific about his publications; at least Odell was so in his return letter dated December 21: "and sundry pieces have been published by us—particularly those under the Signature of Britannicus, and some under different Signatures—and we flatter ourselves that our Essays, especially on the Subject of Continental Money, have not been altogether without effect."[13]

Both the last essay discussed, and another which appeared on April 15, 1780, and speaks at length about continental money, are signed "A Loyal American," which virtually confirms that on at least two occasions Odell and Seabury used that pseudonym. Given the April essay, it is also reasonable to conclude that Clinton paid Britannicus more promptly than expected.

Odell continued to use the newspaper as a forum to disseminate British policy and to express his own opinion when he could. In the March 11 edition of the *Royal Gazette* he was able to record his own thoughts. He subjected a *chansonette* written two years earlier to a "little wholesome discipline in the way of *correction*." It was printed as "Ode For the New Year, 1780." The 1778 version praises Britain—"Freedom's transatlantic throne"—and condemns blind mortals led on by ambition. In the important revised version, Odell specifically identifies the Loyalists' enemy as ministers in Parliament who are unsympathetic to their cause. He bids Britannia, the "scourge of haughty France and Spain" to "rise again" and triumph. He notes that Britain must fight on two fronts, which has weakened her. The rebels are one front. The other is not France and Spain but the divided Parliament:

> If but thy native sons were true,
>   From faction were thy senate free,
> How shou'd the proudest nations rue
>   Their bold attempts to cope with thee![14]

Odell tries to get his message across to the public by using the popular *Rule Britannia* as melody. His poems alone would be read and remembered by few. Simple words set to a thoroughly familiar song would appeal to many. But how much, if any, pressure Loyalists could exert on British home policy was another issue entirely.

The Loyalist Refugee Alone

In March 1780 Odell, now separated from his family for more than three years, wrote a poem to his wife about his profound loneliness, his fears for his family's safety, and his wistful hopes for the future. What can we know about this hard-driving Anglican minister who always seemed to land on his feet? Too few details apart from what we see in his work survive to flesh out his personality. But in this poem we get a rare private look at him: "I had been long a Wanderer, long had tried, / With baffled hope, to stem an adverse tide." This lyric, titled "A Loyalist, in Exile from his Family, Sends a Miniature Picture to His Disconsolate Wife" and dated New York, March 23, 1780, begins:

> Though cruel Fate condemns me still to mourn,
> An Exile, from thy chaste embraces torn;
> From year to year prolongs an Age of grief,
> While Hope deferr'd still mocks my fond belief. . . .

Odell conjures up a terrifying scene in his imagination. He sees the "ruthless tyrant" pointing his lance toward Ann's pillow: "Thy bed surrounded by an orphan train, / Whose tender cries to Heaven ascend in vain!" The nightmare leaves him in "speechless agony" while "Horror" shakes his "trembling frame." Once his "joy was full":

> But soon the rising Storm began to roar,
> And soon the Deluge swept me from the Shore!
> Again I wander, weary and unblest,
> Far from the Paradise I once possess'd.
> Possess'd, alas! like Adam—for a day!
> And now, with heavy heart, alone I stray.

Unlike Adam, Odell cannot count loss of Paradise as his fault: "No guilt is mingled in my cup of gall." He prays that Providence Divine will "Protect the Mother and her Infant care, / Be thou her Guard, her Refuge from despair." He has faith that he will be restored to Paradise when the war is over and thus asks Providence Divine to "Subdue the bloody rage of Civil Strife." Prayer renews his hope:

> the Dawn is near.
> When Peace shall banish Discord's bloody Train,
> And Love his long lost Paradise regain.

He refers to himself as a "person turn'd adrift / Upon a troubled Ocean," a lifeless form" who without Ann "Alone remains to bide the pelting storm." Thus he will take refuge in his imagination "till the howling of the Storm shall cease, Till Civil frenzy hear the Voice of Peace. . . ."[15]

Britannicus Continues

By April 15 Britannicus was back at work in the public domain. He tried to make the "PEOPLE of AMERICA" aware of the repercussions of Congress's decision to declare itself insolvent and to charge the individual colonies with the responsibility of levying taxes to support the war effort. More than 383 million Continental dollars were in circulation, and they were worth virtually nothing: "By the late resolves of the 13th of March last, the Congress, *regardless of all public faith and honour,* have passed a compleat act of *insolvency* in their own favour," and thus have determined "to *break* and *cheat* their creditors, with paying scarcely *sixpence* in the pound." The "unhappy creditors, the deluded, ruined, and devoted victims of their folly and ambition, are not even called upon or consulted." They extended congressmen credit, "which they have traded upon to your destruction." Doctor Franklin urged the circulation of paper money knowing that it would depreciate. Those who wisely recognized that these Continentals could never be redeemed and thus refused to accept them "the bayonet and Tender Laws at last" persuaded.

According to Britannicus, Benjamin Franklin calculated that the war would be over in three or four years because "he imagined Great-Britain would be obliged, from a want of resource herself, and the embarrassments of a wicked opposition, to relinquish her claims upon America." He never dreamed that the war "would *outlive* the *forced* credit of the money." But the "war still rages" and will go on so long as "Great Britain has a shilling to spend."

Now Congress has resolved not to issue "any more bills of credit on their *own* authority" and instead to levy a tax on each state "to provide funds and issue *other* bills in lieu of the present. . . . By this *subterfuge*, after having done all the mischief they could, and subjecting you to anarchy, confusion, and distress: They mean to get their own necks out of the halter, and saddle you hereafter with the public misfortunes." In a word, they "require you to make bricks without straw." The victims cannot furnish funds to redeem the bills they issue to carry on the war. What has changed from the start? This scheme must fail "for the same reason that your funds failed *before* . . . your independence being *yet* in *dispute*," which means that "every inch of ground, and every thing you possess is in *dispute*, and liable to be taken from you, perhaps in the approaching campaign."

It is in vain for you, or any of your political scribblers, (the famous *Crisis* writer, who boasts himself the author of Common Sense, a pedantic Schoolmaster, not worth six pence, nor possessing as much property in the country) to assert that your independence is as established as fate, when the fact is, that at this moment it is more precarious than ever, and from every circumstance, both of a public and private nature, absolutely *lost* to you."

Nevertheless, Congress directs that these new bills "shall be redeemable in *specie, within* five years after the present, and bear an interest of 5 per cent, payable also in specie. . . ." Where is this specie to come from? A loan from any European power is out of the question. If "you mean to save yourselves from utter destruction, or wish to retain what *little* the Congress have been pleased to leave you by their late *paper experiment* and public cheat passed upon you . . . you must not hesitate . . . to refuse every kind of *credit or circulation* to the *new imposition* ordered to be repeated upon you by their late resolves."

Remember, Britannicus warns, "that if you sin again you sin with your eyes open, and will richly merit the perdition that will inevitably await you should you be so lost to all sense of interest, good policy, and regard for yourselves, families, and country, as again to trust that Congress, who by their folly, weakness, wickedness, and ambition, have already brought you to a state of ruin, and by this their new devised scheme, replete with madness tenfold, (should you adopt it,) will again sink you into wretchedness, misery, and irretrievable distress."

Take "a serious view of your affairs," Britannicus advises his readers. The colonists have a right to know the truth. The rebels do not have the adequate means to carry on the war. The probable loss of Charleston and the two Carolinas, which supply "the principal funds on which you rely to support your foreign credit," makes their present situation completely precarious. The British fleet has prevailed over both the French and Spanish fleets; British troops have triumphed in Africa, Europe, and the Mediterranean. Britain "is left now more at liberty to prosecute the war at *home* with *greater* vigour and certainty of success, and *here* with every prospect of decisive advantage."

Disregard what Congress claims; "does not ruin, wretchedness and distress stare you full in the face, look which way you please?" The colonists have it in their power to escape the calamities of war. "A Commission of peace is again lodged in the British Commander in Chief, Sir Henry Clinton—embrace the benevolent invitation of your gracious Sovereign before it is too late, and give praise to Heaven for so great salvation."

Only those Loyalists who approached sainthood would actually have welcomed Clinton's "Commission of peace" for the rebels. That Odell could be counted on to announce Clinton's policy does not mean that he accepted it. Other than losing his main source of income, what would Britannicus accomplish by resigning? Any protest against these benevolent invitations would need to be made directly to the king and his party. For the Loyalists to challenge Clinton, in print or in private, would have been futile, no doubt dangerous.

8 *Odell's Confidence Bolstered*

Charleston, South Carolina, was one of the most important and wealthy towns in the South. On May 12, 1780, it surrendered to Clinton, which was not altogether surprising given the large number of Loyalists in the area. In keeping with the policy of courting the rebels Clinton offered full pardon to anyone who would take an Oath of Allegiance.[1] To those Loyalists like Odell who wanted an immediate end to the war as well as compensation for their losses, Clinton's leniency was infuriating and ill-timed. After all, he had an ideal opportunity to force a conclusion. The morale of the Continental army was lower than at Valley Forge. Washington, despondent about runaway inflation, civilian apathy, and the fact that his own army was on the verge of breaking up, wrote: "I have almost ceased to hope."[2]

For Odell, hope of a British military victory came from another quarter. In May negotiations involving the capture of West Point had resumed. Arnold had come away from his trial relatively unscathed, legally. Humiliated and impoverished however, he judged that any chance of a distinguished military career was lost. With this in mind, he petitioned his longtime friend Washington to assign him the command of West Point. Washington agreed despite objections from the Second Continental Congress.

The Arnold Conspiracy Nudged Forward

During the summer of 1780 Arnold moved what money he had left to London, and wrote to André about the strengths and weaknesses of West Point as he heard about its condition—"Troops and Provision wanting there." After the first visit to the garrison, he informed André of its vulnerability—"It is surprising a Post of so much importance should be so totally neglected"—and offered a plan whereby the British could first capture Rocky Hill, a "wretchedly executed" redoubt, and then take the Point itself.[3] Arnold pressed for an assurance of payment regardless of how the matter would turn out: ". . . twenty thousand pounds Sterling I think will be a cheap purchase for an object of so much importance." He also wanted an annual stipend of five hundred pounds and a personal interview with an officer to rehearse the last details.

Clinton refused to name a specific fee, but Odell stressed Clinton's generosity. On July 24 Odell wrote to Stansbury to inform Arnold that "His Excellency authorizes me to repeat in the strongest terms the assurances so often given to your Partner, that if he is in earnest and will to the extent of his Ability cooperate with us, he *shall* not in any possible event have cause to complain, and essential Services *shall* be even profusedly rewarded, far beyond the stipulated indemnification, &c." The only problem was that Clinton thought that "indemnification (*as a preliminary*) is unreasonable." However, "he has not the smallest doubt but that every thing may be settled to mutual satisfaction when the projected interview takes place at W[est] P[oint]."[4] The intrigue was on the verge of success.

The American Times

On July 21, 1780, Rivington announced the publication of *The American Times,* a poem by Jonathan Odell writing under the pseudonym of Camillo Querno. Querno was the poet laureate and jester to Pope Leo X; Odell, indeed jester and poet laureate for the Loyalist cause, took the occasion to register his impatience with his own "patron," King George III, who had yet to pay him attention. In this satire, on which Odell's literary reputation rests, we find his most complete expression of Loyalist ideology. He believed that man and society functioned best when established institutions were respected, and order prevailed. Criticism was appropriate, and in this poem Odell criticized Parliament. The rebel leadership's wholesale defiance of authority resulted in anarchy and therefore the end of civilization in the colonies. The poem, then, is a multifaceted assessment of rebel evils and British follies as well as Odell's own judgments and laments.

In *The American Times* Odell indulges his anger and gives reign to "acrid rhyme." Both the preface and the opening passages of the poem justify the diatribe. In almost all of his earlier writing, particularly the pieces signed Yorick and Veridicus, Odell characterized his narrator as a plain, honest man wishing no harm to any virtuous person. He saw evil around him, and though he was reluctant to expose it, he felt an obligation to make all aware that vice prevailed and that a return to order and reason was imperative. In the absence of any other poet making the necessary accusations he fulfilled his responsibility. He had been sarcastic. He had chided and mocked and railed. He had also laced his poems and essays with wit and good-natured humor. His writing conveyed an impassioned concern for innocent people caught up in the lies of the ambitious few, a passel of self-centered anarchists who had no thought for the lives they destroyed in their misguided stampede for power. Now he is plainly furious. At this point in the war Odell, one of a handful of people who believed that West Point would soon fall to the British army, was confident.

"Smarting beneath accumulated woes," Odell drops the comic dimension and "hurls verses of ridicule and abuse" at his longtime adversary, the Continental Congress. There is a sense of urgency here; the war is about to end. But the preface is not mere ridicule. Its combination of disdain, reference to the "fugitive nature of the subject," and seasoned thought make it an apt beginning to a major expression of the Loyalist rationale:

> The masters of Reason have decided, that when doctrines and practices have been fairly examined, and proved to be contrary to Truth, and injurious to Society, then and not

before may Ridicule be lawfully employed in the Service of Virtue.

This is exactly the case of the grand American Rebellion; it has been weighed in the balance, and found wanting: able writers have exposed its principles, its conduct, and its final aim. Reason has done her part, and therefore this is the legitimate moment for Satire.

Accordingly the following Piece is offered to the Public. What is found to want of Genius, the Author cannot supply; what it may want of Correction, he hopes the candor of the Public will excuse on account of the fugitive nature of the subject: next year the publication would be too late; for in all probability there will then be no Congress existing.[5]

In the opening passage of *The American Times* Odell, emboldened by knowledge of the fugitive negotiations underway, describes the deplorable state of affairs and his felt mission:

> When Faction, pois'nous as the scorpion's sting,
> Infects the people and insults the King;
> When foul Sedition skulks no more concealed,
> But grasps the sword and rushes to the field;
> When Justice, Law, and Truth are in disgrace,
> And Treason, Fraud, and Murder fill their place;
> Smarting beneath accumulated woes,
> Shall we not dare the tyrants to expose?

The narrator proceeds with clear knowledge of the risk he takes. A "Champion of Virtue," he will bear "without one anxious throb, / The wrath of Congress, or its lords the mob." Drawing imagery again from the metaphor of disease, he memorably delineates his sense of Revolutionary America:

> Bad are the Times, almost too bad to paint;
> The whole head sickens, the whole heart is faint;
> The State is rotten, rotten to the core,
> 'Tis all one bruize, one putrefying sore.

"Anarchy" and "Folly" have inflamed a "cheated populace." Congress with its "paper-dollars" has brought them to "Famine." Once there was domestic life—the plough, the awl, the needle, the shuttle. Now there is "Confusion" and murder. The "legions" of "new-born statesmen" and "senators" who "infest the land" are to blame. This turnabout is all the more grievous when one thinks how close the colonists were to prosperity and all its blessings when Congress instituted "Tyranny":

> Ye western climes, where youthful plenty smil'd.
> Ye plains just rescued from the dreary wild,
> Ye cities just emerging into fame,
> Ye minds new ting'd with learning's sacred flame,
> Ye people wondering at your swift increase,
> Sons of united liberty and peace,
> How are your glories in a moment fled?
> See, Pity weeps, and Honour hangs his head.

Odell borrows a poetic device from Milton's *Paradise Lost* to dramatize the malignancy that has descended on the peaceful "western climes." These "new-born statesmen" and "mushroom generals" are the fallen angels who inhabit Pandemonium, but ones who can leave, assume human shape, and wreak havoc on earth. The narrator asks for and receives "some magic voice, some pow'rful spell, / To call the Furies from profoundest hell":

> They come, they come!—convulsive heaves the ground,
> Earth opens—Lo! they pour, they swarm around;
> About me throng unnumber'd hideous shapes,
> Infernal wolves, and bears, and hounds, and apes;
> All Pandemonium stands reveal'd to sight. . . .

He will record their monstrous deeds. They have managed to infect the people because, like Shakespeare's witches in *Macbeth*, they are "well skill'd in necromantic lore." Busily they toil with "the magic cauldron" and prepare "the cursed drench" that "poisons all the air with horrid stench." We get a detailed description of the "vile ingredients of the pot":

> Dire incantations, words of death, they mix
> With noxious plants, and Water from the Styx;
> Treason's rank flowers, Ambition's swelling fruits,

> Hypocrisy in seeds, and Fraud in roots,
> Bundles of Lies fresh gather'd in their prime,
> And stalks of Calumny grown stale with time;
> Handfuls of Zeal's intoxicating leaves;
> Riot in bunches, Cruelty in sheaves;
> Slices of Cunning cut exceeding thin;
> Kernels of Malice, rotten cores of Sin;
> Branches of Persecution, boughs of Thrall,
> And sprigs of Superstition, dipt in gall;
> Opium to lull or madden all the throng,
> And assa-foetida profusely strong;
> Milk from Tisiphone's infernal breast;
> Herbs of all venom, drugs of every pest,
> With minerals from the centre brought by Gnomes;
> And seethe together till the furnace foams.

This fantastic "potion," this "draught design'd / To cheat the croud," must have stripped a people of their honor and virtue. The narrator's purpose is clear: "Yet tho' the frantic populace applaud, / 'Tis Satire's part to stigmatize the fraud." While the fiends "Cheat male and female, poison age and youth," he will "pursue" them with the goad of truth.

As the hideous shapes from Pandemonium hover about him, he singles out the most villainous and denounces each one: Livingston, Jay, a Belial figure whom Satan owns "for his darling son," Chase, Bob Morris—"Mammon 'tis in hell"—and Gouverneur Morris. Duer, Duane, Cooper, Hancock, and the two Adams are not forgotten.

Part 1 reserves its strength for an attack on Washington, who appears accompanied by "hell's music." He is more evil than any of the "profligate corrupt rich" of Congress, because he has knowingly led innocents to slaughter. The narrator speaks sadly of the pitiful followers in "ragged ranks," of "Falstaff's soldiers, poor and bare; / Or else the rotten regiments of Rag-fair," and asks the "great chief" to "for once permit a private man / To parley" with him. Damnation is absolute:

> Hear thy indictment, Washington, at large;
> Attend and listen to the solemn charge:

> Thou hast supported an atrocious cause
> Against thy King, thy Country, and the laws;
> Committed perjury, encourag'd lies,
> Forced conscience, broken the most sacred ties;
> Myriads of wives and fathers at thy hand
> Their slaughter'd husbands, slaughter'd sons demand;
> That pastures hear no more the lowing kine,—
> That towns are desolate, all—all is thine. . . .

Washington, condemned in "Reason's Court," must assume responsibility for the blood that his "band of ruffians" spill. Often the Quakers who would not bear arms were singled out as enemies and the hanging of the Quakers Roberts and Carlisle is especially reprehensible. But the narrator does not readily perceive Washington's personal motive. Why, when almost famous, did he join with Congress and therefore with shame: "Was it ambition, vanity, or spite," or all three? Finally, having noted, to his own pain and abhorrence, Washington's "frequent sacrilege," "blasphemies," and the "Innumerable crimes" he had defended, Odell pronounces:

> Go, wretched author of thy country's grief,
> Patron of villainy, of villains chief;
> Seek with thy cursed crew the central gloom.

Part I of *The American Times* concludes with an apology to Milton. Odell has found *Paradise Lost* to be "prophetic." In it he has been able to trace the "crimes, the follies of the present age." The comparison is both apt and specific: "What Michael to the first arch-rebel said, / Would well rebuke the rebel army's head; / What Satan to th' angelic Prince replied, / Such are the words of Continental pride." At last comes the prediction compounded of fury and passion:

> I swear by Him, who rules the earth and sky,
> The dread event shall equally apply;
> That Clinton's warfare is the war of God,
> And Washington shall feel the vengeful rod.

Part II of *The American Times* focuses attention on "meaner game": monsters, most notably Pulaski, who fled from Poland after his failed attempt to assassinate the king, and the Presbyterian minister John Witherspoon, president of Princeton and a member of Congress, his name "the curse / of sound religion." Portrait follows damning portrait. Little about the verse or the villains is memorable. As a satirist, however, Odell strengthens his credibility with an even-handed portrait of Henry Laurens, one-time president of Congress.

The narrator does not understand why Laurens rebelled. He was not cursed with an "insatiate lust" for power; he was not foolish enough to believe that the king ruled tyrannically; he was not a bankrupt. He would not "for a trifle sell" his soul; he enjoyed a "clearness" of fame; his private life was commendable. The narrator decides that Laurens acted on his republican principles. Considering that anarchy has ensued, this cannot be forgiven:

> Could these give right to desolate a land?
> Could it be right, with arbitrary will
> To fine, imprison, plunder, torture, kill!
> Impose new oaths, make stubborn conscience yield,
> And force out thousands to the bloody field?
> Could it be right to do these monstrous things,
> Because thy nature was averse to Kings?

A "saucy hiss" from Democracy interrupts him. Hers is a harlot's face. On her breast she wears a "glittering gorget" with two inscriptions that bespeak her fundamental duplicity: "Servant of Servants, in a laurel wreath, / But Lord of Lords is written underneath." She holds a flaming sword and darts "poison'd" with "Circean potions." Some of the "motley train" who attend her read addresses to the people, some threaten—"Rods, scourges, fetters, axes, others hold." She herself is a sorceress whose "magic wand" bends the rabble to her will. Her true nature is one with violence, cunning, persecution, and hypocrisy, although she disguises herself with public spirit, policy, zeal, and religion. The crowds drink from her golden cup and are intoxicated. Yet there remains "a chosen phalanx" who defy her arrows, the Loyalists:

> The sons of Truth inviolate remain.
> Invulnerable champions, sacred band,

> Behind the shield of Loyalty they stand;
> Unhurt, unsullied they maintain their ground,
> And all the host of heav'n their praises sound.

Democracy has infected the rebels. The narrator, staying with the imagery of disease, acknowledges that "too, too many feel her baneful spell." Too many are bled by her shafts, and swollen by her venom. Because the "cruel plague assaults each vital part," he calls on the Reverend Doctor Inglis (rector of Trinity Church in New York), a "wise physician," a "sage of Exculapian art!" His own part is over; he has applied the caustic, made the proud flesh cringe, forced the patient to feel and smart. Inglis can heal: "Direct the diet thou, prepare the purge. / Thou to the bottom probe the dangerous sore, / And in the wound the friendly balsam pour."

The third and final part of *The American Times* opens with the poet's decision to send the "infernal crew" of "coxcomb Congressmen," inept chiefs, and "preachers who, for gospel, discord preach . . . headlong back" to the "Stygian shore." He invites "sober Reason" to "direct the song," but Reason is powerless in this world where "millions hate and hiss" at her. In these seditious times where votes are bought and opinions sold, what chance has the "soft voice" of reason? She has tried and failed:

> When civil madness first from man to man
> In these devoted climes like wildfire ran;
> There were who gave the moderating hint,
> In conversation some, and some in print;
> Wisely they spake, and what was their reward?
> The tar, the rail, the prison, and the cord.

There are still those who "Confront the lies that Congress sends abroad; / Expose the sophistry, detect the fraud," but even armed with "Truth's genuine maxims" they cannot prevail. The "knights of old" who wandered through the world and overcame enchanters, dragons, and giants "Play'd not so deep, so desperate a stake, / As he who draws the pen for Virtue's sake." The problem in this time and place is that "error . . . rallies fresh her force tho' oft repell'd."

Historians have long tried to account for the fact that

Washington's army did hold together despite all odds, and did regroup to fight again despite how seriously they had been hurt. General Nathanael Greene put it this way: "We fight, get beat, rise and fight again."[6] Odell had always been alert to the intricacies of military realities. His narrator also finds endurance to be a key to the rebels' success.

> Cut, hack'd, and mangled, she denies to yield,
> And straight returns with vigour to the field:
> Champions of truth, our efforts are in vain;
> Fast as we slay, the foe revives again.

Odell is not merely a polemist. His pseudonym hinted at his impatience with the king; here he castigates Parliament outright. Parliament abetted the rebels by issuing inflammatory tax laws and thereby created "Times . . . out of joint." The narrator, holding "Truth's radiant mirror" for guidance, and speaking with the "still small voice" of reason, places blame where he judges that it belongs. Echoing William Franklin, who deemed "the opposition of the colonists more mad than the measures of the ministry," the narrator finds both Britain and the Whigs the essence of madness. Odell denounces both Parliament's tax laws and those colonists who "have flown to arms." He can be considered America's first antiwar poet:

> Stand forth, Taxation—kindler of the flame;
> Inexplicable question, doubtful claim:
> Suppose the right in Britain to be clear;
> Britain was mad to exercise it here.
> Call it unjust, or, if you please, unwise;
> The Colonists were mad in arms to rise:
> Impolitic, and open to abuse,
> How could it answer—what could it produce?
> No need for furious demagogues to chafe;
> America was jealous, and was safe.
> Secure she stood in national alarms,
> And Madness only would have flown to arms.

Odell's position is completely clear: Britain's taxation "scheme" would never have succeeded. The mistaken policy would have crumbled under its own weight. He borrows a phrase from his recent Britannicus essay: "Why lift the spear against a brittle reed?" The rebels' reaction to Britain's taxation "scheme" was extravagant, amazing, and thoroughly irresponsible: "This was not Reason—this was wildest rage, / To make the land one military stage." He cannot explain the "strange resolve" that forced farmers, tradesmen, and lawyers to take up arms needlessly except to say again that it was "surely Madness." It pains him "to view the phrenzy of the cheated mob." "Frantic as Bacchannals . . . They rushed to perpetuate the worst of crimes": "Chas'd peace, chas'd order from each bless'd abode."

Odell brings the familiar themes from his Britannicus essays to *The American Times*. The narrator takes Congress to task for issuing paper dollars and for entering into an alliance with France: "Hail to the master-piece of madness, hail." Thus Congress has sealed the rebels' doom. They might as well "Proclaim thro' all the land that Louis rules— / Worship your saint, ye giddy-headed fools."

Conventionally, the satirist apologizes for his angry art and attempts to explain his motivations. In a particularly sincere-sounding passage, directed to the "Illustrious guardians of the laurel hill," the speaker confesses that he has succumbed to the fierce emotions of the time. The disease imagery, which likens the torn body to the bleeding country, continues to prove effective:

> I wish'd for Reason in her calmest mood
> In vain—the cruel subject fires my blood.
> When thro' the land the dogs of havock roar,
> And the torn country bleeds in every pore,
> 'Tis hard to keep the sober line of thought:
> The brain turns round with such ideas fraught.
> Rage makes a weapon blunt as mine to pierce,
> And indignation gathers in the verse.

He wishes words would themselves be the necessary weapon to punish "culprits" and "villains" but recognizes the limitation of his art: "Such are the times—Cease, useless Satire, cease! / Each moment dire barbarities increase." Once again, he looks to Britain to supplant its strategy of mercy, a strategy that has not worked for the Loyalists, certainly, with a military commitment to justice:

> O! may that hour be soon! for pity's sake,
> Genius of Britain, from thy slumber wake,
> Too long has mercy spoke, but spoke in vain:
> Let Justice now in awful terror reign.

As in the earliest poems, he retracts his accusation to the extent of explaining that "slumber" is evidence of virtue.

"Britannia's guardian angel" appears, scolds the rebels for ingratitude, and applauds her own "ceaseless" labor to "reclaim . . . frantic sons from misery and shame" rather than to punish them. She repeats her willingness to "forgive" them for their "errors." *The American Times* closes with a warning: "At length the day of Vengeance is at hand: / Th' exterminating Angel takes his stand." The rebels must now hear "the last summons" and "relent." Those who have remained loyal, "who now lie humbled in the dust," will be rewarded by the king. The guardian angel does not threaten the rebels. Their fate is not spelled out. When America is rid of "dire pollution" and both "heaven and earth are pleas'd" with "due vengeance," America shall "flourish yet again, belov'd, rever'd" by the loving father.

The American Times is Odell's most accomplished poem, and surely the finest Augustan satire to come out of the Revolution; only Trumbull's *M'Fingal* is in the same league. Writing associated with the losing side is typically relegated to obscurity. This, Odell's last major poem, is not read chiefly because it puts forward the Loyalist rationale as he interpreted it, explaining that Parliament's policy of colonial taxation was misguided; that the colonists could eventually prevail within the course of orderly procedure; that the radical Whig leadership—a self-serving group having nothing to lose by creating chaos but their debts—irresponsibly forced armed confrontation with the most powerful military in the world; and that this policy was not simply treasonous but would bring certain ruin to gullible millions who at no time in their history were more prosperous. He denounces Congress, damns Washington, and his poem suffers the fate of literature written in behalf of a failed cause.

A Personal Loss

While *The American Times* began to circulate, the Benedict Arnold conspiracy moved toward completion. Arnold insisted on a personal meeting with one of Clinton's trusted officers so that arrangements could be finalized. André, then an adjutant general, believed that if he were personally involved in the capture of West Point his promotion to lieutenant colonel would be assured. Clinton wanted to send a more experienced soldier, but André prevailed. The plan was for André to meet Arnold at Dobbs Ferry near West Point, discuss the last details, and return to the British lines on the *Vulture*, which was anchored in the river for that purpose. Clinton specifically warned André against taking any papers from Arnold that might incriminate him. In September, just before he set out, André paid Odell forty-two pounds, "presumably for expenses of the Stansbury correspondence."[7]

The conversation between Arnold and André, who used his code name John Anderson for the occasion, lasted through the night. Toward dawn Arnold insisted that André accept maps and information concerning the point. André either ignored or forgot Clinton's advice and acquiesced. For some unknown reason rebels fired at the waiting ship, which quickly sailed well out of range. André, carrying "a confidential statement of Washington's military intentions" between his stockings and his boot, was stranded behind rebel lines. Arnold gave André a pass and left him in the care of a sentry who was to escort him to safety while Arnold returned to West Point. As they approached Tarrytown, the sentry, fearing for his own life in that strip of no man's land, gave André a few Continental dollars and went on his way. André, wearing his British officer's uniform, was stopped shortly thereafter by three ruffians, who demanded money he did not have. They took the gold watch he offered instead, but would not believe that a British officer was not carrying sterling. They stripped him to search and found the papers Arnold had given him. "Of his captors, only Paulding could read. As the naked royal officer watched anxiously, the gigantic yokel labored through the documents. 'This,' he cried, 'is a spy!'"

They took André to Lieutenant Colonel John Jameson, who

sent a messenger to Arnold informing him that one John Anderson had been caught carrying his pass as well as a "parcel of papers . . . I think of a very dangerous tendency," and that the papers in question had been "sent to General Washington."

Historic events tumbled over each other. Washington, together with Hamilton and Lafayette, was on his way to West Point. Arnold and Peggy were at breakfast when Jameson's message arrived. He whispered to her that all was lost, ran through the back door, and made it to the riverbank on horseback, where he leaped aboard his barge and ordered the oarsman to proceed with all haste because he must get to the *Vulture* to deliver a secret message from Washington to her captain. Washington's servant appeared at West Point to announce, "His Excellency is nigh at hand."[8]

Washington was frantic. Clinton offered forty South Carolina gentlemen in exchange for the captured André; Washington refused. By all accounts, André was "a cultivated, charming gentleman," and personally Washington admired him, judging him "more unfortunate than criminal."[9] Nevertheless, he ordered him hanged. André asked for a military execution appropriate to his rank; that is, to be shot. Washington—his critics thought him irrational on this score—refused. André was hanged.

For the Loyalists in New York, André's death was a blow. Often ignored by Clinton, they had turned to his sympathetic aide-de-camp. For Odell, André's death was a genuine personal loss. The two had known each other since Burlington, when André was a prisoner of war and Odell wrote "Birth-day Ode" and "A Farewell" for him. They met again in Philadelphia when André was Howe's aide-de-camp and a leading member of "Howe's Thespians," and Odell was Superintendent of the Printing Presses. They worked on the Clinton-Arnold correspondence, and André made certain that Clinton paid him for the Britannicus essays. They were identified together in the public mind. When Rivington printed *The American Times* he appropriately offered it in the same six-shilling packet that included André's mock epic "The Cow Chase, Complete in Three Cantos." Odell's brief poem commemorating André's death, "To the Memory of Major André," calls him the essence of honor, virtue, and truth, and concludes:

Adorn'd by Science, cherish'd by the Nine,
Prepared alike in Camp or Court to shine,
With loyal zeal and patriot ardor fired,
Dear to his Country, by her foes admir'd,
His murder fill'd with measure of their shame,
And stamp'd with deep disgrace their Leader's name.[10]

9 *Leaving the Colonies*

When Cornwallis surrendered to Washington at Yorktown, the war was almost over despite the presence of several British regiments in New York, in locations near the Canadian border, and in various parts of the South. While Washington warned Americans against celebrating prematurely, war-weary Prime Minister Lord North resigned in March 1782, and there was little enthusiasm in the "disenchanted" Parliament for continuing.[1] During the last months of the Revolution the strained relationship between the British army and the Loyalist refugees in New York City did not change, however. General Clinton, whom Judge Jones called "one of the most irresolute, timid, stupid and ignorant animals in the world,"[2] clashed with the Associated Loyalists. Odell was a board member of this organization founded by William Franklin.

Within weeks of his release from Simsbury Mines, Franklin tried to organize Loyalists into guerrilla bands that would plunder the countryside surrounding New York for foodstuffs, salable goods, and prisoners. On several occasions he presented the plan to Clinton, who routinely ignored it. To circumvent Clinton, Franklin worked in conjunction with former governor William Tyron of New York. Now an emigré in London, Tyron pled their case for two years with the king and Parliament. By December 1780 Franklin had secured the king's approval and funding from Parliament.

The Board of Associated Loyalists

Franklin as president of the Board of Directors of Associated Loyalists issued a declaration, which Rivington printed in the *Royal Gazette* on December 28, 1780. The declaration described the way that the organization functioned, called for volunteers, and emphasized the king's approval of the project. It began by noting that a regular and efficient system for "employing the zeal of that Class of his Majesty's Loyal Subjects" for the purpose of "reducing the rebels" had long been wanted. "His Majesty has therefore been induced to signify his royal pleasure, that a Board be established to oversee his faithful Subjects" in their attempt to capture property, take prisoners, and "put a stop to those distinguished cruelties with which the Colonial Loyalists are generally treated, when they have the misfortune of falling into the hands of the Rebels."

The declaration is most clear as to who will govern. The Associators will operate under the jurisdiction of the Board of Directors, and the Board will direct their activities, distribute plundered goods "among them in such shares" as are specified in the Articles of Association, and regulate prisoner exchange.

Franklin was able to bring enough pressure to bear on Clinton so that, publicly, he had to support the Associators. "In pursuance of his Majesty's gracious intentions," Clinton "has been pleased to issue a Commission" constituting this Board, and has agreed to furnish the Associators with ammunition, provisions, and British ships, Franklin wrote in his declaration. Loyalists were suspicious of Clinton, and Franklin stressed that the Board's authority was absolute unless the Associators act "in conjunction with any of his Majesty's land and sea forces."

The retaliatory policy underpinning the organization was described in the plainest of terms. The directors "pledge themselves to the Associators to omit nothing in their power, to make the enemy feel the just vengeance" in retaliation for "the most ignominious deaths" which "so many worthy Loyalists have already suffered."

Franklin officially appointed Odell assistant secretary on

April 15, 1781. Like the other Board members, he received two hundred pounds sterling from the British government and a share of whatever plunder the Associators brought in. Odell was financially more secure than at any other time since the start of the war.

When the British regulars joined the Loyalist Associators on raiding expeditions, tensions ran high. Associators complained that they did not get their fair portion of the spoils. Franklin had enough support in England to force Clinton to answer the charge. Responding to the king's injunction, Clinton issued an open letter on March 9, 1782, to His Excellency Governor Franklin, president of the Honorable Board of Directors of Associated Loyalists: ". . . it is his Royal Pleasure that I do, in his Majesty's name, give the loyal Refugees the fullest assurances of the continuation of his affection and regard for their happiness; and that in all events they may rely upon the utmost attention being shown to their safety and welfare." The Loyalists may be assured that when they "are joined with the King's troops" there will be no discrimination between them apropos of what has been surrendered.

Given Clinton's sanction, Associators became bolder. Two weeks after the letter appeared they began to send news of their successes to the *Royal Gazette*. An Associator officer reported that his boats captured three sloops and five privateer whale boats. From rebels' ships bound for Philadelphia, Baltimore Associators took the cargo of rum, wine, tobacco, and oil. In the Charleston area Associators caught rebels plundering cattle, and killed or took prisoner two hundred of them.

There was tremendous pressure within the refugee camps to avenge the Loyalist dead. The Associators, organized, armed, and responsible only to the Board, had the power if not the authority to take retribution directly. In April 1782 they secured Clinton's permission to transfer a British prisoner, Captain Huddy of the New Jersey militia, being held in New York back to Monmouth County, New Jersey, for, they said, a prisoner exchange. Captain Lippincott and the Associator party hanged Huddy from a tree in retaliation for the killing of a Loyalist named White in the same county about two weeks before. A "label" pinned to the corpse warned the rebels: "We, the refugees, having long with grief beheld the cruel murders of our brethren and finding nothing but such measures daily carried into execution, we therefore determine not to suffer without taking vengeance for the numerous cruelties; and thus begin, having made use of Captain Huddy as the first object to present to your view; and we further determine to hang man for man while there is a refugee existing. Up goes Huddy for Philip White."[3]

Clinton believed that Lippincott acted on orders from the Board and was outraged by the deception. He stripped the Associated Loyalists of their powers. Franklin left for England. Two days after Odell officially lost his appointment he sent a brief letter signed with his familiar pseudonym Veritas to the *Royal Gazette*, contending that the Board did not have foreknowledge of Lippincott's intention.[4] Whether or not the Board did approve of the hanging of Captain Huddy, the incident dramatizes the intensity of the civil war between the rebels and the Loyalists as well as the tension between the Loyalists and the British army. From start to finish, the Loyalists were caught between forces that they were powerless to control.

Odell and Sir Guy Carleton

On May 5 Sir Guy Carleton arrived in New York to replace Clinton as commander in chief. He hoped to negotiate peace without conceding independence to the colonies. The May 22 edition of the *Royal Gazette* announced that Carleton could effect an "advantageous" reconciliation. This news came, presumably, straight from London and was dated March 8:

Advices by the Packets

It is confidently said that Sir Guy Carleton's commission for treating with the Americans, is more extensive than any powers sent hitherto from this country: and that while it provides for the honour and interest of Great-Britain, it affords the Americans an opportunity of reconciliation on more advantageous terms to themselves than any they can derive from a French alliance.

Carleton had orders in hand from the Rockingham-Shelbourne ministry that granted the colonies independence. But he believed an "honourable" reconciliation possible because, among other reasons, the king was decidedly against independence. He probably assumed that at the right moment he and the king would prevail over the ministry and preserve the empire. And, too, the New York Loyalists assured him the "large majority" of the colonists wanted reunion.[5] Carleton quickly organized to open lines of communication with Washington as soon as possible. Odell joined his staff on May 25, as chaplain to the King's American Dragoons and perhaps on that day as Translator of French and Spanish Papers as well.

What would happen to him if Carleton's plan worked out? Would the British army reestablish the Loyalists among their former enemies? Rivington, it seems, thought not. On July 10 he began his own conciliation campaign:

> To the Public: The Publisher of this Paper, sensible that his zeal for the success of his Majesty's arms, his sanguine wishes for the good of his country, and his friendship for individuals, have at times led him to credit and circulate paragraphs, without investigating the facts so closely as his duty to the Public demanded; trusting to their feelings, and depending on their generousity, he begs them to look over past errors, and depend on future correctness; for henceforth he will neither expect nor solicit their favours longer than his endeavors shall stamp the same degree of authenticity and credit on the Royal Gazette (of New York), as all Europe allow to the Royal Gazette of London.

Circumstantial evidence suggests that at this juncture Rivington became a spy for Washington.[6] Odell continued to work for British authority, specifically for Carleton's plan for "cordial reconciliation."

On August 1 Prince William Henry presented the King's American Dragoons with their standards. Odell, chaplain of the regiment, addressed them at their campgrounds on Long Island. He spoke about reconciliation now that the "horrors inseparable from civil discord" had "convulsed an empire." The country had "become a Scene of distress and confusion, of war and desolation . . . [of] mutual incriminations, relentless proscriptions, murders and assasinations!" It was to be greatly lamented that "once loyal hearts" had "courted" the "ancient Rivals and invenerate Enemies of Britain" to "join this bloody contest between the Children and the Parent." His prayer was "that the time is coming, when the voice of reason shall again be heard, when Envy and Jealousy and unnatural Enmity shall cease, and ancient ties of brotherhood again be felt, and the blessings of peace, on the basis of a generous reunion and cordial reconciliation shall compensate for all our past errors and misfortunes." Britain was "now, as She ever has been, anxious to be at peace with her Children." Her offers were generous and tendered with affection.

What would happen to Britain's loyal children depended on the British army. The Dragoons, a volunteer regiment whose "Officers are to a man AMERICANS," and who, according to Rivington, "feel very sensibly for the sufferings of their Loyal Brethren, who are groaning under the heavy yoke of oppression," knew they could do little for themselves. Their numbers fell off. On the day before Odell asked them to renew their vows in Prince Henry's presence, Rivington needed to advertise for recruits—"Very great encouragement will be given to the Recruits, or to any person who brings a Recruit to the volunteer regiment." To add to the general embarrassment, Prince Henry left for the British West Indies after the ceremony.

Carleton's Activities

On July 31 Carleton received a letter from Shelbourne that told him what he knew months before: he had neither the power nor the authority to negotiate peace without granting independence. Carleton had done so much to bring Washington to the bargaining table before he learned that the ministry had ceded independence that he construed Shelbourne's letter an "act of treachery."[7] Odell shared Carleton's illusions. He never did understand the ministry's rationale.

Carleton appointed Odell his assistant secretary on November 4. Five days later Britannicus's appeal to Lord Shelbourne appeared in the *Morning Chronicle*. It acknowledged that the Shelbourne administration had agreed to independence for America. But, independence can mean "unconditionally free" or it can mean "free from British legislation, but subject to the British Crown, as Ireland." Britannicus preferred the latter alternative. "Shades of emphasis" aside, what Britannicus had wanted "since their act of independence and treaty with France" was an appeal to the "sword" as the "sole umpire" to "terminate the contest. . . ." Either Shelbourne's administration will allow France to "dictate terms of peace" or it will obtain an "honourable and desirable peace . . . by treating the combined fleet of our perfidious enemies, and breaking it. . . ." By an honourable and desirable peace, Britannicus meant "a union of interests with America, short of total independence, and equitable terms from the European powers."

What was in Britannicus's mind? Did he think Shelbourne would replace Carleton with an aggressive military man who would break the back of a war-weary Congress and an exhausted people? It is true that if Carleton had had his way he would have returned to England. He had asked for permission on August 2, two days after he received Shelbourne's letter, and again on October 29. As secretary, Odell surely knew of Carleton's correspondence. Was it possible that the Shelbourne administration would recognize its mistake of granting America independence prematurely, overturn the Conway resolution, which enjoined the military from using force, and take to the field again?

Britannicus should have known that Parliament gave America independence to drive a wedge between America and France. The war in Europe was of far greater concern than the status of far-flung colonies. From the Loyalists' viewpoint, Britain must win the war and keep the army in the colonies while the Loyalists repossessed all that had been taken. Actually, this would not have been possible. Britain was at war with France and Spain and needed all available manpower. Whether or not Odell would have agreed, if Carleton had succeeded in negotiating a "cordial reconciliation" he probably would have withdrawn the army and "washed his hands" of the Loyalists.[8] What other choice would he have had?

An Attempt at Reconciliation

Provisional Articles of Peace were signed in Paris on November 30, 1782. By the First Article, Britain acknowledged the colonies "to be free, sovereign, and independent States," and relinquished all claim to their government, property, and territory. Carleton's job was to oversee the withdrawal of the British forces and the return of the Loyalists to their homes, according to the terms of the Fifth Article: "Congress should earnestly recommend to the Legislatures of the several States" to restore all confiscated estates within British lines, to allow all persons to return to their homes, and arrange to repurchase their property for the same price for which it had been sold "not only with justice and equity, but with that spirit of conciliation, which on the return of the blessings of peace should universally prevail." Obviously the congressional recommendation was completely ignored.[9] Carleton tried to prompt rebel leaders to honor the Fifth Provisional Article, and Odell drafted at least a portion of one letter for the cause. Arguably one of the most revealing Loyalist writings that we have, it is a wonder it was written in the first place. Odell focuses on the need for good will and the need to protect political dissenters as a policy of sound government.

> This Country, so long convulsed by the rage of Civil War, is at length considered as finally dismembered from the British Empire. Provisional Articles have been "agreed upon to constitute a Treaty of Peace"—and if nothing should intervene to hinder the concluding of the Treaty proposed, the United States of North America will now be established in the possession of an uncontroverted and unlimited Independency, with a very great extent of territory. Whether, in point of political happiness, they are, all things considered, to be gainers by such a revolution, is a question that might be left for Experience to decide. But, surely, every good man must wish that their Conduct, in the present critical and important moment, might be directed by that Spirit of prudence, integrity and honor, which alone can promise them the future enjoyment of national prosperity.

Odell cites Britain's generosity when the Provisional Articles were drawn up and defines the Loyalists' terrible circumstance:

> Must it not be a matter of Surprise, then, to all the world, to see a Spirit of determined opposition spreading through the United States, against the very moderate Stipulations that have been made in favor of those Americans, who, during the war, held themselves bound, by the ties of allegiance, to take part with the Government under which they were born and educated.
>
> Sentiments of Loyalty to an established Government are certainly too respectable to merit reproach and persecution, even from those who, with equal Sincerity, are persuaded that a dissolution of the Government, by force, and the founding of a new one, is become *necessary*, and therefore think their duty calls them to attempt it: In such a case they are doubtless, during the contest, under a necessity of guarding, with a jealous vigilance, against all opposition. Humanity, however, must recoil at the idea of extending this concession to the confiscation, proscriptions and executions, which, nevertheless, do seem to be among the mischiefs inseparable from Civil War; but—when the war is at an end, and the Revolution is established by universal consent, are not the Founders of the new Government called upon, by the united voices of Humanity and Wisdom, to heal the wounds of civil Dissension, and to receive into the Class of Citizens all those who, by the legal dissolution of their former ties, are free and willing to return to the Bosom of their Country, to whose Government their past conduct is now a pledge of their future fidelity. To punish such men for their former loyalty is, in fact, no less than to suggest a caution to their own people, in case of any insurrection against the present Government, to beware of hazarding either life or fortune in defence of legal and established authority.

These are "the Dictates of both Wisdom and Humanity." How has it happened then that popular committees have adopted violent resolutions that have been accepted by the people, and in some instances by their principal magistrates and constitutional representatives? These resolutions "will endanger the domestic peace, and injure the public welfare and reputation of the United States." Odell considers the economics of forcing tens of thousands into exile:

> Can it be for the interest of any Government to countenance the expulsion of so many thousands, of whom at least a great majority, might have been useful Citizens, in a Country very far from being over-stocked with Inhabitants! How far the absence of those, who are already gone and preparing to go forever from their Native Country, must lessen her means of internal wealth and Strength; and how far it might increase the weight of taxes on those who have driven them away; are questions that certainly merit the attention of all well-wishers to the prosperity of these Infant States.

Topics of ideological argument can wait for another occasion. The urgent task is "to publish, by way of solemn appeal to the impartial world, a Series of transactions," a record of "Facts that have recently occurred in different parts of this Country, and are supported by solemn and credible Depositions."

As in all previous instances Judge Jones supported Odell's position. Here he elaborates on these "facts": "No sooner did the Loyalists, who had taken protection within the British lines during the war, attempt to return into their respective provinces, and former places of abode, in consequence of this [fifth] article, than they were taken up, and insulted. Some were tarred and feathered, many tied up and whipped in the most inhuman manner, while others were actually hamstringed, and sent back into British lines."[10]

Odell returns to his "unpleasant" duty of having to remind the present government of its obligations, and he does so in most mild terms: "(The motives to this Publication do not proceed from any Spirit of recrimination, but from a sincere desire that the Friends of humanity in the Country, who have the public Interest at heart and are invested with Authority, may be duly appraised, how much their influence appears to be wanted to restrain that illiberal Spirit, which has already been suffered in so many instances to violate the Articles agreed upon to constitute the Treaty of

Peace.)" Three times Odell rewrote this parenthetical appeal to those invested with authority. Here the letter breaks off.[11] No doubt he would have liked to say that once peace was restored the men "naturally" suited for the top of the political and social hierarchy would displace their inferiors and resume their customary places.

Despite the fact that the Loyalists as a group had a great deal to contribute to the new government—they were "useful Citizens" and a resource of "wealth and Strength," as Odell's letter argues—it cost Washington's regime less in every way to force them into exile. Property had been confiscated; legislative positions had been filled. Odell's case for reconciliation was so weak that he gave it up, it seems, before it even began. Nonetheless, the letter bears witness that had the active Loyalists Odell speaks for been given the opportunity to remain at peace in the colonies, they would have.

Carleton named the Loyalist Edward Winslow an advance agent and sent him to explore the possibilities of relocation in Nova Scotia.[12] Throughout the chaotic year 1782 talk revolved about emigration. Every issue of the *Royal Gazette* included advertisements for houses and properties to be sold. There were notices of public auctions where Loyalists virtually gave away what it would not make sense to take. News came from Nova Scotia "To those LOYAL REFUGEES who either have already left, or who hereafter may leave their respective Countries, in search of other Habitations." There were encouraging items about the healthful northern climate as well as names of people to contact. Nonetheless, the mere thought of leaving family, business, friends, and all that was familiar for a wilderness in an unforgiving climate struck terror. By the fall of 1782 Carleton sent 600 apprehensive pioneers, the first of 28,000 emigrés to Nova Scotia.[13]

For a brief time during the fall of 1783, Odell did not feel "resigned" to Nova Scotia.[14] He wrote to the well-connected Winslow asking him to use his influence "respecting" his hopes for an appointment as assistant secretary to a British ambassador, "if such an one is to be sent to this country."[15] At the same time Odell "apparently hoped" to be appointed the first Anglican bishop in the colonies.[16] He had thought about that possibility when William Franklin held the "bait" out to him even before he took holy orders, and on several occasions he joked about it in his poems. But both ambitions came to nothing. Britain did not name an ambassador to the United States and the coveted bishopric went to Samuel Seabury, Odell's collaborator on the Britannicus essays.

Because he had no other viable choice, Odell turned his attention to Nova Scotia where he would have to reestablish himself. During the preceding months he and his colleagues had fleshed out ideas about New Brunswick, the new all-Loyalist colony they wanted to be carved out of Nova Scotia. They were concerned with how it should be structured and how they could solidify their own positions of privilege and authority within it. They were self-serving, but not simply so. Ann Gorman Condon observes in *The Envy of the American States: The Loyalist Dream for New Brunswick*, "But cynicism about Loyalist motives should not obscure how profoundly these men regarded themselves as uniquely qualified to establish a proper hierarchical society in the new colonies and to direct their development in a manner that would produce both internal order and external allegiance to Great Britain."[17]

If the New Brunswick colony were to become a reality, settlers would need a resident bishop,[18] a substantial college,[19] as well as free prime land and the requisite supplies. If Nova Scotia were to remain intact, they would have to find places within Governor Parr's administration. But in either case, as Colonel Gabriel Ludlow (the future mayor of Saint John) explained to Carleton, the Loyalist gentlemen were "unaccustomed to labour" and must have "the immediate assistance of Government" if they are to "exist in an uncultivated country."[20] Ludlow might have added that the Loyalist elite, like most of their American counterparts, needed a ready supply of cheap labor, preferably labor they did not need to pay at all.

British Policy toward Slavery and Servitude

Thousands of black slaves had joined the British because of Lord Dunmore's proclamation in 1775 and Clinton's Philipsburg proclamation in 1779 that promised them "freedom and a farm." The seventh article of the Provisional Articles of Peace demanded that the British desist from evacuating these newly freed slaves when they evacuated the army and the Loyalists. In May 1783 Carleton and Washington met in Orangetown, New York, and vehemently disagreed over the interpretation of the seventh article.

Washington insisted that slaves who fought for the British remained the property of their owners and must not be allowed to leave the colonies. Carleton argued that the Philipsburg proclamation freed all slaves who claimed its protection before November and therefore enjoyed the protection of the British government. To strengthen his negotiating position, he assigned Odell the Herculean task of ascertaining Britain's legal position. The Odell Papers contain more than sixty tracts about slavery. The manuscript is faded, and often illegible, but the work seems to be nothing less than an attempt to trace the history of servitude and slavery under English law since the Anglo-Saxon period by studying court cases, one by one. We do not know what use Carleton made of Odell's efforts. We do know that he insisted that he would only surrender those ex-slaves who arrived behind British lines after November 30. Washington reluctantly concurred and settled for compensation for the loss of the rest.[21]

As a result of Carleton's negotiations, nearly three thousand black veterans immigrated to the Maritimes.[22] Whatever his intentions, the overwhelming majority of these blacks were either reenslaved or became indentured servants or wage slaves: "They were regarded as little more than physical beings, whose function was to fill the lowest levels of the labour force."[23] Thus the interests of the Loyalist gentlemen Ludlow spoke of were served. The Quaker Loyalists determined to persevere on their own, and did so.

Departure

Odell preached his last sermon in the colonies at St. Paul's and St. George's on November 9, 1783, three weeks before the British army withdrew. The anxious Loyalists were leaving behind everything of value. Depressing news from Nova Scotia fostered panic and bitterness. Refugees unable to deal with the loneliness and harsh climate were already beginning to reappear in the colonies. For instance, Joseph Stansbury, Odell's associate during the Benedict Arnold days, had returned to New York in October, having spent less than three months in Nova Scotia.[24] Odell's sermon urged all to be kind to each other on earth and to know that there will be a day when "all violence & hatred & malice shall be unknown."

> The Lord of Life and Glory . . . has assured us that he will esteem every act of true kindness & cordial benevolence done to the meanest of his Servants as done to himself, & that he will acknowledge it as such at the dread tribunal of the final judgment, let us remember how great our obligation to love one another, and to discharge the duties of humanity and benevolence, as that we may be at last partakers of the love and glorious approbation of him who died to redeem us from the vengeance due to our sins, & to open a door for our admission into everlasting life and glory, into a state of endless felicity, where all violence & hatred & malice shall be unknown, & where the diffusion of love eternal shall combine the blessed in a common participation of joy & in united acts of praise & glory to God & to the lamb forever & ever. That this may be the happy, the glorious portion of us all, God of his infinite mercy grant, through Christ our Lord, Amen.[25]

When Carleton left New York for England, Odell went with him. The Odell Papers include the beginning of a poem that describes the crossing and his disconsolate mood. This was no "wild adventure" conceived in "some delirious fit / Of Fancy"; rather he "in many a tranquil hour, / Weighed well the attempt till hope matured to faith." Here in the opening lines, and often during the next months, Odell tells us that he is an American: "Not with a heart unmoved I left thy Shores. / Dear Native Isle!—not without a pang, / As thy fair uplands lessen'd on the view, / Cast back the long involuntary look!"

10 *From London to New Brunswick*

Odell arrived in England in January 1784. Not only was he one of the few who had sufficient money to present his case before the Loyalist Claims Commission in person, but his patron Carleton "continued to dominate English political views of British America."[1] If anyone could catapult Odell into power, it would be Carleton. And unlike the overwhelming majority of Loyalists who could only afford housing in the less expensive cities such as Bristol, Odell lived in Hanover Square, London, the center of political activity. He renewed his friendship with the Reverend Jonathan Boucher and perhaps through Boucher's agency delivered at least two sermons before members of the Society for the Propagation of the Gospel. He seemed to be in an advantageous position when, on March 23, he went before the Loyalist Claims Commission in an effort to secure compensation for services rendered to the British government as well as for losses sustained during the war.

"The Memorial of Jonathan Odell" is addressed "To the Commissioners appointed by Act of Parliament for inquiring into the Losses and Services of the American Loyalists." Odell refers to himself as the "late Rector of Burlington and Mountholly," now "in the 47th year of his Age." He speaks of "a series of Persecutions" that ended his comfortable life in Burlington; his offense was "his open and decided Character as a Loyalist." While in Burlington he had contributed "not a little . . . to promote an abhorrence of such measures as tended to throw the Country into Confusion and draw the People into Acts of Rebellion." When his letters were intercepted in October 1775, "he was arrested by order of the Provincial Congress of New Jersey then sitting at Trenton, before whom he was compelled to appear as a Prisoner, and who endeavoured, by treating him as an Enemy to his Country to make him the Victim of popular resentment."

After the Declaration of Independence usurped all the powers of government,

> your Memorialist was again arrested by the Provincial Congress, and held Prisoner within the limits of his Parish until the 12th of December in the same year, when a Party of Men, armed with fixed Bayonets and conducted by an American Captain from one of the Gallies then lying off the Town of Burlington was landed expressly for the purpose of seizing and confining the person of your Memorialist, in quest of whom they made a diligent Search from house to house avowing their Determination to secure him dead or alive; so that having more than once very narrowly escaped falling into their hands, and finding it was no longer in the power of his Parishioners to screen him even by concealment from the vindictive Malice of his Enemies he was reduced to the necessity of taking refuge within the British Lines, where he continued till the final Evacuation of New York.

During the seven-year exile "from his Family and his Parish your Memorialist has rendered confidential Services of essential Importance to the British Government." He "has been repaid with very flattering Marks of Approbation" and "beneficial Employments." Sir William Howe had appointed him to "superintend the Printing Offices and the periodical Publications at Philadelphia with a Salary at the rate of £50 Sterling a year while the British Army was in possession of that City; and your Memorialist during that time, and afterwards at New York wrote and published in the News Papers sundry occasional Essays with a view to serve the Interests of Truth and Loyalty in that misguided Country."

In January 1778, thirteen months after joining the army, he had been appointed chaplain to one of the British-American Corps, and received "the pay of Chaplain from that time to the 24th of October 1783 when those Corps were disbanded." Sir Henry Clinton had appointed him Assistant Secretary to the Board of Directors of Associated Loyalists in April 1781, for which he received five shillings a day until November 4, 1782, when his appointment was terminated. Sir Guy Carleton had paid him ten shillings a day as translator of French and Spanish Papers and had appointed him Assistant Secretary to the Commander in Chief "with an additional Salary of ten shillings a day commencing the 1st of July in 1783." These appointments continued until "the 24th of Decemb. last when the American Staff was dissolved."

Your Memorialist "therefore considers himself as compensated for the Loss of his Professional Income at Burlington, but from that time he has been unemployed, and is now reduced to count upon the uncertain continuance of £50 a year, hitherto allowed him as Missionary from the Society, and on the expected Half Pay of a Military Chaplain."

He had known for some time that in consequence of a "New Jersey Inquisition Judgment" his personal effects had been sold at public auction in 1779 and his real estate confiscated.

> [Your] Memorialist conceives it his Duty in behalf of himself and his Family to state, that exclusive of the Loss of his Parish at Burlington, the actual Loss of Property thus incurred by your Memorialist in consequence of his Loyal Attachment to the British Government cannot be rated on a fair and candid Estimate at less than Five hundred Pounds Sterling. Conscious therefore of having endeavor'd to his utmost by diligent and faithful Services to merit protection and Support, and being still precluded from his native Country where he has a Wife and four Children to maintain your Memorialist prays that his Case may be taken into your Consideration in order that your Memorialist may be enabled under your Report to receive such Aid or Relief as his Losses and Services may be found to deserve.[2]

While Odell waited for their decision he worked for the Partition Movement and its effort to create New Brunswick. The London Loyalists tried to persuade the British government that

Governor Parr had not executed his responsibilities, that a substantial number of the 28,000 emigrés to Nova Scotia had not been settled on their land, that supplies had not been distributed, and that crops had not been planted. Winslow and his colleagues in Nova Scotia gathered necessary political, economic and geographical data supporting partition and sent it to London, where Odell and other prominent Loyalists "were to press their case before the two great English patrons of the Loyalist cause, Sir Guy Carleton and General Henry Fox."[3] They had little reason to be optimistic. British public opinion was "skeptical" regarding the value of far-flung colonies, and even the sympathetic Lord North-Charles James Fox coalition would not be easily persuaded to reorganize the political structure of Nova Scotia. When William Pitt, who was not a known supporter of Loyalist interests, replaced the North-Fox coalition, Odell and the London Loyalists believed all was lost.[4]

They need not have worried. In March the Committee on Trade and Plantations accepted the Loyalists' accounts and recommendations concerning Nova Scotia and the establishment of New Brunswick, perhaps because Parr's representative did not reach London until long after the committee had concluded its deliberations. Political reorganization in British North America had been achieved on Loyalists' terms.[5] Odell's cheerful "Song" dated April 14 seems to have been written in response to the committee's decision. It begins: "How changed are my feelings from those which possess'd me / When parting with friends and my dear native shore / On leaving behind those who loved and caressed me / Resolved to succeed or to see them no more."[6]

It may have been just before the Loyalist Claims Commission acted on Odell's case that a fearful and unprincipled Odell wrote to his wife instructing her to appeal to the vestry of St. Mary's Church in Burlington.[7] Recall that Odell introduced himself to the commissioners of the Loyalist Claims Commission as "the late Rector of Burlington and Mountholly" who "considered himself as compensated for the Loss of his Professional Income at Burlington." Nevertheless he tells Ann to persuade the vestry that, while it is true that he has been unable to serve his parishioners, he is in fact the rightful minister of St. Mary's and therefore entitled to collect "all rents and issues arising from the church estate." The distinction can be made between "rents and issues arising from the church estate" and "Professional Income," but clearly Odell insists that he is the "rightful minister" when he knows he is not. In May, Ann (whom Odell often called Nancy) wrote that the vestry decided against paying him, and, significantly, that they decided not to invite him to return as minister. Odell's response, dated London, July 5, 1784, mixes anger and disappointment. It begins:

> MY DEAR NANCY
> Your last letter of May 2d, gives me an account of conduct in the Vestry, which I confess surprises me. However I do not mean to upbraid them, if they are not of themselves conscious of their ingratitude toward me, it were in vain to attempt to convincing them, either by argument or expostulations. All I shall say is, let them look to their Church which they must confess I have a right to tell them is a monument of the indefatigable and disinterested Zeal of a Man whose Family had every reason to expect all the kind Returns and friendly attentions in their power especially at a time like that which has torn me so long from them.

Odell insists that she make a "formal demand" for payments due him from the time he was "forcibly driven away by an armed Body." He argues that he is the minister of that church until he "shall either voluntarily resign or be legally dispossessed" of his right, which has not been "in the smallest degree affected by the revolution." Therefore receipts from the church estate belong to him. Odell ends bitterly. He instructs Ann, who holds lawful power of attorney for him, to inform the vestry he shall not "tamely relinquish" his "Claim to rigid Justice," but shall avail himself "of every lawful and Practicable means to compel them to do that which they ought to Blush not to have done of their own accord."[8] Whether one judges Odell more sinned against than sinning, one thing is certain: his plan did not work.

While waiting for the Loyalist Claims Commission to render him "protection and support," Odell tried another possibility. To find out if he had family in the British Isles who could help him to settle there, he wrote to Thomas Odell, a relative in Limerick, Ireland, on June 19, 1784. He asked about his forebears' emigration either from England or Ireland to the colonies. Thomas responded on July 15: "I am inclined to think that all of the name are descendants of one family who came to England with William the Conqueror." The illustrious past has not shaped the present. Thomas goes on to say that he would very much like to visit him in London, but a twenty-eight-year-old father of eight children cannot get away often. Although he mentions that he has asked other relatives about Odell's inquiry, there is no suggestion that anyone plans to see him. Rather "all the gentlemen of the family join him in expressing their concern" that he did not "make his inquiry in person."[9] Information concerning the Odell coat of arms was all that resulted from this exchange of letters. It was most unlikely that he could count on the branch of the Odell family still in the British Isles.

Prosperity at Last

In June the Loyalist Claims Commission awarded Odell the highly influential post of Provincial Secretary to New Brunswick. On July 9 a London Loyalist conveyed the message to Winslow, who wanted the post for himself: "Col. Carleton, Sir Guy's brother, is at length appointed and has accepted. . . . Mr. Odell has the appointment under Col. Carleton."[10] On August 6 Odell sent the news along to Thomas Odell: "I am at present engaged in preparing for my new employment as Secretary of the *New* Province of *New* Brunswick to which the Brother of my Friend and Patron Sir Guy Carleton is appointed Governor."[11] Odell was also appointed Registrar of Records and Clerk of the Council at a salary of one thousand pounds sterling. His future would be prosperous after all.

The Practicalities of Reunion

The Reverend Benjamin Moore, second Episcopal bishop of New York and godfather to Odell's youngest child, writes to Odell that he has been informed of his appointment as Secretary and his plans for "embarking for the *New* Province of New Brunswick in the *new* Land called *Nova* Scotia." Having addressed the letter of

November 15 to St. John's, "supposing *that* to be the place of your Destination," he speaks of the practicalities involved in Odell's reunion with his family. Tact was not Moore's most polished skill: "Welcome once more to the Shores of America. May you now find a place of Rest, if possible more happy & I hope much more permanent, than that which you were compelled to meet on the Banks of the Delaware." He has heard that Ann and the children are well. However: "You will hardly expect to see them this winter at Nova Scotia. Would it not be practical for you to pay us a visit in the spring, send for your family to New York, & embark here for your own country? How came that Expression 'own country' to escape my Pen?"

In what sounds like a warning to Odell not to argue further with St. Mary's about payment, Moore begins his brief discussion of church news from Burlington: although "I am again fixed in the Church in this City, upon Terms as degrading as Spite & Jealousy could make them, . . . I have sacrificed a good deal for the sake of Peace & Harmony; & I am determined, nothing shall be wanting, on my Part, to preserve what we have at last obtained."[12] It would have been pointless for Odell to persevere with St. Mary's in any case. Not one active Loyalist from New Jersey was allowed to return after the war.[13] The vestry had chosen his successor.[14] When he arrived at Halifax in November 1784, Odell was neither American nor Canadian. He was a Loyalist.

In New Brunswick

Odell, the best educated and one of the most politically prominent of the New Brunswick Loyalists, "attained a leading position from the beginning."[15] Soon after he arrived in the province with Governor Carleton, he settled in Fredericton, the capital, where his family joined him the following year. He built a substantial home and eventually owned 642 acres. He was directly involved in the establishment of the University of New Brunswick and was named a warden of Trinity Church in Saint John. He exerted political influence all his life and even arranged to have his son, William Franklin Odell, succeed him as Provincial Secretary although Downing Street objected to nepotism on "general principles."[16] In a word, Odell was among the most successful of the New Brunswick Loyalists. Nothing about his life, however, asks that we see him as the "Loyalist tradition" would have us.

According to this tradition, the colonial elite immigrated after the war to British North America. Endowed with family connections, education, and wealth, these genteel champions of British values presided over the development of "model" conservative communities on the very border of seditious, republican America. Whereas the anarchists to the south might think of them as driven exiles "drifting off into a black despair of North American nothingness,"[17] they were God's chosen whose enviable lives and solid works would reflect glory on the British Crown. They "rejected all things American,"[18] defined themselves as builders of colonies, and looked to the future with confidence born of conviction.

Contemporary scholarship has proved the Loyalist tradition a myth. The complex of distortions lingers in the popular imagination and can be summed up in words like these from the 1844 inscription on William Franklin Odell's tombstone: "Born in New Jersey in a time of trouble and revolt, he inherited his father's loyalty, and was from his earliest years associated with that band of faithful men who forsook their native land and took refuge in the forests of New Brunswick rather than violate the allegiance they had sworn." As Odell's argument with the vestry of St. Mary's amply demonstrates, emigration was not a matter of allegiance, kept or broken. Whether a Loyalist returned home or went into exile almost always depended on his neighbors' attitudes. Both Odell and Samuel Seabury were active and visible Loyalists. Seabury stayed, but Odell could not.

The Loyalist elite did not reject "all things American." Rather, they maintained active correspondences with conservative Americans, the Federalists, because of personal ties and mutual political concerns, primarily the events leading up to the War of 1812 as well as the war itself.[19] Odell's experience supports this view. He and Clement Clark Moore, Reverend Benjamin Moore's son, exchanged letters. Their main interest was rhetoric and grammar. Odell discussed matters relevant to his work, *An Essay on the ele-*

ments, accents and prosody of the English language. (Jonathan Boucher found a London publisher for it.) Moore wrote "Twas the Night before Christmas" and sent Odell a copy.

Moore refers to an "antigallican" song Odell sent him, surely "Song for the 4th of June 1808." By then a great deal of anti-French sentiment existed in conservative circles on both sides of the border. Odell denounced France as the "fierce usurper . . . leagued with Hell" and predicted that Canada would remain peaceful. There is no evidence that Odell sent Moore a copy of "A Second Salute to Neighbor Madison," dated 1814, but there is no reason to think he did not. The Federalists would agree with Odell when he villified "Nap" and "Mady," those "possess'd with a tearing ambition," those "Destroyers of peace and good order."[20]

What was it like for Odell in New Brunswick? The village of Fredericton "remained largely unconnected by roads with the outside world" during his lifetime.[21] In 1784 he told Boucher he would write to him in London. His letter, dated 1802, explains that he had not written sooner because nothing had happened in this "frozen retreat" that was "worthy of your attention." He goes on: "It is now near eighteen years that I have at times thought of this promise, and always with a sincere determination to perform it—but seldom with anything at hand that appeared like to afford you either amusement or interesting information."[22]

This was not genial self-effacement; it seems that New Brunswick did not satisfy his expectations. In 1789 Odell petitioned the House of Assembly for financial assistance. Unable to collect his salary "owing to the Infant State of the Province," he observes: ". . . Your Memorialist can with great truth declare that the Emoluments of his Office have hitherto been far less than he had reason to expect. . . ."[23]

The New Brunswick economy depended to a considerable extent on its cheap labor force. The precarious economy faced a crisis in 1790. Many hundreds of free blacks planned to immigrate to Sierra Leone to escape degradation. Odell, now a slave owner himself, used his administrative authority to block the exodus.[24]

Thomas Peters, representing angry free blacks, brought a Petition of Grievances from New Brunswick to the British cabinet in 1790. He was introduced to the sympathetic directors of the

Sierra Leone Company, who invited Peters and as many who wanted to go with him to immigrate to the colony of Sierra Leone. The British government would bear the cost of transportation. New Brunswick's white establishment was predictably outraged by the plan.

Carleton appointed Odell as a recruiting agent. Blacks who wanted to emigrate had to apply to him and his associates. The agents demanded to see certificates of freedom that had been issued nine years before. Because many certificates had been lost or were too old to read, this "move effectively rendered numbers of New Brunswick blacks ineligible for emigration." The historian James St. G. Walker also charges Odell and his associates with other deceptions aimed at preventing blacks from leaving. Despite harassment blacks signed up in substantial numbers, thereby confirming Peters' accusation that the promises made to the veterans were not kept.[25] More than one thousand people, having overturned the will of the royal governor and members of His Majesty's Council, immigrated to Sierra Leone.

New Brunswick did not become the political oligarchy Odell thought it should. The House of Assembly, made up of elected representatives, was not content to be a "mere ratifying body."[26] This first assembly elected in the new province used its power of the purse to challenge the authority of the appointed governor and council. Carleton retaliated; he accused the assembly of preferring "republican Systems."[27] Each body claimed the other violated the Constitution.

The second assembly was more antagonistic than the first. Carleton dismissed the representatives and called for an election.[28] The aggressive third assembly sent a petition to the king in 1797 in an attempt "to defend their rights as Englishmen against an overweening executive power."[29] Two years later Carleton asked to be allowed to resign because he had lost all his influence.[30] In response, the British government offered hope that harmony would be restored. By 1801 the locally elected assembly had come to a "shaky compromise" with the royally appointed executive—the council and governor.

Unstopped, finally, by the Loyalist elite, the strength of the elected representatives continued to grow. Imagine how anachronistic Odell sounded when, on February 14, 1814, he admonished the House:

> Every British Subject is, or ought to be, taught—"to fear God and to honor and obey the King," and all that are put in authority under him. And so long as he walks peaceably within these sacred limits of religion and loyalty, he is entitled to his full enjoyment of all the blessings which flow from the Laws and the Constitution of his Country—that happy Constitution which he is bound to cherish and to revere, as being both fixed by Sanctions even of divine Authority. "To speak evil of Dignities" is therefore, in his estimation, to affront the Majesty of Heaven. But this does not preclude the free and respectful exercises of his legal Right, to consider *public Men* and *public Measures*, without exception, as Subjects of public observation and discussion.

Odell was not taken seriously.[31]

The Odell Papers do not supply enough information for a particularized narrative of his New Brunswick years. But there is enough, such as the 1814 speech just cited, to convince us that Odell never moved off dead-center Loyalist ideology. Consider "The Vacant House," an autobiographical poem written in August 1804. Governor Thomas Carleton had retired to England the year before. As Odell walks through the empty house, he is all but overcome with a sense of loss. His thoughts return to the Revolution: "And fierce Rebellion drove me from the Shore, / Which I was destin'd to behold no more. / From Anna far, and from her Infant train, / Nine years exiled, . . ." He then thinks of "Carleton's kind protecting care," and how Carleton took him from the "Wreck" and placed him in "a safe Asylum," New Brunswick.

"O England! why recall him from the field, / Just when Rebellion was prepared to yield?" These lines deserve to be thought through, because they define the limits of Odell's perception. In May 1782 Carleton did defy Shelbourne's order to evacuate the army from New York. He arranged for regiments in the south to reinforce his army so that he could negotiate with Washington from a position of strength. But Washington's "cool response" to his letters and the "continued refusal of American leaders to respond positively to any of [his] peace overtures," led Carleton to report to Shelbourne on June 18: "hitherto I have not found the least disposition in the rulers of the provinces to come into pacific measures."[32] Odell was wrong; rebellion was not prepared to yield. Nor did England recall Carleton from the field. Although he twice asked for permission to resign, he stayed on in New York for fifteen months to oversee the withdrawal of the army.

Perhaps Odell is referring to Carleton's tenure as commander of the British army in Canada, 1775–77. During the summer of 1776 Carleton was to move his army southward and join Howe's thirty thousand troops moving from New York City up the Hudson. If Washington attacked them, they would destroy him. If he retreated, they would occupy New England, effectually isolating the region. Cut off from the cradle of revolution, the rest of the colonies would inevitably capitulate. Whether the strategy would have worked can be debated.[33] That Carleton was on the verge of success when Burgoyne replaced him cannot be. Rather, Carleton wasted the opportunity to pursue a fleeing army in October 1776 with the result that the British army's position was logistically poor in 1777. When John André, a prisoner of war of the Canadian campaigns, met Odell in Burlington in May 1776, it is possible that André overestimated Carleton's ability. Yet Odell, never far from British headquarters, must have heard the corrected versions.

It is not simply that Odell's loyalty to Carleton obscured his judgment. Rather, he failed to take account of the larger issues. If Carleton had succeeded in 1777, how could Britain trade with hostile colonies? If Carleton had succeeded in 1782, how would the Loyalists have survived without the protection of the British army? Loyalist ideology supplies answers, but they are not the right ones. Odell's own experience should have taught him the obvious—people who acquire privilege, by birth or by design, hold on to it. Errors in judgment aside, the events of Odell's life during the war years add to our understanding of the Revolution as a civil war; his poems and essays synthesize Loyalist ideology, an area of study that increasingly commands attention, if not always approval.

Appendix

Funeral Notice: The Order of the Procession

Chief Mourner: William Franklin Odell
Mourners: Members of His Majesty's Council, Members of the Assembly, Principal Officers of Government, The Magistrates and Gentlemen of the Bar, The Gentlemen of the Army and Departments, The Gentlemen of the Town, The Military

The Inscription on Odell's Tombstone

25 September 1737–25 November 1818
He was educated for the profession of physic and surgery, and in the successive stages of his life he continued to explore the depths of science and to traverse the fields of literature. But, without neglecting any branch of usefulness, he undertook a higher task, and in 1767 was ordained and appointed to the spiritual charge of Burlington, in the Province of New Jersey. As he feared God, so he honored the King, and in the disturbances which led to the Independency of the United States he espoused the cause of the Government with openness, with decision, and with zealous warmth. Hence he was persecuted and proscribed; and in 1776 driven out from his family and home, his occupation and means of sustenance. His principles and qualifications procured him the notice of persons in command at the seat of war, and during its continuance he faithfully executed many important and confidential trusts. At the close of the Rebellion he took refuge in the Mother Country, where

his sufferings were remembered and his services appreciated. He was called to a seat in His Majesty's Council in this Province, then newly erected, with the appointment of the Secretary, Registrar of Records, and Clerk of the Council. The duties thus devolving upon him he unremittingly and faithfully discharged for upwards of thirty years, assisting also upon emergency in the church. After the relinquishment of his appointment, he kept on his wonted course to the end. Religious, loyal, upright, charitable, prompt in friendship, persevering in good offices. He is now mourned in proportion as he was cherished and respected, by his family, by his friends, by the public, and by the poor.

Notes

1. Odell's First Ministry

1. "Pedigree of Odell, of United States and Canada 1639–1894," Odell Papers, New Brunswick Museum, Saint John, New Brunswick, unnumbered. The town records of Concord, Massachusetts, show that William Odell, Jonathan Odell's first American ancestor, lived in that colony in 1639. Soon after he moved to Fairfield, Connecticut, as the owner of a considerable estate. William's son John received at least two land grants from Fairfield. He in turn deeded some or all of that land to his son Samuel Odell, who was named an ensign of the General Assembly. Samuel's son John married Temperance Dickinson of New Jersey.

2. Jonathan Odell to a relative in Limerick, England, June 19, 1784, London, Odell Papers.

3. Willard Sterne Randall, *A Little Revenge: Benjamin Franklin and His Son* (Boston: Little, Brown, 1984). 193.

4. Carl Bridenbaugh, *Mitre and Sceptre, 1689–1775* (New York: Oxford University Press, 1962), 205.

5. "Welcome Home After the Peace in 1763. Addressed to the 22nd Regiment," Odell Papers; Winthrop Sargent, *The Loyal Verses of Joseph Stansbury and Doctor Odell* (Albany, N.Y.: J. Munsell, 1860), 106; Joan J. Anderson, "A Collection of the Poems of Jonathan Odell with a Biographical and Critical Introduction" (Master's thesis, University of British Columbia, 1961), 3. "To Britannia in the Year 1763," Odell Papers; Anderson, "Poems of Odell," 2.

6. Arthur Lyon Cross, *The Anglican Episcopate and the American Colonies* (Cambridge, Mass.: Harvard University Press, 1924), 269–70.

7. Ibid., 269. Thomas Bradbury Chandler was the prominent Anglican minister of St. John's Church in Elizabethtown, New Jersey. Publicly he did not discuss the political implications of the bishop question, but there were of course political dimensions that he acknowledged in a letter to the

bishop of London. Of the Appeal he writes, "It expresses the Opinion of the Clergy in most of the Colonies, of the Case of the American Church of England, and represents some of the Reasons and Facts, upon which their Opinion is founded." He goes on, cautiously, to suggest his awareness of the complexity involved: "There are some other Facts and Reasons, which could not be prudently mentioned in a Work of this Nature, as the least Intimation of them would be of ill Consequence in this irritable Age and Country: such of our Superiors, if there be any such, as are governed altogether by political Motives, to espouse the Cause of the Church of England in America, than any contained in the Pamphlet. But I must content myself with having proposed those only which could be mentioned safely, and leave the Event to Divine Providence" (p. 345). Cross reprints the complete letter to Bishop Terrick, the same bishop who ordained Odell a deacon (pp. 345-356).

8. Brindenbaugh, *Mitre and Sceptre*, 190.

9. Leonard Woods Labaree, *Conservatism in Early American History* (Ithaca, N.Y.: Cornell University Press, 1959), 64.

10. Bernard Bailyn, *The Ideological Origins of the American Revolution* (Cambridge, Mass.: Belknap Press, 1967), 97.

11. Sargent, *Loyal Verses*, 193.

12. George Morgan Hills, *History of the Church in Burlington, New Jersey* (Trenton, N.J.: William S. Sharp, 1876), 303.

13. Ibid., 291.

14. Ibid., 292.

15. Ibid., 296.

16. "On the Anniversary of a Friend's Marriage," Odell Papers; Anderson, "Poems of Odell," 7. "To the Ladies of Burlington Bank," Odell Papers, under the pseudonym "Orlando"; Anderson, "Poems of Odell," 16. "The True History of the Golden Age," Odell Papers; Anderson, "Poems of Odell," 18.

17. "Pope's Garden at Twickenham," Odell Papers; Sargent, *Loyal Verses*, 108; Anderson, "Poems of Odell," 5. "Song From Milton's Allegro, With Two Addition Stanzas, Written at Sea, Anno 1767," Odell Papers; Anderson, "Poems of Odell," 8.

18. Philip A. Wadsworth, ed., *Selected Works of La Fontaine* (Carbondale: Southern Illinois University Press, 1950), 205. For La Fontaine, the vizier's contentment has to do with the pleasures of contemplation in which the "cares which courts involve" have no part. Marianne Moore's translation of La Fontaine follows:

> As, might I loiter with tempting queries to solve
> Where the Muses touch my lyre, forget the care
>   which courts involve;

> And ponder the livelong day lofty thoughts
>   which never tire,
> With my hours at command for what the stars
>   inspire;

Marianne Moore, trans., *The Fables of La Fontaine* (New York: Viking, 1954), 262.

19. Janice Potter, *The Liberty We Seek: Loyalist Ideology in Colonial New York and Massachusetts* (Cambridge, Mass., and London: Harvard University Press, 1983), 24.

20. Ibid., 63.

21. "When A Man of True Spirit, in Speaking or Writing," as well as Odell's letter to the editor, signed Veridicus, appear in a clipping in the Odell Papers. Both appear in the April 8–25, 1768, edition of the *Pennsylvania Chronicle*.

22. Larry R. Gerlach, *Prologue to Independence: New Jersey in the Coming of the American Revolution* (New Brunswick, N.J.: Rutgers University Press, 1976), 110.

23. Ibid., 149.

24. "Pope's Garden at Twickenham," Odell Papers; Anderson, "Poems of Odell," 5; Sargent, *Loyal Verses*, 108–10. Sargent dated and titled the poem "On Pope's Garden at Twickenham 1765." His introductory note reads: "These verses must have . . . been written during Odell's residence at London: the allusions to Pope's works need no explanation."

25. Paul Fussell, *The Rhetorical World of Augustan Humanism: Ethics and Imagery from Swift to Burke* (Oxford: Clarendon Press, 1965), 284.

2. Burlington amid Violence

1. Cross, *Anglican Episcopate*, 124–25.

2. Thomas B. Vincent, ed., *Narrative Verse Satire in Maritime Canada* (Ottawa: Tecumeseh Press, 1978), xviii.

3. Gerlach, *Prologue to Independence*, 162.

4. Ibid., 266.

5. Hills, *Church in Burlington*, 300.

6. Ibid., 302. During the next months similar resolutions were passed in New Jersey and New York.

7. The director of the American Philosophical Society, Whitfield J. Bell, Jr., prepared a biographical sketch of Odell in August 1967. It is unpublished and can be found among the Odell Papers.

8. Labaree, *Conservatism*, 113.

9. Moses Coit Tyler, *The Literary History of the American Revolution*, 2 vols. (New York and London: G. P. Putnam's Sons, 1897), 1:457.

10. Ibid., 2:54.

11. Wallace Brown, *The King's Friends: The Composition and Motives of the American Loyalist Claimants* (Providence, R.I.: Brown University Press, 1965), 168.
12. Kenneth Silverman, *A Cultural History of the American Revolution* (New York: Thomas Y. Crowell, 1976), 306.
13. Ibid., 307.
14. Lorenzo Sabine, *Biographical Sketches of Loyalists during the American Revolution with an Historical Eessay* (1864; reprint, New York: Kennikat Press, 1966), 2:215. During the next month similar resolutions were passed in New Jersey and New York.
15. Stephen Botein, "Printers and the American Revolution," in Bernard Bailyn and John B. Hench, eds., *The Press & the American Revolution* (Worcester, Mass.: American Antiquarian Society, 1980), 37-38.
16. Sabine, *Biographical Sketches*, 2:217.
17. Ibid., 2:218.
18. Clarence Edwin Carter, ed., *The Correspondence of General Thomas Gage with the Secretaries of State, 1763-1775* (New Haven, Conn.: Yale University Press, 1931), 2:387-88.
19. Ibid., 2:390.
20. Ibid., 2:422.
21. Norman Gelb, *Less than Glory: A Revisionist's View of the American Revolution* (New York: G. P. Putnam's Sons, 1984), 81.
22. George Washington Nordham, *George Washington and Money* (Washington, D.C.: University Press of America, 1982), 26.
23. John C. Fitzpatrick, ed., *The Writings of George Washington* (Washington, D.C.: U.S. Government Printing Office, 1931-44), 4:122.
24. Fred Lewis Pattee, ed., *The Poems of Philip Freneau* (1902; reprint, New York: Russell and Russell, 1963), 1:174-75.
25. Hills, *Church in Burlington*, 304.
26. Jonathan Trumbull, *Poetical Works* (Hartford, Conn., 1829), appendix 2, 231. The most accessible edition of *M'Fingal* is in Edwin T. Bowden, ed., *The Satiric Poems of Jonathan Trumbull* (Austin: University of Texas Press, 1962). All citations in my text refer to the canto and line number.
27. Samuel G. Goodrich, ed., *Jonathan Trumbull's "M'Fingal"* (Hartford, Conn.: Lincoln and Stone, 1820), 7. Trumbull wrote the poem at the insistence of John Adams, who also abhorred anarchy.
28. Ira D. Gruber, *The Howe Brothers and the American Revolution* (New York: Atheneum, 1972), 56.
29. Hills, *Church in Burlington*, 308-9.
30. Ibid., 309.
31. Ibid., 314.
32. Ibid., 310.
33. Cited by Wallace Brown, *King's Friends*, 121.

3. Revolution Comes to Burlington

1. Robert McClure Calhoon, *The Loyalists in Revolutionary America, 1760-1781* (New York: Harcourt Brace Jovanovich, 1965), 353.
2. Gruber, *Howe Brothers*, 107.
3. Ibid., 83.
4. Benjamin Quarles, *The Negro in the American Revolution* (Chapel Hill: University of North Carolina Press, 1961), 19. On November 7, 1775, on board the *William* in Norfolk harbor, the Earl of Dunmore announced: "I do hereby declare all indentured servants, Negroes, or others, free, that are able and willing to bear arms, they joining His Majesty's troops, as soon as may be, for the speedily reducing of the colonies to a proper sense of their duty to His Majesty's crown and dignity." Rebel slaveholders in every colony were afraid to arm their slaves. On October 13, 1775, the Continental Congress passed a resolution barring blacks from the army, but Dunmore's policy was so effective that on December 31 Washington instructed recruiting officers to accept free blacks. Because the Continental army was increasingly plagued by a shortage of manpower, Washington went further, ignoring his advisors, and enlisted slaves. Tens of thousands joined the Revolution, almost all in noncombatant roles. Dunmore's efforts and Washington's probably canceled each other out.
5. Gruber, *Howe Brothers*, 79.
6. *Pennsylvania Evening Post*, February 6, 1776.
7. P. S. Cafferty, "Loyalist Rhapsodies: The Poetry of Stansbury and Odell" (Ph.D. dissertation, George Washington University, 1971), 100-101.
8. Potter, *Liberty We Seek*, 45.
9. Hills, *Church in Burlington*, 310; Sargent, *Loyal Verses*, 9; Anderson, "Poems of Odell," 21. In another poem written in 1776 Odell points to one of the most famous who has fallen prey to misguided ambition. "Inscription for a curious Chamber Stove," his most often reprinted poem, praises the "celebrated Doctor Franklin" for his achievement in science and then singles out his flaw: he coveted *"political* fame" and thus abetted sedition. Thomas B. Vincent, *Jonathan Odell, An Annotated Chronology of the Poems, 1759-1818* (Kingston, Ontario: Loyal Colonies Press, 1980), 5. Vincent identifies the numerous sources: *Gentleman's Magazine* (London) (April 1777); *Pennsylvania Evening Post* (Philadelphia), November 29, 1777; Odell Papers; Jonathan Boucher, *A View . . . of the American Revolution* (London, 1797), 449; William Smith, *The Life and Letters of William Smith* (Philadelphia, 1803), appendix; Sargent, *Loyal Verses*, 5; Anderson, "Poems of Odell," 21; and Cafferty, "Loyalist Rhapsodies," 139.
10. Hills, *Church in Burlington*, 310-11.
11. Odell Papers; Sargent, *Loyal Verses*, 7; Anderson, "Poems of Odell," 23; Cafferty, "Loyalist Rhapsodies," 97.
12. Odell Papers; Cafferty, "Loyalist Rhapsodies," 109.
13. Hills, *Church in Burlington*, 317.

14. Cafferty, "Loyalist Rhapsodies," 105.
15. Hills, *Church in Burlington*, 312.
16. Odell Papers; Anderson, "Poems of Odell," 20.
17. Hills, *Church in Burlington*, 312.
18. Ibid., 317.
19. Odell Papers; Anderson, "Poems of Odell," 25.
20. Calhoon, *Loyalists in Revolutionary America*, 353.
21. Gruber, *Howe Brothers*, 124.
22. Ibid., 21.
23. Ibid., 126.
24. Tyler, *Literary History*, 2:63.
25. Odell Papers: Anderson, "Poems of Odell," 29.
26. Gruber, *Howe Brothers*, 135.
27. John Shy, "The American Revolution: The Military Conflict Considered as a Revolutionary War," in *Essays on the American Revolution*, edited by Stephen G. Kurtz and James H. Hutson (Chapel Hill: University of North Carolina Press; New York: W. W. Norton, 1973), 134.
28. Gruber, *Howe Brothers*, 136.
29. Odell Papers; Cafferty, "Loyalist Rhapsodies," 153-54.

4. Confrontation and Flight

1. John Jackson, ed., *Margaret Morris: Her Journal with Biographical Sketch and Notes* (Philadelphia: George S. MacManus, 1949), 42-47.
2. Ibid., 42.
3. Ibid., 44.
4. Ibid., 44.
5. Ibid., 89-90.
6. Ibid., 47.
7. Ibid., 47.
8. Hills, *Church in Burlington*, 321n.
9. Jackson, *Morris Journal*, 92.
10. Ibid., 48-49.
11. Ibid., 50.
12. Ibid., 53.
13. Ibid., 54-65.
14. Hills, *Church in Burlington*, 316.
15. Ibid., 315.
16. Ibid., 317.
17. Ibid., 316.
18. Thomas Jones, *History of New York during the Revolutionary War*, edited by Edward Floyd De Lancey (New York: New York Historical Society, 1879), 1:126-28. Joseph Galloway testified before the House of Commons Committee on the American Papers. He was asked for his opinion on

Howe's action at the Delaware River in 1776. This interchange was printed by Rivington in the *Royal Gazette* on October 30, 1779:

> *Q* Whether, in your opinion, the river Delaware might have been crossed by Sir William Howe when he came down to Trenton with the army, and your reasons for that opinion.
>
> *A* There does not appear to me to have been any difficulties to have prevented the British army from passing the Delaware in December, 1776 when Sir Wiliam Howe was at Trenton. I have said that Washington's force was but small.

19. Jackson, *Morris Journal*, 68.

5. Odell for the Loyalists and General Howe

1. Winthrop Sargent, *The Life and Career of Maj. John Andre* (Boston: Ticknor and Fields, 1861), 209.
2. Calhoon, *Loyalists in Revolutionary America*, 374–75.
3. Cafferty, "Loyalist Rhapsodies," 111.
4. Robert Middlekauff, *The Glorious Cause: The American Revolution, 1763–1789* (New York: Oxford University Press, 1982), 368.
5. Cafferty, "Loyalist Rhapsodies," 115.
6. North Callahan, *Royal Raiders: The Tories of the American Revolution* (Indianapolis: Bobbs-Merrill, 1963), 103.
7. Jackson, *Morris Journal*, 175.
8. Odell Papers; Vincent, *Jonathan Odell*, 8.
9. Potter, *Liberty We Seek*, 26.
10. Cited by Callahan, *Royal Raiders*, 106.
11. Middlekauff, *Glorious Cause*, 365.
12. Hills, *Church in Burlington*, 318.
13. Middlekauff, *Glorious Cause*, 389.
14. William Howe, *The Narrative of Lieut. Gen. Sir William Howe* (London: H. Baldwin, 1781), 57.
15. Odell Papers; Cafferty, "Loyalist Rhapsodies," 122.
16. Middlekauff, *Glorious Cause*, 391.
17. Cafferty, "Loyalist Rhapsodies," 117.
18. Odell Papers. Howe's appointment of Odell as chaplain appears in a notice dated Headquarters, January 25, 1778. While in Philadelphia Odell preached at least three sermons: two at Philadelphia College Hall (one on Easter Day) and another at St. Peters to the Fuzileers on April 12, 1778.
19. Carl Van Doren, *Secret History of the American Revolution* (New York: Viking Press, 1941), 456–57; Odell Papers.
20. Stansbury Papers in the Peter Force Collection, Library of Congress. Cafferty cites Sargent's comment that Stansbury's original version of the

poem "offers renewed evidence of the disesteem Sir William Howe felt during his occupation of Philadelphia" (p. 199). In his own transcription of the poem Cafferty offers other variations that Sargent printed from Stansbury's longhand copy. He also traces Burgoyne's part in Howe's military campaign and repeats speculations as to the identity of Howe's mistress (pp. 203–4).

21. David Hawke, *The Colonial Experience* (Indianapolis: Bobbs-Merrill, 1966), 472.

22. Wesley S. Griswold, *The Night the Revolution Began: The Boston Tea Party, 1773* (Brattleboro, Vt.: Stephen Greene Press, 1972), 52. Adams's statement was predictable. Generations earlier, their English counterparts wrested power from the aristocrats who made up the Lords of Trade. The Board of Trade, a subcommittee of the Privy Council of Parliament, replaced them, with the result that British merchants dictated policy and reaped profits once reserved for the nonmerchant class. Colonists typically followed British footsteps in every phase of life, albeit years later. By the 1760s and the 1770s they had caught up with the thinking of the British merchant class. Successful businessmen like John Hancock, who had spent years in England learning the shipping trade, were not about to settle for a Board of Trade that treated colonial merchants as though they were servants to the Lords of Trade.

23. Howe, *Narrative*, 30; cited by Anderson, "Poems of Odell," 300.

24. Jones, *New York during the Revolutionary War*, 1:237–61.

25. Odell Papers.

26. Brown, *King's Friends*, 115.

6. Odell in Clinton's New York

1. Sargent, *Maj. John André*, 209.
2. Wilbur C. Abbot, *New York in the American Revolution* (New York and London: Charles Scribner's Sons, 1929), 254.
3. Sargent, *Maj. John André*, 209.
4. Pattee, *Poems of Freneau*, 2:7.
5. Abbot, *New York*, 252.
6. Sargent, *Maj. John André*, 206.
7. Letter from Odell to André dated December 18, 1779, cited by Van Doren, *Secret History*, 457.
8. Odell Papers.
9. Odell Papers; Anderson, "Poems of Odell," 64.
10. Odell Papers; Anderson, "Poems of Odell," 63. This prologue is the only one that can be dated with any certainty. "Chrononohotonthologos" was staged four times. Only once, on January 9, 1779, did it appear with Samuel Foote's two-act comedy, "Taste," at the John Street Theatre. Possibly this was Odell's "first Essay" after all. It tells us "our Stage is new," which probably refers to the Theatre Royal that opened in New York on

January 6, 1778, according to the January 10 edition of the *Royal Gazette*. On the other hand, Rivington advertised the play, *The Tragedy of Douglas*, as written by a character in the cast. The prologue speaks of this offering as "No new production." Yet the newspaper does not mention it in an earlier issue.

11. Odell Papers; Anderson, "Poems of Odell," 63–64.

12. Potter, *Liberty We Seek*, 107–8.

13. Letter from Odell to Andre, December 21, 1779, cited by Van Doren, *Secret History*, 457–58. Van Doren notes Clinton's approval (p. 216).

14. Don Higginbotham, *The War of American Independence* (New York: Macmillan, 1971), 229.

15. James Thomas Flexner, *George Washington in the American Revolution, 1775–1783* (Boston: Little, Brown, 1968), 324. When Clinton sent eight thousand troops to defend the West Indies, Washington wanted to attack the weakened army in New England. Specifically he asked (he could not order) d'Estaing to attack six thousand British regulars on an island off Rhode Island. John Sullivan, under Washington's command, had nine thousand men at Newport. As d'Estaing made ready, the British installations' lookouts reported the approach of a British fleet. D'Estaing ordered his men back to the ships to chase the British. A storm came up that battered the French fleet and there never was a confrontation. Meanwhile, Sullivan had been left to deal with the British land troops alone.

16. Robert Middlekauff, *The Glorious Cause: The American Revolution, 1763–1789* (New York: Oxford University Press, 1982), 432.

17. Edmund Burke, *Speech on Conciliation with America*, edited by Hammond Lamont (Boston: Ginn, 1897), 18.

18. Odell Papers.

7. Working in Vain for the Cause

1. Van Doren, *Secret History*, 457.

2. James Thomas Flexner, *The Traitor and the Spy: Benedict Arnold and John Andre* (New York: Harcourt, Brace, 1953), 232.

3. Cafferty, "Loyalist Rhapsodies," 26–27.

4. Van Doren, *Secret History*, 202–3.

5. Ibid., 448–55.

6. Odell Papers; Winthrop Sargent, *The Loyalist Poetry of the Revolution* (Philadelphia, 1858), 38; Anderson, "Poems of Odell," 35.

7. Potter, *Liberty We Seek*, 151.

8. Odell Papers; Sargent, *Loyal Verses*, 45; Anderson, "Poems of Odell," 46. Influential Loyalists began to campaign for possibilities that might bring about a rebel defeat. Given the unwillingness or inability of the British army to end the war, the formation of Loyalist regiments was a necessity. In a number of quarters, this had been deemed mandatory from the start. From time to time Loyalists wrote letters to the *Royal Gazette* calling

for volunteers to turn out for a regiment. Generally the writer began by castigating "fellow Refugees" for their "indolent and languid inactivity," urged them "to take up arms, against our cruel and inveterate enemies, the rebels, by whom we have been plundered, insulted, and persecuted, in a most barbarous manner," reminded them that if "the rebellion is not suppressed we must flee to the remote corners of the globe," and concluded with the assurance that if the refugees act with "a becoming and spirited resolution," then "his Majesty's commander, in chief, will . . . grant us all the favour, and indulgence that we can reasonably hope for." The wording is from a letter Rivington printed on April 11, 1778. Securing Clinton's "approbation" was the stumbling block. Like his predecessor William Howe, Clinton as a fact of policy did not want to arm, train, supply, or encourage the Loyalists in this pursuit. Loyalist regiments formed at their own expense. Given the general poverty of the refugees, it was a difficult process. Nevertheless, there were numerous Loyalist regiments in the field during the last years of the war.

William Rankin's plan to recruit not a regiment but a secret Loyalist army was the most ambitious of these various undertakings. During the spring of 1779 Rankin negotiated with Clinton, with André acting as the liaison. By June Rankin claimed that he had more than seven thousand men who were willing to arm themselves in preparation for the capture of a major rebel arsenal in Carlisle, Pennsylvania. He wanted Clinton to send a fleet to support them. Clinton refused, but Rankin continued to press his case. He was soon joined in his effort by William Franklin, who had distinguished himself in the French and Indian War. Franklin offered to lead a Loyalist force from New York and join Rankin's army in Carlisle.

9. Christopher Ward, *The War of the Revolution* (New York: Macmillan, 1952), 2:690.

10. Anderson, "Poems of Odell," 56n.

11. Odell Papers; Sargent, *Loyal Verses*, 51; Anderson, "Poems of Odell," 51.

12. Van Doren, *Secret History*, 69.

13. Ibid., 456–58.

14. *Royal Gazette*, March 11, 1780. The original appears in the Odell Papers; Sargent, *Loyal Verse*, 58; Anderson, "Poems of Odell," 57.

15. Odell Papers; Anderson, "Poems of Odell," 59.

8. Odell's Confidence Bolstered

1. Robert Middlekauff, *The Glorious Cause: The American Revolution, 1763–1789* (New York: Oxford University Press, 1982), 449–50.

2. Flexner, *Traitor and the Spy*, 313.

3. Van Doren, *Secret History*, 461.

4. Ibid., 464.

5. I have relied on the edition printed in Sargent, *Loyalist Poetry of the*

Revolution, 1–37. Sargent's own note says that the poem "is here printed from the text given in The Cow Chase &c., (N.Y. 1780), collated with an earlier copy in the Fisher MSS" (p. 151). The lines from the Fisher manuscript read "Should Atley summon to his savage bar, / To tremble at his rod be from us far." Sargent identifies Atley as "one of the court that convicted Roberts and Carlisle" (p. 152). Oddly enough, he does not include these two lines in the text of the poem itself. My own copy from Rivington's press, dated July 21, 1780, also excludes these lines.

Another version, called *The Times, A Satirical Poem*, is significantly shorter. I have two copies of this version, evidently from the same press in New Jersey, as the bottom of the title page reads "New Jersey: Printed But Not Published." The author is identified: "By The Rev. Mr. Odell." One copy comes from the John Work Garrett Library, Evergreen House, Baltimore. The name Mr. Odell has been crossed out and "Daniel Batwell of York Pa." has been written in its place. The same hand also wrote the title, "By Camillo Querno, Poet Laureate to the Congress." The text itself is filled with corrections, and the final five pages of this copy, titled "Additions from the MSS," are more than six hundred lines. William Gwynn signed on the side of the title page.

Daniel Batwell (1730–83) preached a sermon at York Town, Philadelphia, on July 20, 1775, titled "A General Fast Throughout the Twelve United Colonies Being the Day Recommended By The Honorable Continental Congress For A General Fast." He prays for Congress if "to preserve our rights and privileges be the sole aim. . . ." There must be "no sparks of disloyalty" and no rupture between the king and his subjects. To my knowledge, this is the only extant writing by Daniel Batwell.

On the other copy, one hand inserted "Jonathan" before "Odell," and another crossed out Odell and wrote "The author's real name was Smith he was a Reverend gentleman who resided sometime in York, in Pennsylvania." A third hand, again William Gwynn, signed on the side of the title page.

The Reverend William Smith, who was the provost of the College and Academy of Philadelphia, delivered a sermon titled "An Funeral Oration In Memory of General Montgomery and of the Officers and Soldiers Who Fell with Him, December 31, 1775 Before Quebec; Drawn Up (and Delivered February 19th, 1776) at the Desire of the Honorable Continental Congress." The sermon, like Odell's, contains allusions to the classics and cites passages of poetry. According to Sabine, *Biographical Sketches*, 2:316–17, John Adams was at first impressed by Smith's demeanor, but called his oration "an insolent performance." Smith's stance was unfavorably viewed by the supporters of the Declaration of Independence, against which he wrote and acted. There is no reason to ascribe authorship to Smith simply because he was a Loyalist.

Kenneth Rede discusses the possibilities of authorship in "A Note on the Author of *The Times*," *American Literature* 2 (March 1930): 79–82. Rede has examined the Batwell manuscript, which differs from my own in that

William Gwynn has autographed the first fly leaf. Rede supplies additional information about Batwell by quoting the Reverend Samuel Fitch Hotchkin in *Country Clergy of Pennsylvania* (Philadelphia: P. W. Ziegler, 1890), 293-94:

> Rev. Daniel Batwell succeeded Dr. Andrews (at York) in 1774. In the Revolution, Dr. Batwell was a loyalist and prayed for King George. This caused resentment and he was therefore dragged from his horse and thrice plunged into Codorus Creek.
>
> When Mr. Batwell returned to his home at Huntington, armed men from York brought him back and put him in prison on a charge of being concerned in a conspiracy to destroy the Continental Magazine in Pennsylvania. Dr. Batwell memorialized Congress at York on October 2, 1777, asking release. His physician, Dr. Jameson, stated that he was so emaciated by a complication of disorders, that his life would be endangered unless he was removed from the jail. The matter was referred to the President and the Supreme Executive Council of the State. Mr. Batwell was released from jail, but still remained in custody. Soon, he was freed even from this, and returned to England where he was rewarded by the king with a good parish in which he served until his death.

Rede conjectures that Batwell may have been the "long disguised writer" of *The Times* because "his signature appears on the title page, that corrections and additions, presumably, in his hand appear on all but two pages of the text in the Garrett collection . . . he was the author of other productions of the period, and a known loyalist; all these appear to lend weight to the suggestion" (p. 82). I do not know of Batwell's "other productions," and have no reason to consider him the author of *The Times*.

Rede also traces complexities according to the card made by the Library of Congress. The bibliographers, following Sabine, *Biographical Sketches*, 13:523, credit Odell as author of *The Times*. Rede notes that "in addition, they note that the volume 'appeared also under the title "*The American Times A Satire* . . . *by Camillo Querno (pseud.)* . . . 1780.' Still further they note that the work is 'ascribed also to George Cockings,' and that in their copy there are manuscript additions, 10 pages at the end and a 'note on title page: The author's real name was Smith, he was a reverend gentleman who resided some time in York, in Pennsylvania.'" Rede does not pursue the matter. I would add two comments. First, the preface to George Cocking's "War: An Heroic Poem" (April, 1774) sounds too officious to have anything to do with what we know Odell wrote: "Readers, of whatever rank, or denomination, if ye should receive any pleasure from, and approve the following lines, as to their general design, it is the summit of my ambition." Second, the Library of Congress also owns a complete copy of *The American Times*. It is included among four poems printed by Rivington on July 21, 1780, in André's memory. The first poem is André's "Cow-

Chase," and the last page presents a portrait made from a drawing André did of himself. This is the version that Sargent printed in *Loyal Verses*. On the subject of authorship he supplied this judgment in a note: "That he [Odell] was the writer of *The American Times* (under the pseudonym of Camillo Querno) . . . is a fact of which I have now no doubt, although it is not there so stated, and although it has been attributed to the Rev. Dr. Myles Cooper" (p. 105). I will leave the accomplishments of the Reverend Cooper to someone more adventurous than myself, and go on to consider the major difference between the complete version and the short one.

The short version, whether Smith or Batwell or Cockings or Cooper had anything to do with it, has been cut by more than six hundred lines. Five couplets have been omitted, but it is the omission of five long descriptive passages that changes the character of the short version altogether. The first omitted passage cuts deeply into part 1:

> Hail, Faction, wayward queen, whose charms retain
> Such opposites—the sordid, and the vain:
> Who jar in all things else, in thee unite;
> Robert the greedy, Gouverneur the light;
> And if another contrast we display,
> Still both are thine, the serious and the gay.
> There is a man, all spirit, life, and ease,
> Whose native humour never fails to please;
> There is a man devout, reserv'd austere,
> Whose grave demeanor other men revere;
> These, whom their various turns forbad to meet,
> Have met in Congress in communion sweet;
> There mirth put off, and gravity resign'd,
> The two sworn brothers stand in treason join'd;
> Io triumphe, sing the dev'lish fiends,
> Discordant natures whose seduction blends.
> But still the question agitates mankind,
> Could Duer be over-reach'd, Duane be blind?
> Thy sprightly genius, Duer, coulds't thou controul,
> The flow of wit, the sallies of the soul,
> Abandon every muse, and every grace,
> For eminence among a savage race?
> Coulds't thou, Duane, give up thy favourite church,
> And leave religion weeping in the lurch,
> Bid truth and decent piety adieu,
> For dire promotion o'er a godless crew?
> In Jotham's famous apologue we read,
> Not so the fruit-trees wiser far decreed;
> Shall we, said they, our wine and oil desert,
> Which decorate the face, and cheer the heart,

Quit peace and plenty, elegance and ease,
To reign scrub monarchs over barbarous trees?
'Twere strange—but stranger, Honour to resign,
And govern, legion-like, the herd of swine.

What group of Wizards next salutes my eyes,
United comrades, quadruple allies?
Bostonian Cooper, with his Hancock join'd,
Adams with Adams, one in heart and mind.
Sprung from the soil, where witches swarm'd of yore,
They come well skill'd in necromantic lore;
Intent on mischief, busily they toil,
The magic cauldron to prepare and boil;
Array'd in sable vests, and caps of fur,
With wands of ebony the mess they stir;
See! the smoke rises from the cursed drench,
And poisons all the air with horrid stench.

Celestial muse, I fear 'twill make thee hot
To count the vile ingredients of the pot:
Dire incantations, words of death, they mix
With noxious plants, and Water from the Styx;
Treason's rank flowers, Ambition's swelling fruits,
Hypocrisy in seeds, and Fraud in roots,
Bundles of Lies fresh gather'd in their prime,
And stalks of Calumny grown stale with time;
Handfuls of Zeal's intoxicating leaves;
Riot in bunches, Cruelty in sheaves;
Slices of Cunning cut exceeding thin;
Kernels of Malice, rotten cores of Sin;
Branches of Persecution, boughs of Thrall,
And sprigs of Superstition, dipt in gall;
Opium to lull or madden all the throng,
And assa-foetida profusely strong;
Milk from Tisiphone's infernal breast;
Herbs of all venom, drugs of every pest,
With minerals from the centre brought by Gnomes;

Was this the potion, this the draught design'd
To cheat the croud, and fascinate mankind?
O void of reason they, who thus were caught;
O lost to virtue, who so cheap were bought;
O folly, which all folly sure transcends,
Such bungling sorc'rers to account as friends.

Yet tho' the frantic populace applaud,
'Tis Satire's part to stigmatize the fraud.

> Exult, ye jugglers, in your lucky tricks;
> Yet on your fame the lasting brand we'll fix.
> Cheat male and female, poison age and youth;
> Still we'll pursue you with the goad of truth.
> While in mid-heav'n shines forth the golden flame,
> Hancock and Adams shall be words of shame;
> Whilst silver beams the face of night adorn,
> Cooper of Boston shall be held in scorn.

The other long passages come from part III:

> But knights of old, who wander'd thro' the world,
> And fell destruction on enchanters hurl'd;
> Slew fiery dragons, giants overcame,
> And sav'd from ruin many a peerless dame;
> Play'd not so deep, so desperate a stake,
> As he who draws the pen for Virtue's sake.
>
> For once the monster slain, the spell was broke;
> And joy succeeded to the daring stroke:
> The ladies bless'd their lovers with their charms,
> And the knight rested from his feats of arms.
>
> But error may not with such ease be quell'd;
> She rallies fresh her force tho' oft repell'd.
> Cut, hack'd, and mangled, she denies to yield,
> And strait returns with vigour to the field:
> Champions of truth, our efforts are in vain;
> Fast as we slay, the foe revives again.
> Vainly th' enchanted castle we surprize;
> New monsters hiss, and new enchantments rise.
> . . . .
> Expose an opal to the solar ray,
> And mark the beams that momentary play:
> See the gay stone, in mimic robes array'd.
> Glow in the red or in the purple fade;
> In swift progression vary to the sight,
> And run thro' all the different modes of light.
> Go then, and count the colours as they rise;
> Tell, if thou canst, the numbers of the dyes;
> Each combination of the fluid mass;
> Nor let the shifting of a sun-beam pass.
> This once accomplish'd, thy sagacious pen
> May note the phrenzies of impatient men.
> The bands of faith and loyalty who break,
> And roam the fields of popular mistake.
> Truce with these flow'rs—the Times are out of joint;

> Hence trifling—come we closer to the point:
> Some must attendant on th' eternal King,
> Truth's radiant mirror for my guidance bring.
> I ask not now the thunder and the fire;
> The still small voice is all that I desire.

Winthrop Sargent, Moses Coit Tyler, and Thomas B. Vincent, three scholars who have studied Odell's work most closely to date, credit him with the authorship of *The American Times*. I also believe that Odell wrote *The American Times*, which was printed by Rivington on July 21, 1780, and reprinted by Sargent in 1858. Why someone excised the lines above to create *The Times* and then tried to restore them remains a puzzle.

We can speculate about Odell's specific sources, which go a long way toward indicating authorship. He probably was working with the material that made up *The American Times* for quite a while. According to Rivington, it was written "several months" after Pulaski's death on October 11, 1779. Odell started writing either during the spring when the Arnold conspiracy began in earnest, or perhaps months earlier. He might have tried out his material in three pieces that then appeared in the *Royal Gazette*. The first piece, dated January 23, 1779, and signed "A Dreamer," expounds on an "observed phenomenon." When men "degrade themselves from the character of *rational* beings," they assume the appropriate bestial characteristics. The soul of Louis XVI, for instance, has "transmigrated into a half-starved *jackass*." On the other hand, poets like Pope, the melodious *"Swan of Twickenham,"* are rewarded. The speaker dreams of a "crowd of shades" punished with sentences of damnation. First is Chief Justice M'Kean, condemned to be hounded eternally by the souls of the Quakers Roberts and Carlisle. Deane becomes a monkey, General Lee an adder, and Livingston a wolf. Jay is turned into a rattlesnake, and the whole Continental army "ordered to put on the shape of the *timid Hare*, whose disposition they already possessed."

A Dreamer elicited a friendly response from Somnolentus on January 30. He too dreamed of judges passing sentence on villains, namely on all the French ministers of state and, significantly, on "some of the leaders of *Opposition* in the British Parliament." Acknowledging Minos as his guide, Somnolentus reports that in his dreams King Louis howls in "the dialect of an enraged Gremalkin," rages at Count d'Estaing, and then apologizes to him for "not hazarding an action with Lord Howe, whom he called a *sauvage Anglois*." Congress persuades the simpleton *Charon* to accept Continental dollars and ferry them to Hell. Payne [Paine] is particularly obnoxious. He has assumed the "form of a *Musketo*." The sound of rattles, made by members of Congress as they change into rattlesnakes, awakens him.

On February 10, A Dreamer concludes the exchange of visions. He gives most of his attention to Mr. Payne, who has metamorphosed into a dog, and he explains that the ancient Greeks reserved the epithet, a dog, for the most impudent of their enemies. A Dreamer goes on to explain Homer's epithet, which would be literally translated *"Dog's face,* but which Mr. Pope . . . has rendered no less forcibly *'thou dog in forehead.'* " Sancho Panza's proverbs are used to describe the art of congressional lying, and Sam Adams, a student of Machiavellian policy, is compared to Catiline and Cromwell.

The references to Pope's translation of Homer and Sancho Panza's proverbs, as well as the Hobbesian images of rattlesnakes and wolves and allusions to Catiline and Machiavelli, recall the books in Odell's library. He referred to Minos in "Le Songe d'un habitant du Mogul," used "Timid Hare" in his poem about Schuyler's Peacock Expedition, and focused a great deal of energy on Paine in "The Word of Congress." Odell of course might not have been either A Dreamer or Somnolentus. Yet it would be an extraordinary coincidence for all three Milton admirers to be familiar with Odell's work and to say that members of Congress are hell born and enter the poem, in the words of *The American Times,* as "hideous shapes, / Infernal wolves, and bears, and hounds, and apes." And, too, all three authors hurl ridicule at the villains and sentence them.

Among the general influences on *The American Times,* consider three volumes Odell owned: Richard Glover's *Leonidas,* in which the valiant few succeed against many barbarians; Samuel Butler's *Hudibras,* which concerns the misadventures of the pompous Presbyterian knight in his conflict with King Charles I; and possibly Charles Churchill's *The Rosciad,* in which actors who can neither act nor think pass beneath the narrator's contemptuous gaze.

6. Cited by Norman Gelb, *Less than Glory: A Revisionist's View of the American Revolution* (New York: G. P. Putnam's Sons, 1984), 85.

7. Van Doren, *Secret History,* 320.

8. Flexner, *Traitor and the Spy,* 358–67.

9. John André, *Major André's Journal, Operations of the British Army under Lieutenant Generals Sir William Howe and Sir Henry Clinton, June 1777 to November 1778* (Tarrytown, N.Y.: W. Abbatt, 1930), 9.

10. Odell Papers; Anderson, "Poems of Odell," 62.

9. Leaving the Colonies

1. Robert Middlekauff, *The Glorious Cause: The American Revolution, 1763–1789* (New York: Oxford University Press, 1982), 571.

2. Jones, *New York during the Revolutionary War,* 2:221.

3. Van Doren, *Secret History,* 430–31.

4. *Royal Gazette,* November 4, 1782.

5. Paul H. Smith, "Sir Guy Carleton, Peace Negotiations, and the Evacuation of New York," *Canadian Historical Review* 3 (1969), 253.

6. James Rivington was allowed to remain in New York after the British army left. The *Salem Gazette* on December 25, 1783, reported an " 'undoubted fact' that Rivington was protected in person and property by a

guard as Americans entered the city" and that he was "allowed to remain in the country after the Peace of 1783 for reasons best known to the great men at the helm." Rivington survived Washington's entrance into the city, but his newspaper did not, although he changed its name to *New-York Gazette, and Universal Advertiser* on December 10, 1783. Whether Rivington was a spy or perhaps a double agent during the war will remain a mystery. Certainly his life was filled with danger. But a series of failed investments that he made in behalf of his sons and friends brought him to ruin. At the age of 72 he entered debtor's prison. Catherine Snell Crary, "The Tory and the Spy: The Double Life of James Rivington," *William and Mary Quarterly* 16 (January 1959): 61–72.

7. Smith, "Sir Guy Carleton," 262.
8. Ibid., 264.
9. Jones, *New York during the Revolutionary War*, 2:242.
10. Ibid., 2:244.
11. Odell Papers.
12. Esther Clark Wright, *Loyalists of New Brunswick* (Fredericton, New Brunswick, 1945), 88–90.
13. Ann Gorman Condon, *The Envy of the American States: The Loyalist Dream for New Brunswick* (Fredericton, New Brunswick: New Ireland Press, 1984), 88.
14. Ibid., 34.
15. William Odber Raymond, ed., *The Winslow Papers* (Saint John: Sun Printing, 1901), 148.
16. Alfred G. Bailey, "Jonathan Odell," *Dictionary of Canadian Biography*, vol. 5, 1801–1820 (Toronto: University of Toronto Press, 1983), 630.
17. Condon, *Envy of American States*, 53.
18. Odell and other Clergymen of New York to Sir Guy Carleton, March 21, 1783, Headquarters Papers, No. 7182, cited in Condon, *Envy of American States*, 56; Bailey, *Dictionary of Canadian Biography*, 5:630.
19. Bailey, *Dictionary of Canadian Biography*, 5:630.
20. Condon, *Envy of American States*, 67.
21. James W. St. G. Walker, *The Black Loyalists: The Search for a Promised Land in Nova Scotia and Sierra Leone, 1783–1870* (New York: Holmes and Meier, 1976), 11.
22. Condon, *Envy of American States*, 191.
23. Walker, *Black Loyalists*, 57; William A. Spray, *The Blacks in New Brunswick* (Fredericton, New Brunswick: Brunswick Press, 1972), 16. Spray comments: "With the loyalists were several thousand Black people. Some came as slaves or indentured servants, others as free Blacks or Black loyalists. In documents, the loyalists always preferred to refer to their slaves as 'servants.' However, the status of the majority of Blacks who were listed as 'servants' was certainly no different than that of those listed as slaves."
24. Anderson, "Poems of Odell," 36. Joseph Stansbury eventually became a "reconstructed" Loyalist. It was a long process. After the end of the war

he destroyed all of his political verse except a copy of "God Save the King." On the back he wrote lines of reconciliation beginning: "Now this war at length is o'er, / Let us think of it no more." He moved with his family to Burlington, but was arrested that same week. He promised to leave the state within ten days and was released. In August 1783 Stansbury sailed for Nova Scotia without his wife and children. In October he sailed for England. Despite his part in the Benedict Arnold intrigue, he was not able to secure a pension from the Loyalist Claims Commission. He then returned to Philadelphia with plans to resume his business. A rock with a letter attached and thrown through his window intimated that "it would not be possible for him to live in Philadelphia, although, as was also hinted, it might be possible for him to die there." By 1793, however, he was "so accepted by the community" that he ran in a city election. He decided, finally, on New York, where he "quietly took up allegiance to the newly formed United States" (Cafferty, "Loyalist Rhapsodies," 34–38).

25. Odell Papers.

10. From London to New Brunswick

1. Condon, *Envy of American States*, 115.
2. "The Memorial of Jonathan Odell," March 23, 1784, in the Loyalist Claims Commission, Audit Office Transcripts, Examinations in Nova Scotia, XVI, 397–410. These papers are held by the New York Public Library.
3. Condon, *Envy of American States*, 71.
4. Ibid., 115.
5. Ibid., 117.
6. Odell Papers; Cafferty, "Loyalist Rhapsodies," 239.
7. If the letter was written after the committee made its decision, Odell may have believed that Carleton's fall from power would adversely affect his own future.
8. Hills, *Church in Burlington*, 320–21.
9. Odell Papers.
10. William Odber Raymond, ed., *Winslow Papers* (Saint John: Sun Printing, 1901), 213.
11. Odell Papers; Anderson, "Poems of Odell," iv.
12. Benjamin Moore to Jonathan Odell, November 15, 1784, Odell Papers.
13. Brown, *King's Friends*, 116.
14. Hills, *Church in Burlington*, 323.
15. Alfred G. Bailey, "Jonathan Odell," *Dictionary of Canadian Biography*, vol. 5, 1801–1820 (Toronto: University of Toronto Press, 1983), 630.
16. Odell Papers; Anderson, "Poems of Odell," xv.
17. Jane Errington and George Rawlyk, "The Loyalist-Federalist Alliance of Upper Canada," *American Review of Canadian Studies* 14, no. 2 (Summer 1984), 158.
18. Errington and Rawlyk, "Loyalist-Federalist Alliance," 157.

19. Ibid., 159.
20. Odell's other poems and songs concerning events leading up to the War of 1812 and the war itself include "To the Memory of Lord Nelson" (July 1806), "Hull's Incursion into Canada" (September 1812), "Monsieur Hull, of his late Expedition" (October 1812), "The Battle of Queen's Town, Upper Canada" (November 1812), "The Agonizing Dilemma" (November 1812), and "A Cheering Salute to Our Neighbor Madison" (January 1814). For a full discussion of "The Agonizing Dilemma" see Vincent, *Narrative Verse Satire*, 173–85.
21. Bailey, *Dictionary of Canadian Biography*, 5:631.
22. Odell Papers; Anderson, "Poems of Odell," xiii.
23. Cited by Condon, *Envy of American States*, 155–56.
24. Walker, *Black Loyalists*, 123.
25. Ibid., 123.
26. Condon, *Envy of American States*, 169.
27. Cited by Condon, *Envy of American States*, 161.
28. Ibid., 163.
29. Ibid., 164.
30. Ibid., 171.
31. Odell Papers. If we are to believe Edward Winslow, Odell's arrogance made him unique among the old guard Loyalists: "His habits & manners are such as in the days of superstition might have suited a High priest of the order of Melchisedec, but are ill calculated for a civil department. His hauteur is so disgusting that he has become completely obnoxious. . . ." Winslow to Daniel Lyman, March 12, 1800, cited by Bailey, *Dictionary of Canadian Biography*, 5:630. It should be remembered that Winslow coveted Odell's appointment as secretary to the province. He took heart from rumors in 1784 that the appointment was temporary.
32. Cited by Smith, "Sir Guy Carleton," 260.
33. Robert Middlekauff, *The Glorious Cause: The American Revolution, 1763–1789* (New York: Oxford University Press, 1982), 338.

Bibliography

Primary Sources

Anderson, J. J. "A Collection of the Poems of Jonathan Odell with a Biographical and Critical Introduction." Master's thesis, University of British Columbia, 1961.

André, John. *Major André's Journal, Operations of the British Army under Lieutenant Generals Sir William Howe and Sir Henry Clinton, June 1777 to November 1778*. Tarrytown, N.Y.: W. Abbatt, 1930.

Cafferty, P. S. "Loyalist Rhapsodies: The Poetry of Stansbury and Odell." Ph.D. dissertation, George Washington University, 1971.

Carter, Clarence Edwin, ed. *The Correspondence of General Thomas Gage with the Secretaries of State, 1763–1775*. New Haven, Conn.: Yale University Press, 1931.

Clark, Harry Hayden, ed. *Poems of Freneau*. New York: Harcourt, Brace, 1929.

Freneau, Philip. *Poems Written and Published during the American Revolutionary War*. New York: Scholar's Facsimiles and Reprints, 1976.

Galloway, Joseph. *Cool Thoughts on the Consequences to Great Britain of American Independence*. London: J. Wilkie, 1780.

———. *Letters to a Nobleman on the Conduct of the War in the Middle Colonies*. Reprint. Boston: Gregg, 1972.

Hills, George Morgan. *History of the Church in Burlington, New Jersey*. Trenton, N.J.: William S. Sharp, 1876.

Howe, William. *The Narrative of Lieut. Gen. Sir William Howe*. London: H. Baldwin, 1781.

Jackson, John, ed. *Margaret Morris: Her Journal with Biographical Sketch and Notes*. Philadelphia: George S. MacManus, 1949.

"The Memorial of Jonathan Odell," March 23, 1784. Loyalist Claims Commission, Audit Office Transcripts, Examinations in Nova Scotia, XVI, 397–410. New York Public Library, New York.

Moore, Marianne, trans. *The Fables of La Fontaine*. New York: Viking, 1954.
Morris, Margaret. *Private Journal Kept during a Portion of the Revolutionary War, for the Amusement of a Sister*. Philadelphia, 1836. Reprint. New York: Arno Press, 1969.
Odell, Jonathan. Papers. New Brunswick Museum, Saint John, New Brunswick.
Pennsylvania Chronicle, 1767–68.
Philadelphia Evening Post, 1779.
Royal Gazette, 1780–82.
Sargent, Winthrop. *The Loyal Verses of Joseph Stansbury and Doctor Odell*. Albany, N.Y.: J. Munsell, 1860.
———. *The Loyalist Poetry of the Revolution*. Philadelphia: Collins, 1858.
Stansbury, Joseph. Papers. Peter Force Collection. Library of Congress, Washington, D.C.
Trumbull, John. *M'Fingal*. New York: John Buel, 1795.
Van Doren, Carl. *Secret History of the American Revolution*. New York: Viking, 1941.
Vincent, Thomas B. *Jonathan Odell: An Annotated Chronology of the Poems, 1759–1818*. Kingston, Ontario: Loyal Colonies Press, 1980.

Secondary Sources

Abbot, Wilbur C. *New York in the American Revolution*. New York and London: Charles Scribner's Sons, 1929.
Ahlstrom, Sydney E. *A Religious History of the American People*. New Haven, Conn.: Yale University Press, 1972.
Anderson, Troyer Steele. *The Command of the Howe Brothers during the American Revolution*. New York and London: Oxford University Press, 1936.
Aptheker, Herbert. *The Negro in the American Revolution*. New York: International Publishers, 1940.
Austin, Mary Stanislas. *Philip Freneau: The Poet of the Revolution*. Detroit, Mich.: Cale Research Co., 1968.
Axelrad, Jacob. *Philip Freneau*. Austin: University of Texas Press, 1967.
Bailyn, Bernard. *The Ideological Origins of the American Revolution*. Cambridge, Mass.: Harvard University Press, Belknap Press, 1967.
———. *Pamphlets of the American Revolution, 1750–1776*. Cambridge, Mass.: Harvard University Press, 1965.
Bailyn, Bernard, and Hench, John B., eds. *The Press and the American Revolution*. Worcester, Mass.: American Antiquarian Society, 1980.
Bakeless, John. *Turncoats, Traitors and Heroes*. Philadelphia and New York: J. B. Lippincott, 1959.
Beer, George Louis. *British Colonial Policy, 1754–1765*. Gloucester, Mass.: Peter Smith, 1958.

Beers, Henry A. *The Connecticut Wits*. New Haven, Conn.: Yale University Press, 1920.
Bercovitch, Sacvan. *The American Jeremiad*. Madison: University of Wisconsin Press, 1978.
Billias, George A. *George Washington's Opponents*. New York: William Morrow, 1969.
Bowden, Edwin T., ed. *The Satiric Poems of John Trumbull*. Austin: University of Texas Press, 1962.
Bowden, Mary Weatherspoon. *Philip Freneau*. Boston: Twayne, 1976.
Bowler, Arthur R. *Logistics and the Failure of the British Army in America*. Princeton, N.J.: Princeton University Press, 1975.
Bowman, Allen. *The Morale of the American Revolutionary Army*. Washington, D.C.: American Council on Public Affairs, 1943.
Bowman, Larry G. *Captive Americans: Prisoners during the American Revolution*. Athens: Ohio University Press, 1976.
Bradley, Arthur G. *United Empire Loyalists*. London: Thornton, Butterworth, 1932.
Brebner, J. B. *Neutral Yankees of Nova Scotia*. Toronto: McClelland and Stewart, 1969.
Bridenbaugh, Carl. *Mitre and Sceptre: Transatlantic Faiths, Ideas, Personalities, and Politics, 1689–1775*. New York: Oxford University Press, 1962.
Brown, Wallace. *The Good Americans: The Loyalists in the American Revolution*. New York: William Morrow, 1969.
———. *The King's Friends: The Composition and Motives of the American Loyalist Claimants*. Providence, R.I.: Brown University Press, 1966.
Calhoon, Robert McClure. *The Loyalists in Revolutionary America 1760–1781*. New York: Harcourt Brace Jovanovich, 1965.
Callahan, North. *Royal Raiders: The Tories of the American Revolution*. Indianapolis: Bobbs-Merrill, 1963.
Cohen, Lester H. "Explaining the Revolution: Ideology and Ethics in Mercy Otis Warren's Historical Theory." *William and Mary Quarterly* (April 1980): 200–18.
Commager, Henry Steele, and Morris, Richard B. *The Spirit of 'Seventy-Six*. 2 vols. Indianapolis and New York: Bobbs-Merrill, 1958.
Condon, Ann Gorman. *The Envy of the American States: The Loyalist Dream for New Brunswick*. Fredericton, New Brunswick: New Ireland Press, 1984.
Cowie, Alexander. "John Trumbull as a Revolutionist." *American Literature* 3 (November 1931): 287–95.
Crary, Catherine S. *The Price of Loyalty: Tory Writings from the Revolutionary Era*. New York: McGraw-Hill, 1973.
———. "The Tory and the Spy: The Double Life of James Rivington." *William and Mary Quarterly* 16 (January 1959).
Cross, Arthur Lyon. *The Anglican Episcopate and the American Colonies*. Cambridge, Mass.: Harvard University Press, 1924.

Cunliffe, Marcus. *George Washington*. London: Collins, 1959.
Davidson, Philip. *Propaganda and the American Revolution*. Chapel Hill: University of North Carolina Press, 1941.
Eggleston, George, ed. *American War Ballads and Lyrics*. New York: G. P. Putnam and Sons, 1889.
Emerson, Everett, ed. *American Literature, 1764–1789: The Revolutionary Years*. Madison: University of Wisconsin Press, 1977.
Errington, Jane, and Rawlyk, George. "The Loyalist-Federalist Alliance of Upper Canada." *American Review of Canadian Studies* 16 (Summer 1984): 157–76.
Ferguson, James G. *Power of the Purse*. Chapel Hill: University of North Carolina Press, 1964.
Fisher, Sydney George. *The True History of the American Revolution*. Boston: Gregg, 1972.
Flexner, James Thomas. *George Washington in the American Revolution, 1775–1783*. Boston: Little, Brown, 1968.
———. *The Traitor and the Spy: Benedict Arnold and John Andre*. New York: Harcourt, Brace, 1953.
Flick, Alexander C. *The American Revolution in New York*. Port Washington, N.Y.: Kennikat Press, 1967.
———. *Loyalism in New York during the American Revolution*. New York: Columbia University Press, 1901.
Foner, Philip S. *Blacks in the American Revolution*. Westport, Conn.: Greenwood, 1975.
Fulton, Richard M. *The Revolution That Wasn't*. Port Washington, N.Y.: Kennikat Press, 1981.
Furnas, J. C. *The Americans: A Social History of the United States 1587–1914*. New York: G. P. Putnam's Sons, 1969.
———. *Considerations upon the American Inquiry*. London, 1779.
Fussell, Paul. *The Rhetorical World of Augustan Humanism: Ethics and Imagery from Swift to Burke*. Oxford: Clarendon Press, 1965.
Gerlach, Larry R. *Prologue to Independence: New Jersey in the Coming of the American Revolution*. New Brunswick, N.J.: Rutgers University Press, 1976.
Gipson, L. H. *The Coming of the Revolution*. New York: Harper and Row, 1954.
Granger, Bruce I. *Political Satire in the American Revolution*. New York: Cornell University Press, 1960.
Greene, Jack P., ed. *The Reinterpretation of the American Revolution, 1763–1789*. New York and London: Harper and Row, 1968.
Griswold, Wesley S. *The Night the Revolution Began: The Boston Tea Party, 1773*. Brattleboro, Vt.: Stephen Greene Press, 1972.
Gruber, Ira D. *The Howe Brothers and the American Revolution*. New York: Atheneum, 1972.

Herodotus, T. *The Establishment of the Establishment: Living History*. Oklahoma City: Lance Books, 1975.
Higginbotham, Don, ed. *Reconsiderations on the Revolutionary War: Selected Essays*. Westport, Conn., and London: Greenwood Press, 1978.
Howard, Leon. *The Connecticut Wits*. Chicago: University of Chicago Press, 1943.
Hyman, Harold M. *To Try Men's Souls: Loyalty Tests in American History*. Berkeley and Los Angeles: University of California Press, 1960.
Jones, Thomas. *History of New York during the Revolutionary War*. Edited by Edward Floyd De Lancey. 2 vols. New York: New York Historical Society, 1879.
Kobre, Sidney. *The Development of the Colonial Newspaper*. Pittsburgh: Colonial Press, 1944.
Kurtz, Stephen G., and Hutson, James H., eds. *Essays on the American Revolution*. Chapel Hill: University of North Carolina Press; New York: W. W. Norton, 1973.
Labaree, Leonard Woods. *Conservatism in Early American History*. Ithaca, N.Y.: Cornell University Press, 1959.
Leary, Lewis. *That Rascal Freneau: A Study in Literary Failure*. New Brunswick, N.J.: Rutgers University Press, 1941.
Linsley, Rev. George T. "The Episcopate of Samuel Seabury." *Episcopal Historical Tracts*. Hartford, Conn.: Church Missions Publishing, 1925.
Lundin, Leonard. *Cockpit of the Revolution: The War for Independence in New Jersey*. Princeton, N.J.: Princeton University Press, 1940.
Maier, Pauline. *From Resistance to Revolution: Colonial Radicals and the Development of American Opposition to Britain, 1765–1776*. New York: Alfred A. Knopf, 1972.
———. *The Old Revolutionaries: Political Lives in the Age of Samuel Adams*. New York: Alfred A. Knopf, 1980.
Marsh, Philip M. *The Works of Philip Freneau: A Critical Study*. Metuchen, N.J.: Scarecrow Press, 1968.
Martin, James Kirby. *Men in Rebellion*. New York and London: Macmillan, 1976.
Miller, Perry. *The Life of the Mind in America from the Revolution to the Civil War*. New York: Harcourt, Brace and World, 1965.
Mitchell, Broadus. *The Price of Independence*. New York: Oxford University Press, 1974.
Moore, Frank. *Songs and Ballads of the American Revolution*. New York: Hurst, 1905. Reprint. New York: Arno Press, 1969.
Mott, Frank Luther. *American Journalism*. New York: Macmillan, 1941.
Nelson, William H. *The American Tory*. London: Oxford University Press, 1961.
Noll, Mark A. *Christians in the American Revolution*. Washington, D.C.: Christian College Consortium, 1977.

Norton, Mary Beth. *The British-Americans: The Loyalist Exiles in England 1774–1789*. Boston: Little, Brown, 1972.
Paine, Thomas. *The Works of Thomas Paine*. New York: W. H. Wise, 1925.
Parrington, Verrnon Louis. *The Colonial Mind, 1620–1800*. New York: Harcourt, Brace, 1927.
Pattee, Fred Lewis, ed. *The Poems of Philip Freneau: Poet of the Revolution*. 3 vols. 1902. Reprint. New York: Russell and Russell, 1963.
Pickering, James H., ed. *The World Turned Upside Down: Poetry and Prose of The American Revolution*. New York and London: Kennikat Press, 1975.
Potter, Janice. *The Liberty We Seek: Loyalist Ideology in Colonial New York and Massachusetts*. Cambridge, Mass., and London: Harvard University Press, 1983.
Prescott, Frederick C., and Nelson, John H., eds. *Prose and Poetry of the Revolution*. New York: Thomas Y. Crowell, 1925.
Randall, Willard Sterne. *A Little Revenge: Benjamin Franklin and His Son*. Boston and Toronto: Little, Brown, 1984.
Royster, Charles. *A Revolutionary People at War: The Continental Army and American Character, 1775–1783*. Chapel Hill: University of North Carolina Press, 1979.
Sabine, Lorenzo. *Biographical Sketches of Loyalists during the American Revolution with an Historical Essay*. 1864. Reprint. New York: Kennikat Press, 1966.
———. *The Loyalists of the American Revolution*. Reprint. Springfield, Mass.: Walden, 1957.
Sargent, Winthrop. *The Life and Career of Maj. John André*. Boston: Ticknor and Fields, 1861.
Savelle, Max, and Middlekauff, Robert. *A History of Colonial America*. New York: Holt, Rinehart and Winston, 1964.
Scheer, George F., and Rankin, Hugh F. *Rebels and Redcoats*. Cleveland and New York: World, 1957.
Schlesinger, Arthur M. *The Colonial Merchants and the American Revolution*. New York: Fredrick Ungar, 1966.
———. "Liberty Tree: Geneology." *New England Quarterly* 25 (December 1952): 435–58.
———. *Prelude to Independence: The Newspaper War on Britain, 1764–1776*. New York: Alfred A. Knopf, 1966.
Shy, John W. "The Legacy of the American Revolutionary War." In *Legacies of the American Revolution*, edited by Larry R. Gerlach. Logan: Utah State University Press, 1978.
Silverman, Kenneth, ed. *Colonial American Poetry*. New York: Hafner, 1968.
———. *A Cultural History of the American Revolution*. New York: Thomas Y. Crowell, 1976.
Simmons, R. C. *The American Colonies from Settlement to Independence*. New York: David McKay, 1976.

Smith, Page. *The Shaping of America: A People's History of the Young Republic*. Vol. 3. New York: McGraw-Hill, 1980.
Smith, Paul H. *Loyalists and Redcoats: A Study in British Revolutionary Policy*. Chapel Hill: University of North Carolina Press, 1964.
———. "Sir Guy Carleton, Peace Negotiations, and the Evacuation of New York." *Canadian Historical Review* 3 (1969): 245-64.
Stinchcombe, William C. *The American Revolution and the French Alliance*. Syracuse N.Y.: Syracuse University Press, 1969.
Stout, Neil R. *The Perfect Crisis: The Beginning of the Revolutionary War*. New York: New York University Press, 1976.
Sweet, William W. "The Role of the Anglicans in the American Revolution." *Huntington Library Quarterly* 11 (November 1947): 51-70.
Thomas, P. D. G. *British Politics and the Stamp Act Crisis: The First Phase of the American Revolution, 1763-1767*. Oxford: Clarendon Press, 1975.
Tisdale, E. *The Satiric Poems of John Trumbull*. Austin: University of Texas Press, 1962.
Tyler, Moses Coit. *The Literary History of the American Revolution 1763-1783*. 2 vols. New York and London: G. P. Putnam's Sons, 1897. Reprint. New York: Frederick Ungar, 1957.
Ubbelohde, Carl. *The Vice Admiralty Courts and the American Revolution*. Chapel Hill: University of North Carolina Press, 1960.
Van Tyne, Claude Halstead. *England and America: Rivals in the American Revolution*. New York: Russell and Russell, 1969.
———. *The Loyalists in the American Revolution*. Gloucester, Mass.: Peter Smith, 1959.
Vincent, Thomas B., ed. *Narrative Verse Satire in Maritime Canada, 1779-1814*. Ottawa: Tecumseh, 1978.
Walker, James W. St. G. *The Black Loyalists: The Search for a Promised Land in Nova Scotia and Sierra Leone, 1783-1870*. New York: Holmes and Meier, 1976.
Ward, Christopher. *The War of the Revolution*. New York: Macmillan, 1952.
Willard, Margaret Sheeler, ed. *Letters on the American Revolution*. Port Washington, N.Y.: Kennikat Press, 1968.
Williams, George Washington. *A History of Negro Troops in the War of the Rebellion, 1861-1865*. New York: Bergman, 1968.
Williams, Harry T. *The History of American Wars from Colonial Times to World War I*. New York: Alfred A. Knopf, 1981.
Williams, Stanley T. *The Beginnings of American Poetry (1620-1855)*. New York: Cooper Square Publishers, 1970.
Wood, Gordon S. "Conspiracy and the Paranoid Style: Causality and Deceit in the Eighteenth Century." *William and Mary Quarterly* (July 1982): 401-41.
Zimmer, Anne Y. *Jonathan Boucher: Loyalist in Exile*. Detroit, Mich.: Wayne State University Press, 1978.

Index

Adams, John, 48, 76, 85, 95, 99, 101, 166 n.27, 170 n.22, 172 n.5; Episcopate Controversy, 4; in *The American Times*, 121. *See also* Writ of Assistance
Adams, Samuel: in The American Times, 121
American Philosophical Society, 22, 24, 165 n.7
Anderson, Joan, xii, 163 n.5, 164 n.17, 165 n.24, 167 n.11, 168 nn.16, 19, and 25, 170 n.23, 170 nn.9 and 10, 171 n.11, 171 nn.6 and 8, 172 nn.10, 11, 14, and 15, 179 n.10, 180 n.24, 181 nn.11 and 16
André, John, 81, 82, 117, 128–29, 159, 171 n.8, 174 n.5, 179 n.9; liaison in Benedict Arnold intrigue, 96; letter to Arnold, mid-June 1779, 97; liaison between Odell and General Clinton, 98; uses pseudonym John Anderson, 98, 128, 129; meeting with Arnold and its consequences, 128–29; "The Cow Chase, Complete in Three Cantos," 129
Anglican bishop in America: possibility, xii, 3, 4, 5; Dean Jonathan Swift mentioned, 6; heated controversy, 7; in "What the Deuce," 12–13; in "When a Man of True Spirit," 14; and Archbishop Secker, 15; land reserved for, 21; in "Tis Large Indeed," 45–46; Margaret Morris on Odell's aspirations, 59–60; Odell's aspirations, 142–43
Anglican church, 3, 5, 6, 11, 13, 20, 21, 31, 45, 47; Odell writes poems for, 7; as subject of Odell's poems, 12–14, 45–47; in "Tis Large Indeed," 45–47. *See also* Episcopate Controversy; Episcopate Convention; Odell: Letters from Odell to the Secretary of the S.P.G.; Society for the Propagation of the Gospel (S.P.G.)
Anglican ministers, 3, 5, 6, 7, 11, 31; considered Loyalists, 23; and the Oath of the King's Supremacy, 45; in "Tis Large Indeed," 46–47
Arnold, Benedict, xiii, 77; initiates conspiracy, 94–98; in "The Congratulation," 103; assumes command at West Point, 116; and Odell's letters, 117; meets with John André, 128; eludes George Washington, 129
Associated Loyalists, 132–35

Association, the, xii, 22–23, 24, 26
Associators, 133–35
Augustan ideology. *See* Loyalist ideology

Baltimore, Md., 54
Batwell, Rev. Daniel, 172 n.5
Bernard, Governor Francis, 12
Boston, Mass., 34, 37; Britannicus on, 87; in "The Word of Congress," 102; *See* Siege of Boston
Boucher, Rev. Jonathan, 8, 23, 148, 156
Brandywine, Battle of, 69, 70
Britannicus (pseud. Odell and Samuel Seabury): "An Answer," 73–76; on Sir Francis Drake, 103–4; appeal to earl of Shelbourne, 138; Britannicus essays, 84–91, 98, 102, 106–7, 111–13; and *The American Times*, 126; on essayists' fees, 107–9, 129. *See also* A Loyal American
British army, xi, xiii, xiv, 3, 87, 95, 98–99, 104, 118; under General Gage, 26; in *M'Fingal*, 29; Loyalists dependent on, 30; effect on Odell's tone, 34; occupies Boston, 34; Loyalists not used as soldiers in, 35–36; in "The Tory Hunt," 37–38; Loyalists feel need for show of force by, 38; prisoners of war and "Birth-Day Ode," 40; prisoners of war and "A Farewell," 41; in "Tis Large Indeed," 48; victories at Fort Washington and Fort Lee, 51; in "Yoric's Address," 51, 54; Odell on the British army and General Howe, 60–62; in garrisoned New York, 64; in "Song," 66; Rivington reports high morale, 71; General Clinton settles in New York, 77; and "amateur theatricals," 81; Britannicus on, 86, 90; and *The American Times*, 127; and the possibility of reestablishing the Loyalists, 136, 137. *See also* Burke, Edmund
Buel, John: editor of Trumbull's *M'Fingal* (1792), 30
Burgoyne, Gen. John, 27, 85, 169 n.20; in "New Year's Verses 1778," 72
Burke, Edmund, 87
Burlington, N.J., 6, 20, 21, 36, 42, 43, 44, 52, 54–62 passim, 67, 68, 69, 81, 108, 129, 159, 161; "The Memorial of Jonathan Odell," 148, 150, 151; Benjamin Moore and church news, 154
Butler, Samuel: *Hudibras*, 179 n.5

Cafferty, Pastora San Juan, xii, 167 nn.7, 9, 11, and 12, 168 nn.14 and 29, 168 n.20, 169 nn.3, 5, 15, 17, and 20, 171 n.3, 181 n.6
Calhoon, Robert, xiv, 34, 167 n.1, 168 n.20, 169 n.2
Cambridge mission, 5
Carleton, Gen. Sir Guy, xiii, 40, 94, 143, 144, 145, 148, 151, 153, 154, 158–59, 181 n.7; defends Quebec, 36–37; arrives in New York to negotiate peace, 135–36; in "The Tory Hunt," 38; and earl of Shelbourne's letter, 137; asks to return to England, 138; and the Fifth Provisional Article, 139; sends the first Loyalists to Nova Scotia, 142; and an all-Loyalist colony, 143; in "The Memorial of Jonathan Odell," 150
Carleton, Governor Thomas, 154, 157; appointed governor of New Brunswick, 153; and the House of Assembly, 157
Carlisle, Abraham, 122, 178 n.5

Index

Chandler, Rev. Thomas Bradbury, 3, 11, 17; letter to Secretary of the S.P.G., 31, 163 n.7
Charles I (King of England), 179 n.5
Charleston, S.C., 80, 113, 116; battle of, 113, 116; battle in the afterword of "Le Feu de Joie," 106
Chase, Samuel: in *The American Times*, 121
Chesapeake Bay, Md., 69; in "The Congratulation," 102
Churchill, Charles: The Rosciad, 179 n.5
Church of England. *See* Anglican church
Clinton, Gen. Henry, xiii, 27, 77, 80–83, 84, 87, 95, 109, 128, 171 n.15, 171 n.8; Britannicus on, 86–87; Commission of Peace, 113; Oath of Allegiance, 116, 117; and "amateur theatricals," 81; and Benedict Arnold, 95–97, 117; and the Britannicus essayists, 107–8; in *The American Times*, 122; and John André, 128, 129; Thomas Jones on, 132; Associated Loyalists, 132–35 (*see also* Franklin, William); replaced by Sir Guy Carleton, 135; Philipsburg proclamation, 143; "Memorial of Jonathan Odell" on, 150
Condon, Ann Gordon, 143, 180 nn.13, 14, 17, 20, and 22, 181 nn.1, 3, 4, and 5, 182 nn.23, 26, 27, 28, 29, and 30
Congregationalist church, 4, 5, 13, 100
Continental army and militia, 3, 27, 36, 48, 70, 98, 167 n.4; verge of collapse, 51; low morale, 59, 116; and West Point, 94; desertion, 103; in "Le Feu de Joie," 104–6; in *The American Times*, 124–25

Continental Congress, 22–23, 37, 38, 39, 40, 49, 66, 90, 94, 97, 105, 116, 127; and James Rivington, 25–26; rejects peace talks, 48; flees to Baltimore, 54; intimidates the Loyalists, 61; Odell on, 70, 72, 76; Britannicus on, 85, 88–90, 94–95, 99–102, 107, 111–13; and Benedict Arnold, 94–95, 97, 116; in "The Word of Congress," 99–102; in "The Congratulation," 102–3; in "Le Feu de Joie," 104–6; in *The American Times*, 118–27; and the Fifth Provisional Article, 139–42
Continental money, xiii, 27, 49, 85, 102, 103, 109, 128; in "The Law, in Days of Yore," 50; in "Canto," 67–68; Britannicus on, 88–90; Odell identifies as Britannicus's subject, 109; in *The American Times*, 119–20, 126; Britannicus on Benjamin Franklin's paper money policy, 111–13
Conway Resolution, 138
Cooper, Rev. Samuel: in *The American Times*, 121
Cornwallis, Lord Charles, 51; awaits General Howe's permission, 61–62; surrenders at Yorktown, 132

Dartmouth, William Legge, second earl of, 27
Deane, Silas, 178 n.5
Declaration of Independence, 49, 51; Odell on, 42, 45, 61, 149
Delaware River, 40, 43, 51, 52, 54, 61, 62, 66, 67, 70, 154, 168 n.18
Donop, Col. Carl von, 54–56, 57, 67
Drake, Sir Francis: Britannicus on, 103–4
A Dreamer (pseud. Odell?): on sources for *The American Times*, 178 n.5

Duane, James: in *The American Times*, 121
Duer, William: in *The American Times*, 121
Dunmore, John Murray, fourth earl of, 167 n.4; proclamation of 1775, 143

Episcopate Controversy, xii, 4, 5, 6, 7, 11, 13, 20, 21, 31, 45
Episcopate Convention, 11
Estaing, Charles Hector Theodate, comte d', 85, 104, 106, 107, 171 n.15, 178 n.5; Britannicus on, 90, 107; Odell asks Benedict Arnold about strength of, 98; and Savannah, 104; in "Le Feu de Joie," 104–6
Evans, Cadwalader, 22

Federalists, 28, 155, 156
Fifth Provisional Article, 139, 140. *See also* Provisional Articles of Peace
Foote, Samuel: "Taste," 170 n.10
Fox, Charles, 151; North-Fox coalition, 151
Fox, Gen. Henry, 151. *See also* Partition Movement
Franklin, Benjamin, 22, 24, 48, 84, 87, 99, 102, 167 n.9; in "The Word of Congress," 101; Britannicus on fiscal policies, 111–12
Franklin, Elizabeth, 6, 66
Franklin, William, 2, 6–7, 20, 21, 24, 28, 42, 48, 57, 68, 102, 125, 134, 135, 142, 171 n.8; sponsors Odell for Anglican orders, 3; and the New Jersey General Assembly and Lord Hillsborough, 15–16; ends relationship with Benjamin Franklin, 22; petitions George Washington to visit his wife on her deathbed, 66; Simsbury Mines, 41, 132; in "Song," 66; in New York, 81; awarded government pension, 82; letter to General Clinton, November 19, 1778, on Odell's behalf, 108; and Board of Associated Loyalists, 132–35
Franklin, William Temple, 102
Fredericton, New Brunswick, Canada, xiii, 154, 156; House of Assembly, 157–58
French Alliance, xiii; rumors, 13, 88, 98; Britannicus on, 84–87, 90–91, 106; in "The Word of Congress," 99, 102; in "The Congratulation," 102–3; in *The American Times*, 126; and Sir Guy Carleton's commission, 135. *See also* Treaty of Amity and Commerce
French and Indian War (Seven Years War), 3–4, 13, 27, 36, 85, 105–6; subject of "An Answer," 74; William Howe during, 30; in "Birth-Day," 40; mentioned in "A Farewell," 41
Freneau, Philip: "A Voyage to Boston," 27–28; "Sir Harry's Invitation," 80–81; "On the Rising Glory of America," 83–84

Gage, Gen. Thomas, 74; and Parliament, 26–27; writes to Dartmouth, 27; in *M'Fingal*, 29
Galloway, Joseph: on William Howe, 168 n.18
George III (King of England), 4, 35, 36, 40, 65, 117–18; in "Tis Large Indeed," 47; inclinations according to General and Admiral Howe, 49; in *The American Times*, 123, 127; and the Associated Loyalists, 132–34; against independence, 136

Index

Germain, Lord George, 77
Germantown, Pa., battle of, 70
Gernard, Conrad, 86, 95
Glover, Richadd Leonidas, 179 n.5
Greene, Gen. Nathanael, 125
Gruber, Ira D., 30, 166 n.28, 167 nn.2, 3, and 5, 168 nn.21, 22, 23, 26, and 28
Gwynn, William, 173 n.5, 174 n.5

Halifax, Canada, 34, 38, 154
Hamilton, Alexander, 129
Hancock, John, 76; in *The American Times*, 121, 170 n.22. *See also* Smuggling
Henry, Prince William, 136, 137
Hessians, 35, 48, 54–56, 57, 58, 59
Hills, Rev. George, 31, 164 nn.12, 13, 14, and 15, 165 nn.5 and 6, 166 nn.29, 30, 31, and 32, 167 nn.9, 10, and 13, 168 nn.15, 17, and 18, 168 nn.8, 14, 15, 16, and 17, 169 n.12, 181 nn.8 and 14
Hillsborough, Wills Hill, first earl of, 16, 20. *See also* Franklin, William
Hotchkin, Samuel Fitch, 174 n.5
Howe, Admiral Lord Richard, 42, 44, 50, 51, 66, 69–71, 72, 73, 77, 78; on the uselessness of a hostile British America, 35; peace commissioner, 48–49
Howe, Gen. William, xiii, 27, 35, 37, 42, 50, 66, 68, 72, 76, 81, 87, 95, 129, 149, 159, 168 n.18, 169 nn.14 and 18, 169 n.20, 170 n.23, 171 n.8, 178 n.5; peace commissioner, 48–49; Sword and Olive Branch policy denounced, 64–66, 86–87; in "New Year's Verses 1778," 71–72; and Valley Forge, 76–77; *Mischianza*, 77; "The Memorial of Jonathan Odell," 148; reputation as a soldier in 1775, 30; departs Boston for Halifax, 34; withdraws from the Long Island area, 38; New York strategy, 44; offers Oath of Allegiance, 51; denounced by Odell and Thomas Jones, 61–62; authority to grant pardons, 64, 69, 70; in "Song," 65; after Battle of Brandywine, 69; and "An Answer," 75; Britannicus on, 86–87; and the Britannicus essayists, 107–8
Huddy, Joshua, 134, 135. *See also* Associates
Hutchinson, Governor Thomas, 12

Inglis, Rev. Charles, 26, 124

Jackson, John: editor of Margaret Morris's *Journal*, 56, 168 nn.1–7, nn.9–13, and n.19, 169 n.7
Jameson, Lt. Col. John, 128, 129, 174 n.5. *See also* Arnold, Benedict
Jay, John: in *The American Times*, 121
Jefferson, Thomas, 99
Johnson, Samuel, 8
Jones, Judge Thomas, 61, 168 n.18, 170 n.24, 179 n.2, 180 nn.9 and 10; on General Howe's advantage over George Washington, 77; on the *Mischianza*, 77; on General Clinton, 132; on the Fifth Provisional Article, 141

Lafayette, Marie Joseph Paul Ives Roch Gilbert du Motier, marquis de, 85, 129
La Fontaine, "Le Songe d'un habitant du Mogal," 9–10, 164 n.18
Laud, Archbishop, 4
Laurens, Henry: in *The American Times*, 123

Lee, Gen. Arthur, 178 n.5
Lincoln, Gen. Benjamin: in "Le Feu de Joie," 104–5
Lippincott, Captain, 134, 135 See also Associators
Livingston, Governor William, 68; in *The American Times*, 121, 178 n.5
Long Island area, 65, 86; General Howe withdraws, 38; farmers, 64; Britannicus on, 86–87; King's American Dragoons' campground, 136
Loudon, Samuel: editor of Packet, 26
Louis XVI (king of France), 95, 104, 178 n.5; in "Le Feu de Joie," 106; A Loyal American (Britannicus) on, 107
Lovelace, Richard: "To Lucasta in Prison" parodied, 46
A Loyal American (pseud. Odell and Samuel Seabury), 106, 109. See also Britannicus
Loyalists' circumstances: and the Association, 22–26; and General Gage, 26; and the Siege of Boston, 27; in Trumbull's *M'Fingal*, 29; in Freneau's "A Voyage to Boston," 27–28; and British army's departure from Boston, 34; and the Howes' rationale, xiii, 33–36, 48–49, 69–70; and George III, 36; Peacock Expedition, 37; in "The Tory Hunt," 37–38; in "Song for a Fishing Party," 39; in "The General Warrant," 41–43; in "Tis Large Indeed," 44–48; in "The Law, in Days of Yore," 49–50; in "Yoric's Address," 50–51; and pardons for the rebels, 48, 69, 113, 116; and Tory hunters, 57–60, 62, 97; in General Howe's garrisoned New York, 64–65; in "Song" for St. George's Day, 65–66; in "Song" for the king's birthday, 66; and confiscation of property, 67–68, 77–78; in untitled song, 70–71; in General Clinton's garrisoned New York, 80–81, 132; Britannicus voices outrage on, 86–87; and expectations, 87–88; in "The Word of Congress," 98–102; and Loyalist militiamen, 104, 171 n.8; in *The American Times*, 118–27; and Sir Guy Carleton's plan for "cordial reconciliation," 136, 137, 138; and the Fifth Provisional Article, 139–42; and move to Canada, xiii, 142, 144; and the creation of a Loyalist colony in New Brunswick, 143, 150–51. See also Associated Loyalists; Associators

Loyalist Claims Commission, xiii, 148, 150, 152, 153; "The Memorial of Jonathan Odell," 148–50

Loyalist ideology, xii, xiii, 11–12, 27, 38–39, 49–50, 158, 159; on Continental currency, 49–50; in "Canto," 67–68; in "Colonel Buckeridge's Prologue," 84; in "The Word of Congress," 99–102; in "Le Feu de Joie," 105–6; in *The American Times*, 118–27; and the Fifth Provisional Article, 142; Loyalist tradition in the Maritimes, 155–56. See also Loyalists' circumstances

Ludlow, Col. Gabriel, 143, 144
Lyman, Daniel, 182 n.31

M'Fingal, 28–30, 127, 166 nn.26 and 27. See also Trumbull, Jonathan
M'Kean, Chief Justice Thomas, 178 n.5
Massachusetts circular letter, 15, 16

Matlack, Timothy: in "The Word of Congress," 101
Mayhew, Jonathan, 5
Mifflin, Gen. Thomas: in "The Word of Congress," 101
Milton, John, 7, 120, 122, 179 n.5
Montgomery, Gen. Richard, 36, 66, 173 n.5
Moore, Rev. Benjamin, 153–54, 155, 156
Moore, Clement Clark, 155, 156
Moore, Marianne, 164 n.18
Morris, Gouverneur: in *The American Times*, 121
Morris, Margaret, 6, 52, 62, 66–67; on Hessians, the Pennsylvania fleet, and Odell's escape, 54–60
Morris, Governor Robert: in *The American Times*, 121

New Brunswick, Canada, 150, 153, 156, 157, 158; Committee on Trade and Plantations, 151; House of Assembly, 157–58. See also Partition Movement
New Haven, Conn., 25. See also Sears, Issac; Sons of Liberty
New Jersey General Assembly, 15–16, 20, 41; circular letter, 16. See also Franklin, William
New Jersey Provincial Congress, 30, 31, 41, 42, 43, 44, 45; Inquisition for High Treason, 77–78, 150; "Memorial of Jonathan Odell," 149
New York, 23, 66, 69, 77, 129, 132, 134, 135, 144, 145, 149, 153, 154, 158, 159; and General Howe's garrison, 64; and General Clinton's garrison, 80–81. See also Calhoon, Robert
New York Constitutional Gazette, 27
New York Gazette, 49
New-York Gazetteer, 24, 25
Newport, R. I., 3, 25, 85, 90, 171 n.15

North, Prime Minister Lord Frederick, 132, 151; North-Fox coalition, 151
Nova Scotia, Canada, 142, 143, 144, 153; Odell's alternate plans, 142; Governor Parr discredited, 151; Committee on Trade and Plantation, 151

Oath of the King's Supremacy, 5, 45; in "Tis Large Indeed," 45, 47
Odell, Rev. Doctor Jonathan. *See also pseudonyms:* Britannicus; A Dreamer (?), A Loyal American; Osborne, James; Overhill, Jasper; Querno, Camillo; Veridicus; Veritas; V.S.; Yoric (Yorick)

Personal Life
Ancestry, 2, 163 n.1; parents, 2; physician, 2, 161; ordination, 3, 6; personal library of, 7–8; Episcopate Controversy poems, 9–17; resumes practicing medicine, 21; marries Ann de Cou, 21; Mary Odell and William Franklin Odell born, 21; entertains captured British officers, 40–41; suspected of spying, 41–43; N.J. Provincial Congress orders eight-mile parole, 43; negotiates with Hessian commandant Colonel von Donop, 54–56; eludes Tory hunters, 57–60; writes about Loyalists' desperate and "defenceless condition," 60–61; established in Philadelphia, 71; Inquisition for High Treason confiscates his property, 77–78; writes prologues for the New York theater, 82–84; collaborates with Samuel Seabury in the Britannicus essays, 84–91; and Benedict

Odell, Rev. Doctor Jonathan (*Cont.*) Arnold, 94–98; asks fee for Britannicus essays, 107–9; Britannicus resumes, 111–13; the Arnold conspiracy resumes, 116–17, 128–30; addresses American Dragoons, 136–37; Britannicus appeals to earl of Shelbourne, 138; and the Fifth Provisional Article, 139–42; writes to Edward Winslow about the future, 142; arrives in England with Sir Guy Carleton, 148; petitions the Loyalist Claims Commission, 149–50; works for Partition Movement to create all-Loyalist colony of New Brunswick, 150–51; instructs Ann to petition the vestry of St. Mary's for lost income, 151–52; appointed Provincial Secretary to New Brunswick, 153; an old guard New Brunswick Loyalist, 154–59; inscription on tombstone, 161–62

Churches Served
St. Mary's, 6; repaired, 6–7, 21; closed, 42, 45; in "Tis Large Indeed," 45, 47; "The Memorial of Jonathan Odell," 148–50; Odell asks wife to petition the vestry, 151–52; Benjamin Moore's advice on, 154; vestry of, 155
Church at Mount Holly, 21; closed, 42, 45; in "Tis Large Indeed," 45, 47
Trinity Church, Saint John, New Brunswick, Canada, 154

Family
Ann de Cou (wife), xiii, 21, 41, 68, 70, 108, 151; in "The General Warrant," 41–43; "The Way to Keep Him," 70; in "A Loyalist in Exile," 110–11; letter to, July 5, 1784, 152
children: Mary, 21, 42, 108; in "The General Warrant," 41–43; William Franklin, 21, 42, 108, 154; tombstone inscription, 155, 156, 161
Thomas Odell (cousin), letter to, June 9, 1784, 152–53

Essays
An Essay on the Elements, Accents, and Prosody of the English Language, 8, 155–56
"An Answer to the DECLARATION of the GENERAL CONGRESS" in the *Pennsylvania Evening Post: February 17, 1778:* on representation, petition of grievance, ungrateful Americans, 72–73; *February 21, 1778:* French and Indian War financial assistance, France no longer a threat, America must share war debt cost, 73–74; *February 24, 1778:* Stamp Act crisis blamed on Lord Rockingham whose faction abetted a war, 74; *March 13, 1778:* Land Bank of 1741, ruinous paper money policies, 75; *March 25, 1778:* taxation and smuggling, Vice Admiralty Courts, 75–76
"To the Inhabitants of the revolted Colonies in America. On the Alliance with France," *Royal Gazette*, January 6, 1779; British fleet superior to d'Estaing's, France's history of deception, on the Opposition party in Parliament, decries England's Sword and Olive Branch policy, 84–87
"5. To the Inhabitants of the re-

volted Colonies in America. On the Continental Money," *Royal Gazette*, February 27, 1779: Congressional leaders knew paper money would create havoc, Continental dollar depreciated at rate of more than twenty to one, Congress cannot borrow money, 88–90
"To the Inhabitants of the revolted Colonies in America," *Royal Gazette*, April 21, 1779: British army will not withdraw, France will not replace d'Estaing's ruined fleet, questions France's motives, 90–91
"To the Inhabitants of the several (revolted) British Colonies in America," *Royal Gazette*, December 8, 1779: French duplicity, the Treaty of Amity and Commerce, d'Estaing claims Savannah for Louis XVI, dissolve Congress and call a free election, 106–7
"PEOPLE of AMERICA," *Royal Gazette*, April 15, 1780: Congress declares itself insolvent, Benjamin Franklin's paper money policy, rebels and financial ruin, General Clinton's commission of peace, 111–13
Response to the Fifth Provisional Article of the Provisional Articles of Peace, "This Country, so long convulsed by the rage of Civil War," 139–42

Letters from Odell
to England, seized, contents unknown, 30–31, 45
to the Secretary of the S.P.G., 6–7, 20–21, 31, 42, 45; January 7, 1777, 60–61; January 25, 1777, 61; August 18, 1777, 68–69
to John André, 96; July 18, 1779, 97–98; July 21, 1779, 98; December 18, 1779, 108; December 21, 1779, 117
to Joseph Stansbury, July 24, 1780, 117
to Ann Odell, July 5, 1784, 152
to Thomas Odell, June 19, 1784, 152–53; August 6, 1784, 153
to Jonathan Boucher, 1802, 156

Letters to Odell
from Ann Odell, May 2, 1784, 152
from Thomas Odell, July 15, 1784, 153
from Rev. Benjamin Moorse, November 15, 1784, 153–54

Petitions
"The Memorial of Jonathan Odell": the "late Rector of Burlington and Mount Holly," arrested by order of the Provincial Council of New Jersey, flees enemies, exiled from "Family and his Parish" seven years, published essays in Philadelphia and New York, chaplain to a British-American corps, Assistant Secretary to the Board of Associated Loyalists, translator of French and Spanish Papers, Assistant Secretary to Sir Guy Carleton, half pay of military chaplain only certain salary, his real estate confiscated and personal effects sold at public auction in consequence of New Jersey Inquisition Judgment, on behalf of his wife and four children petitions for 500 pounds sterling, 149–50
Memorialist to House of Assembly in 1789, 156, 157–58

200 | Index

Odell, Rev. Doctor Jonathan (*Cont.*)

Poems

The American Times, xiii; contents: satire justified in preface, deplorable state of affairs characterized, congressional leaders scorned, George Washington singled out, anarchy lamented, reason and moderation celebrated though they could not prevail, taxation policies deemed "madness," Britain must make a military commitment, 118–28; authorship queries and textual variations, 175 n.5. *See also* Loyalist ideology

"Birth-Day Ode" (celebrates George III's birthday, 1776, for POWs), 40–41, 45, 129

"Canto" (rebels in power in Burlington), 67–68

"Colonel Buckeridge's Prologue" (prologue in the Rising Glory tradition), 83

"The Congratulation, a Poem" (scorns Continental currency, the French Alliance, and Congress), 102–3

"A Farewell" (in honor of POWs transferred from Burlington to Maryland), 41, 129

"Le Feu de Joie" (celebrates military victory at Savannah), 104–6

"The General Warrant" (Odell suspected of spying), 41–43

"How Changed Are My Feelings from Those Which Possess'd Me," April 14, 1783 (probable response to the political reorganization of British North America), 151

"Immediately After the Tragedy of Chrononhotonthologos, A Prologue Intended for the Farce Called Taste" (prologue suited to please Clinton's coterie), 83, 170 n.10

"Inscription for a Curious Chamber Stove" (on Benjamin Franklin), 167 n.9

"INSTUM ET TENACEM PROPOSITI VIRIM," translation: "No Civil Frenzy, No Dark Frown" (response to eight-mile parole), 43–44

"The Law, in Days of Yore, How Harsh!" (Continental currency), 49–50, 88

"A Loyalist, in Exile From His Family, Sends a Miniature Picture to His Disconsolate Wife" (separated three years, Odell agonizes over his family), 110–11

"Not with a Heart Unmoved I Left Thy Shores" (on leaving the colonies for England), 145

"Ode for the New Year, 1778" (contemns ambitious "blind mortals"), 109

"Ode for the New Year, 1780" (considers unsympathetic ministers in Parliament the enemy), 109–10

"Of Protestant Friends," October 8, 1777 (Loyalists become optimistic when General Howe occupies Philadelphia), 70–71

"On the Anniversary of a Friend's Marriage" (occasional), 7

"On Mr. Pope's (Now William Stanhope's) garden at Twickenham" (homage, ends Episcopate Controversy involvement), 16–17

"Pope's Garden at Twickenham" (homage), 7

"A Second Salute to Neighbor Madison, 1814" (War of 1812), 156, 182 n.20

Index

"Song," June 4, 1777 (optimistic about British military resolve), 66

"Song for a Fishing Party Near Burlington, On the Delaware, in 1776" (Loyalist ideology), 39

"Song for the 4th of June 1808" (France denounced), 156

"Song for St. George's Day, April 23, 1777" (on Howe's military "ineptitude"), 65–66

"Song From Milton's Allegro, With Two Addition Stanzas Written At Sea, Anno 1767" (homage), 7

"Le Songe d'un Habitant du Mogal" (Episcopate Controversy), 9–11, 179 n.5

"Tis Large Indeed–'Tis Monstrous Large He Cried" (response to eight-mile parole), 44–48, 49

"To the Ladies of Burlington Bank," 7

"To the Memory of Major André" (eulogy), 129–30

"The Tory Hunt" (Peacock Expedition), 37–38

"The True History of the Golden Age," 7

"UNTHANKFUL Man, Perversely Blind" (Augustan world view), 8–9, 10

"The Vacant House" (reflects on the past now that Governor Carleton has retired to England), 158

"The Way to Keep Him" (affection for Ann), 70

"Welcome Home After the Peace of 1763" (celebrates end of French and Indian war), 4

"What the Deuce is the Matter?" (Episcopate Controversy), 12–14

"When a Man of True Spirit, in Speaking or Writing" (Episcopate Controversy), 12, 13–15

"The Word of Congress" (French Alliance, "roast" of Congressional leaders, rebel propaganda, Thomas Paine's authorship of *Common Sense* questioned), 98–102

"The World's A Stage and All the Men and Women Merely Players" (prologue scorns New York social whirl), 82–83

"Yoric's Address" (expresses contempt for Whigs now that war is almost over), 50–52

Public Career

Deputy Chaplain of the Royal Fuzileers, 68, 108; in "The Memorial of Jonathan Odell," 150

Chaplain to the First Battalion of Pennsylvania Loyalists, 71

Superintendent of the Printing Presses and Periodical Publications, xiii, 71, 72, 129; in "The Memorial of Jonathan Odell," 149

Secretary to the Corporation for the Relief of the Widows and Orphans of Deceased Clergymen, 7

Assistant Secretary to the Board of Associated Loyalists, 132–34; in "The Memorial of Jonathan Odell," 150

Chaplain to the King's American Dragoons, 136

Translator of French and Spanish Papers, 136; in "The Memorial of Jonathan Odell," 150

Assistant Secretary to Sir Guy Carleton, xiii, 137–38; in "The Memorial of Jonathan Odell," 150

Odell, Rev. Doctor Jonathan (*Cont.*)
Provincial Secretary to New Brunswick, xiii, 153, 162
Registrar of Records, 153, 162
Clerk of the Council, 153, 162

Sermons
in Philadelphia, 1778, 169 n.18
St. Paul's, January 3, 1779, 82
St. Paul's and St. George's, March 21, 1779, 90
"Address to the King's American Dragoons," 136
on leaving the colonies, November 9, 1783, 145
two sermons preached to the Society for the Propagation of the Gospel, 1784, 148

Osborne, James (pseud. Odell), 96. See also Arnold, Benedict
Overhill, Jasper (pseud. Odell), 96. See also Arnold, Benedict

Paine, Thomas, 22, 101, 102; in "The Word of Congress," 101; Britannicus on, 112, 178 n.5, 179 n.5
"Paoli Massacre," 70
Parliament, 132; ministers, 5; and tax laws, 6; and General Gage, 26–27; Trumbull and William Franklin on taxation policies, 28; Britannicus on misrule of, 86; in "Ode for the New Year, 1780," 109; rumors about negotiating peace, 90, 97; in *The American Times*, 125, 127; and ceding independence, 138
Parr, Governor, 143, 151
Partition Movement, 150–51
"The Pausing American Loyalist" (anon.), 23
Peace of Paris (1763), 3–4, 13, 26; in "An Answer," 74; A Loyal American on, 107. See also French and Indian War
Peacock Expedition, 37, 42. See also Odell: Poems, "The Tory Hunt"; Schuyler, Phillip
Pennsylvania Chronicle, 8, 9, 12, 13, 16, 27; edited by William Goddard, 9; addressed by Odell, 15
Pennsylvania Council, 95, 97
Pennsylvania Evening Post, 3, 7, 71, 72, 75
Peters, Thomas: Petition of Grievances from New Brunswick to the British Cabinet, 156–57
Philadelphia, Pa., 52, 54, 61–62, 66, 67, 69, 70, 76, 77, 81, 82, 95, 97; Britannicus on, 87; Stansbury takes the Oath of Allegiance and Adjuration, 95; in the afterword of "Le Feu de Joie," 106
Philipsburg proclamation, 143, 144
Pitt, William, 151
Pope, Alexander, 7, 8, 9, 10, 16, 17, 165 n.24, 178 n.5, 179 n.5
Potter, Janice, 11–12, 39, 165 nn.19 and 20, 167 n.8, 169 n.9, 171 nn.7 and 12
Princeton, N.J., battle of, 65
Provisional Articles of Peace: Fifth Article, 139, 140; Thomas Jones on, 141; Seventh Article, 143–44
Puff, Peter: character in "Tis Large Indeed," 44–48; in "The Law, in Days of Yore," 49–50; in "Immediately After the Tragedy of Chrononhotonthologos," 83. See also Sewall, Jonathan
Pulaski, Count Casimir: in *The American Times*, 122–23, 178 n.5

Quakers: families in Burlington, 6; Roberts and Carlisle hung, 122; and black veterans in the Maritimes, 144

Querno, Camillo (pseud. Odell), 117. *See also The American Times*

Rankin, William, 171 n.8
Rede, Kenneth, 173 n.5, 174 n.5
Rittenhouse, David: in "The Word of Congress," 100
Rivington, James, 24–26, 81, 88, 102, 105, 117, 129, 133, 136, 137, 168 n.18, 170 n.10, 171 n.8, 173 n.5, 174 n.5, 178 n.5, 179 n.6; *New-York Gazetteer* and the Association, 24–26; printer to the king, 65; reports British army's high morale, 71; on conciliation, 136; and *New York Gazette, and Universal Advertiser*, 179 n.6. *See also New-York Gazetteer; Royal Gazette*
Roberts, John, 122, 178 n.5. *See also* Quakers
Rockingham, Charles Watson-Wentworth, second marquess of: in "An Answer," 74; Rockingham-Shelbourne ministry and General Carleton, 136
Royal Gazette, 65, 71, 81, 84, 88, 90, 98, 103, 104, 106, 109, 133, 134, 135, 170 n.10, 171 n.8, 172 n.14, 179 n.4; news on Nova Scotia, 142. *See also* Rivington, James
Rutledge, Edward, 48

Sandy Hook, N.J., 42; in "The Congratulation," 102
Sargent, Winthrop, xi, xii, 71, 164 n.17, 165 n.24, 167 n.9, 169 n.1; 169–170 n.20; 172–175 n.5, 178 n.5
Sauvages, Boissier de, 22
Savannah, S.C., battle of, 98, 104; in "Le Feu de Joie," 104–6; A Loyal American on (Britannicus), 106, 107

Schuyler, Gen. Philip, 37–38, 42. *See also* Peacock Expedition
Seabury, Samuel, 23, 73, 84, 88, 90, 108, 109, 155; ordained first Anglican bishop in North America, 143. *See also* Britannicus
Sears, Issac, 25, 26. *See also* Sons of Liberty
Secker, Archbishop Thomas, 3, 5, 15, 20. *See also* Episcopate Controversy
Seventh Provisional Article, 143–44. *See also* Provisional Articles of Peace
Sewall, Jonathan: "A Cure for the Spleen," 44. *See also* Puff, Peter
Seymoure, Commodore Thomas, 54, 55, 56. *See also* Morris, Margaret
Shelbourne, William Petty Fitzmaurice, earl of 137, 158, 159; Rockingham-Shelbourne ministry, 136; Britannicus on independence, 138
Shippen, Peggy, 95, 129
Shrewsbury, N.J., 42, 45. *See also* Odell: Poems, "The General Warrant"
Siege of Boston, 27, 95. *See also* Calhoon, Robert; Howe, William
Sierra Leone, 156, 157
Slaves, 156; *Royal Gazette* covers news, 81, 167 n.4, 180 n.23; and Lord Dunmore's proclamation, 143; and General Clinton's Philipsburg proclamation, 143; Odell on, 144. *See also* Seventh Provisional Article
Smith, Rev. William, 173 n.5
Smuggling, 75, 76. *See also* Writs of Assistance
Society for the Propagation of the Gospel (S.P.G.), 5, 6, 7, 20, 21; Odell on, 69; Odell's sermons for, 148

Sons of Liberty, 23, 24, 25, 26, 87
Stamp Act, 5, 11, 15, 16; subject of "An Answer," 74
Stansbury, Joseph, xi, xii, 117, 128, 144, 169 n.20, 180 n.24; "New Year's Verses, 1778," 71–72; and Benedict Arnold, 95–98, 117; returns from Nova Scotia, 144–45
Staten Island, N.Y., 42, 48
Sterne, Laurence, 38. *See also* Odell: Poems, "The Tory Hunt"; Yoric
Stiles, Rev. Ezra, 3
Sullivan, Gen. John: in "The Word of Congress," 101; 171 n.15
Swift, Dean Jonathan, 6, 8

Tea Act, 25
Terrick, Bishop Richard, 164 n.7
Townshend duties, 6, 11, 13, 15
Treaty of Amity and Commerce, 88; Britannicus on, 88, 106, 107. *See also* French Alliance
Treaty of Paris: A Loyal American on, 107. *See also* Peace of Paris
Trenton, N.J., battle of, 59, 61, 65; in "Canto," 67; in "Memorial of Jonathan Odell," 149; Galloway on General Howe, 168 n.18
Trumbull, Jonathan: *M'Fingal*, 28–30, 127, 166 nn.26 and 27; "An Essay on the Uses and Advantages of the Fine Arts," 83
Tyler, Moses Coit, xi–xii, 165 nn.9 and 10, 168 n.24, 178 n.5
Tyron, Gov. William, 132. *See also* Associated Loyalists

University of New Brunswick, 154

Veridicus (pseud. Odell), 118, 135, 165 n.21; "UNTHANKFUL man, perversely blind," 8–9, 10; "Le Songe," 9; "What the Deuce," 12; "When a Man of True Spirit," 13; letter to editor Goddard, 14, 15
Veritas (pseud. Odell), 135
Vice Admiralty courts, 76. *See also* Writ of Assistance
V.S. (pseud. Odell): "Pope's Garden," 16
Vulture: fires on John André, 128; Arnold escapes to, 129

Walker, James St. G., 157, 180 nn.21 and 23, 182 nn.24 and 25
Warren, Mercy, 34
Washington, George, xiii, 23, 36, 38, 48, 66, 68, 69, 77, 84, 87, 94, 95, 104, 116, 125, 128, 129, 132, 136, 137, 158, 159, 167 n.4, 171 n.15, 179 n.6; on Continental soldiers at Siege of Boston, 27; "The Blockhead" celebrates takeover of Boston, 34; retreat through New Jersey, 51, 54, 59, 61; issues proclamation from Morristown, N.J., headquarters, 62; rumors about earldom, 64; the "Paoli Massacre," 70; and Valley Forge, 76; and d'Estaing, 85; in *The American Times*, 121–22, 127; and Benedict Arnold and John André, 94–95, 129; in "The Congratulation," 102; and the Fifth Provisional Article, 142; and the Seventh Provisional Article, 144
West Point, xiii, 94, 98, 116, 117, 118, 128, 129
Whig mobs, xii, xiii, 11; and Samuel Seabury, 23; and the *New-York Gazetteer*, 25; and Inglis's "The True Interest of America," 26; in *M'Fingal*, 29
White, Philip, 135. *See also* Associated Loyalists
Whitefield, George, 21
White Plains, 65; Britannicus on, 87

William the Conqueror, 153
Winslow, Edward, 151, 153, 182 n.31; explores relocation possibilities in Nova Scotia, 142; Odell writes about future, 142
Witherspoon, John, in *The American Times*, 123
Writ of Assistance, 76. *See also* Adams, John

Yoric or Yorick (pseud. Odell): and "Birth-Day Ode," 41; and "The Tory Hunt," 37–38; and "A Farewell," 41; and "Tis Large Indeed," 44–48, 49; and "The Law, in Days of Yore," 49–50; and "Yoric's Address," 50–52; "Song" (June 4, 1777), 66; revises "New Year's Verses, 1778," 71–72; and "The World's A Stage and All the Men and Women Merely Players," 82–83; characterized, 118
Yorktown, battle of, 132

The Author

Cynthia Dubin Edelberg is Associate Professor of English at Cleveland State University. Her research interests include contemporary American poetry and fiction and American war poetry. She is the author of *Robert Creeley's Poetry: A Critical Introduction*.